The Lawyer,
The Public,
and
Professional
Responsibility

The LAWYER, The PUBLIC, and PROFESSIONAL RESPONSIBILITY

F. Raymond Marks

with Kirk Leswing

Barbara A. Fortinsky

Chicago   American Bar Foundation

1972

This book is dedicated to
Susan, James, and Thomas Marks

Publication of this volume by the American
Bar Foundation signifies that the work is regarded
as valuable and responsible. The analyses, conclusions, and opinions expressed are those of the
author and not those of the American Bar Foundation
or its officers and directors.

Library of Congress Catalog Card Number: 70–187–314

PRINTED IN U.S.A.

American Bar Foundation

The American Bar Foundation is the legal research affiliate of the American Bar Association. Its institutional mission is to conduct research that will enlarge the understanding and improve the functioning of law and legal institutions. The Foundation's work is supported by the American Bar Association, the American Bar Endowment, The Fellows of the American Bar Foundation, and by outside funds granted for particular research projects.

Table of Contents

ᴘᴀʀᴛ ᴛʜʀᴇᴇ

Preface

This book resulted from a study, made by the American Bar Foundation, of the public interest responses of the private bar. The study was funded in major part by a grant from The Ford Foundation. Opinions expressed herein are those of the authors and should not be construed as representing the opinions or policies of either the American Bar Foundation or The Ford Foundation. Similarly, conclusions drawn from the data are the authors' conclusions, as is the analysis used to reach those conclusions.

The lawyers whom we interviewed gave generously of their time and shared with us the insights they had derived from thinking about and practicing public interest law. We are indebted to each of them. A list of their names and firms appears in the Appendix.

A book of this kind is always the product of interchange with and enrichment from colleagues and others. A few people, however, merit special mention. We can never thank them enough. One of my colleagues, Barlow F. Christensen,

Preface

read, critically commented on, and contributed throughout to the several drafts of the manuscript. In my judgment, his understanding of the problems of the American legal profession is unequaled by any other scholar.

Prior to the submission of the report to The Ford Foundation, Kathleen McCourt read and edited each draft for sense as well as style. Her insights were helpful.

Fe Logan and Jo Muster, often under pressure, deserve special recognition for their untiring typing. So also do Pat Gorai and Richard Clifton, who were of special help in preparing the manuscript.

Jean Luther has been the nurturing and fussing editor from the date of the report to The Ford Foundation, March 1, 1971, to the ultimate production of this book. Her skill and judgment have contributed much to the book; her patience and determination have contributed much to my state of mind.

Finally, the felt presence of Dallin H. Oaks, the Executive Director of the American Bar Foundation, must be acknowledged. Dallin Oaks embodies, by his integrity and standard of excellence, the best qualities of a director of a research institute. His trust in us was invaluable. His standard of excellence influenced *us* greatly, but there was no attempt to influence the content of the work. He has seen to it that both administrative and moral support were available to those engaged in the research enterprise. He was particularly helpful in his comments about the penultimate draft of this book, and was equally objective about those conclusions with which he agreed and those with which he disagreed. He has left the Foundation to assume the Presidency of Brigham Young University, and his presence will be missed.

The love, patience, and support given me by my wife, Sharon Dunkle Marks, was and continues to be both a joy and an inspiration.

F. Raymond Marks
Project Director

PART ONE

The Context of
Public Interest Response

Introduction

Recent developments in the private sector of the legal profession[1] suggest that either the profession has begun a process of "agonizing reappraisal" or it is making token gestures to appease both the sound and fury of current social and political upheaval and the discomforting tensions located within the person of the practicing lawyer. It is too early to tell which.

New forms of organization have emerged; among them are the public interest law firm, the "community," "public interest," and "pro bono" departments, sections, or partners within major establishment law firms, and the law commune. The forms are new, but the underlying issues are old. The question of professional responsibility to the public has been raised with cyclical regularity—particularly over the past one hundred

1. In this book we define the private bar—the private sector of the legal profession—as covering all deployment of legal skills, techniques, and talent not distributed, supported, or offered under the auspices of government. The public sector of the bar is governmental deployment at all levels—local, state, and federal. For a fuller explanation of our working definition of the private bar, see page 52, *infra*.

3

years. So, too, have questions about the ways in which the profession can meet this responsibility.

The questions are not merely institutional. They are personal—excruciatingly personal—when asked by the individual lawyer. He not only has to deal with levels of responsibility as defined and accepted by the profession, he also has to define himself in relation to society and deal with the questions of what he would like to do and what he should do. He must resolve or ignore the possible conflict between his view of the lawyer's role and the rewards which presently reflect the way law in fact is practiced. He must ask the ultimate question: Am I a professional in the true sense of the word if I do not accept public responsibilities which I perceive to be part of my role?

The organization of the legal profession and the predominant system for delivery of legal services by meeting price demand in the marketplace have, to a great extent, frustrated satisfactory answers to both the institutional and the personal questions. Economic self-interest has been seen as an opposite of—or at least in conflict with—service of the public interest. And unhappily there is no indication that either the organizational or marketing features of the legal profession have changed sufficiently to encourage hope for satisfactory answers. On the contrary, despite the sincere and remarkable efforts of a small percentage of the private bar, despite a new type and degree of pressure from the young lawyers just now emerging from law schools, and because of the trends toward concentration and bigness within the profession as a whole— trends which reflect similar ones in the worlds of business and finance—there is cause to despair over whether permanent and satisfactory answers to these questions have been found or, under the circumstances, can be found. Law firms, like business organizations—or, perhaps, like *other* business organizations—have been getting larger. Today's middle-size firm is big by yesterday's standards. The large firms of today are beyond the limits of the imagination of twenty years ago. As clients have grown in numbers, and enterprise in degree of economic concentration, so too have the economic units which serve them—the law firms. The increasing demands for legal services by business interests have caused those services to become both highly organized and specifically reactive to the clients' needs for specialized services.

We do not mean to suggest, however, that all is lost, that there is no hope for lasting answers about the role and behavior of lawyers with respect to public interest and public responsibility. Some of the new sounds and sights are too healthy and too bold a departure to allow for such resignation. We simply mean that the new sounds, new energies, and new forms and styles of address to the public interest or *pro bono publico* questions must be viewed with a critical eye. Judgments will have to be made as to whether the new forms are compatible in the long run with existing patterns of professional organization—and professional ethos—and whether such efforts can be sustained by dependence on voluntarism.[2] The possibility must be entertained from the outset that a more radical change in professional institutions may be necessary even to sustain present levels of effort. Redefinition of role and responsibility may be involved.

2. Brennan, J., "The Responsibilities of the Legal Profession," *The Path of the Law from 1967* (A. Sutherland ed., 1968), warns that "dabbling" in public interest work or reliance upon permissive support for voluntary efforts will not be enough to discharge the bar's responsibility to the public.

chapter 1

The Profession and the Public: Historical Antecedents

This book, the result of a study undertaken by the American Bar Foundation, under a grant from the Ford Foundation, is an examination of the nature, the causes, and the viability of the innovative responses of the private bar to new demands for representation and new challenges requiring the deployment of lawyer skills. Originally the study was designated as "the *pro bono* project." The data for the study were obtained principally from interviews with lawyers engaged, full or part time, in conscious response to public need. After completing the field work, we had a strong feeling that the term *pro bono* obscured more than it revealed—from the viewpoints both of the researcher and of those involved who too lightly used the term, ignoring what it had come to mean, i.e., voluntary dispensation of skills on a nonfee basis. The term "public interest," which is used with greater frequency to refer to the new forms of endeavor, seems to be more explicative, but it, too, obscures; it oversimplifies. An understanding of the emergence of a public interest language and of the historical back-

The Lawyer, the Public, and Professional Responsibility

ground of present effort provides some important clues not only for testing the initial assumption that something new and innovative is occurring within the private sector of the legal profession but also for determining what kinds of tasks are seen by the profession—particularly by those operating public interest and *pro bono* efforts—to be demanded by unrepresented or underrepresented groups and interests or indicated by contemporary social, political, and economic circumstances. A self-portrait of the legal profession is involved.

"*Pro bono publico,*" shortened to "*pro bono,*" is a term that the profession has long used to refer to that portion of a lawyer's efforts or work which has a public quality or aim. Its literal translation from Latin is: "for the good of the public." More often than not it has been used to designate work for which the lawyer is not paid or paid at a rate lower than a lawyer or firm applying the term customarily receives. Free and *pro bono*, therefore, have been used synonymously. Furthermore, the term has not always been applied to the legal representation of clients. Frequently it has been used to designate hours spent or work done "for the public" on projects remote from the lawyer's skill base (but not necessarily remote from his influence base), such as serving on the boards of symphony orchestras, opera associations, hospitals, and school districts—even umpiring in Little League.[1] Time spent by lawyers in a more direct application of their skills which, nevertheless, was not spent on behalf of particular clients has also received the *pro bono* label. Many respondents in our study designated time spent serving as a bar association officer or on a bar association committee as *pro bono* work.[2]

After we examined lawyers' usage of the term *pro bono,* it seemed clear that the term, as it has been applied in the past, involved an intricate separation in the user's mind of the

1. All these examples were cited to us by respondents as types of *pro bono* commitments of either the respondents themselves or partners in their firms. See also E. Smigel, *The Wall Street Lawyer: Professional Organization Man?* 10 (1964).

2. It is assumed that the applying, on behalf of community boards, of lawyer skills by lawyers, such as cited at note 1 *supra,* is *pro bono* work.

central money-making operations of the lawyer from either a higher view of law as a public calling or from the lawyer's life *qua* citizen of the community. The very existence and use of the term *pro bono* signals a bifurcated view. The *pro bono* outlook is lofty; the term has a patrician sense which seems to go beyond its Latin quality. In this sense the lawyer sees himself working for his society. He is called by a higher duty; his work is voluntary; and it is noble.[3] More important, however, he views *pro bono* work as something he would *not* do in the ordinary day-to-day pursuits of his profession. This attitude merits examination, because, despite the bifurcated view, there have been in the past some underlying and silent assumptions that the public's business has been accomplished by the everyday professional pursuit for gain. These assumptions play a crucial role in understanding the emergence of both the language and the reality of public interest work.

The traditional view of a lawyer's role in a society with a legal system based on the common law relies heavily on the adversary method. A single interest—a single side of any conflict—is represented by the lawyer. He is an advocate in the true sense of the word. He is neither judge nor jury; he is not even a social conscience. He is simply an advocate. Accordingly, he does not relate his conduct to the social rules produced by the cases he handles. He is interested solely in seeing to it that the interest of the party he represents is as ably advanced as is humanly and professionally possible.[4] If this is done—on both sides of any adversary conflict—it follows,

3. In many respects the lawyers' *pro bono* "duties" resemble the attention of the upper class and upper middle class to the poor, the sick, and the delinquent at the turn of the century. Matched against notions of work for the "deserving poor" we can locate notions of a proper deployment of *pro bono* effort. See A. Platt, *The Child Savers* (1969).

4. Attention will have to be paid to the development of standards of professional conduct—from the early Canons of Professional Ethics (1908) through the new Code of Professional Responsibility (1969)—because this line of external and self-limitation, critical to any definition of professionalism, represents a departure from a role model defined solely in terms of client interest. Implicit in the fact of a code, and explicit in its statement, is a recognition that both higher principle and the interest of the public may serve to limit the extent of action on behalf of a client.

The Lawyer, the Public, and Professional Responsibility

according to the central assumption of the traditional view, that the result will be both acceptable and just. In particular, the justness of result has been seen as absolutely dependent on the lawyer's single-minded representation of his client. The lawyer in this way has accepted responsibility for the process only, not the result. Neutral principles have been seen as taking care of result. In short, the traditional lawyer has seen himself as serving the public interest by simply doing his daily job of representing only one side of a controversy. In fact, he reasons that if he does anything but serve the singular interests of his clients he is disserving the public interest.[5] It follows, of course, that no special effort is required to serve the public interest. Service to the public is necessarily a by-product of the adversary system.

Viewed in this context, early conceptions of *pro bono* work are more understandable. Since under this conception there was no demonstrable need to intervene in the workings of the legal system on behalf of the public, work such as community service, fund raising, or other charitable endeavors tended to be outside the practice of law.[6] However, one area of the legal enterprise, improvement of the quality and ethical structure of the bar and the bench, was seen as requiring professional representation on behalf of the public. Efforts in this direction were viewed sometimes in terms of the public interest and sometimes in terms of the self-interest of the bar. The perspective of the lawyers who sought professional improvement was important because when they viewed their

5. A. Fortas, "Thurman Arnold and the Theatre of the Law," 79 *Yale L.J.* 988, 996 (1970), mourns the passing of the lawyer's ethic that the individual client's interest, no matter who the client, is the *sole* standard of the lawyer's job. Fortas, in contrast to many earlier lawyers, did see the need to actively supplement this central standard with a requirement that lawyers be obliged to serve the entire community, including the unpopular, the needy, the unjust.

6. *Pro bono* work of this character readily lends itself to strategies of self-interest, too. Service on charity boards is considered an "ethical" way for a lawyer to indirectly advertise his wares. Law firms can define as "promotional" or "business getting" time spent on such boards.

role as discharging an obligation to the public they tended to characterize their efforts as *pro bono* work; when they viewed their efforts as relating to the parochial problems of the bar, they generally would not apply the *pro bono* description.

Early organized efforts of the private bar were therefore toward improving the quality and moral character of both lawyers and judges. Even when viewed as a problem internal to the bar, such efforts, by implication, entailed a recognition of the needs of society, of the public. And they indicated a further recognition, albeit implicit, that the legal profession owed a duty to the general public, which went beyond duty to clients. Recognition of this fact and response to it still appear to be fundamental to the acquisition and maintenance of professional status.[7]

The period of revival of professional legal organizations,[8] beginning about 1870, brought with it attention to and, in some instances, articulation of the issues involved in professional responsibility to the public. There had been previous bar organizations, but they had, for the most part, focused on problems of internal education and dissemination of information; they provided libraries and lectures for lawyers. In other words, early professional organization in the United States dealt with only one aspect of professionalism—the acquisition and improvement of the skill base. Improvement of professional skills does of course bear on responsibility to the public, but it can be accomplished internally, without either explicit demand from the public or explicit response to the public.

7. R. Pound, *The Lawyer from Antiquity to Modern Times* 5 (1953), states:

There is much more in a profession than a traditionally dignified calling. The term refers to a group of men pursuing a learned art as a common calling in the spirit of public service—no less a public service because it may incidentally be a means of livelihood. Pursuit of the learned art in the spirit of a public service is the primary purpose.

K. Llewellyn, "The Bar Specializes—With What Results," 167 Annals 177 (May 1933), similarly defines a profession in terms of "service ahead of gain."
8. Pound, *id.* at 251.

The Lawyer, the Public, and Professional Responsibility

This characteristic distinguishes the older forms of professional organization from those of the revival period and after.

Organizations of the revival period were responses to external as well as internal cries of despair over the sad state of both bench and bar. The legal profession was just emerging from what Roscoe Pound has referred to as the "Era of Decadence."[9] This era—from 1836 to 1870—was marked by a breakdown in the education and training of lawyers and a breakdown in those limited-scope professional organizations which did exist.[10] Moreover, perhaps because of these factors, there was widespread and open and notorious corruption among judges and lawyers.[11] The organization of the Association of the Bar of the City of New York in 1870 was a response to the public and professional outcry against these conditions. This association has been characterized as the first modern bar association started for the purpose of promoting "the practice of a learned art in the spirit of public service and advancing the administration of justice according to law."[12] Professional rebirth and articulated public need were inextricably intertwined in its organization.

A relatively small number of New York City lawyers—235 out of 4,000 lawyers then practicing—signed the call for organization. The signers agreed that the reasons for which they were uniting included their belief that

> organized action and influence of the Legal Profession, properly exerted, would lead to the creation of more intimate relations between its members than now exist, and would, at the same time, *sustain the profession in its proper position in the community and thereby enable it, in many ways, to promote the interests of the public.*[13] [Emphasis supplied.]

9. *Id.* at 223–49.
10. *Id.*
11. G. Martin, *Causes and Conflicts: The Centennial History of the Association of the Bar of the City of New York 1870–1970,* at 3–15 (1970).
12. Pound, *supra* note 7, at 249.
13. Martin, *supra* note 11, at 15.

The Profession and the Public: Historical Antecedents

Samuel J. Tilden, addressing the first meeting of the Association in February 1870, warned of possible parochial tugs on such an organization that could frustrate the higher professional calling. He said:

> Sir, [I] should be not unwilling that the Bar should combine to restore any power or influence which it has lost, except such power and influence as it may have deservedly lost. As a class, as a portion of a community, I do not desire to see the Bar combined, except for two objects. The one is to elevate itself—to elevate its own standards; the other object is for the common and public good. For itself, nothing; for that noble and generous and elevated profession of which it is the representative, everything.
>
> Sir, it cannot be doubted—we can none of us shut our eyes to the fact—that there has been, in the last quarter of a century, a serious decline in the character, in the training, in the education, and in the morality of our Bar; and the first work for this Association to do is to elevate the profession to a higher and a better standard. If the Bar is to become merely a method of making money, making it in the most convenient way possible, but making it at all hazards, then the Bar is degraded. If the Bar is to be merely an institution that seeks to win causes and to win them by backdoor access to the judiciary, then it is not only degraded, but it is corrupt.[14]

The same bifurcation—self-interest versus public interest—that is observable throughout our study (albeit at times under different labels) is apparent during the birth of modern bar associations, including that of the American Bar Association in 1887.[15] Constitutions, by-laws, and formal statements favored responsibility to the public. Discharge of this responsibility was something else—the reality and degree waxed and waned over the ensuing 100 years.

Bar association efforts, both past and present, even when explicitly addressed to the question of the profession's respon-

14. *Id.* at 37–38.
15. S. Baldwin, "The Founding of the American Bar Association," 3 *A.B.A.J.* 658 (1917).

sibility to the public, have for the most part been aimed at the general uplifting of the working level of the legal system, specifically by requiring better minimal skills and moral character of the system's major participants, the judges and lawyers. The bar's work for and on behalf of the public has not usually been in the nature of interceding for particular kinds of interests or groups. The system, working as it should (with quality participation) has been seen to be capable of producing just rules and due attention to public need. In short, bar associations have aimed their efforts for the public at the quality of the system as it is, not at structurally changing the system, supplementing it, or in any way compensating for its inadequacies. Even at this abstracted level, however, it has been implicit that the legal system is operated in trust for the public.

While accepting the view that the public's interest is automatically served by single-minded representation of client interest, and perhaps because of such acceptance, lawyers began to recognize the consequences of the inequality of access to legal representation. They began to grapple with the fact that the act of accepting or rejecting clients involves the discharge of a public duty. If the advocate is seen as representing the public interest through the process of representing his clients, special care need be taken that no man or no interest be denied an advocate. This awareness of a responsibility to the public regarding access first centered on issues concerned with representing the criminal defendant and the unpopular client—not always mutually exclusive categories.[16] Central to representation of both the criminal defendant and the unpopular client is an acceptance of the position that duty to a broader interest overrides personal predilection if the integrity of the judicial process is to be preserved. In the case of the criminal defendant, legal defense came to be seen as an imperative for the preservation of the concept of due process and the vital pre-

16. M. Ernst and A. Schwartz, "The Right to Counsel and the Unpopular Cause," 20 *U. Pitt. L. Rev.* 727 (1958).

sumption of innocence until proven guilty.[17] Similarly, the integrity of the judicial process was seen to require defense for the unpopular cause or party. (Of course, for the person who is both unpopular and a criminal defendant the issues are intensified.)

The broader issue, however, related to letting specific conflicts and disputes be resolved in the courts rather than in the public forum. Presumably, the provision of an impartial mechanism for the resolution of conflict is the ideal to which the profession is committed. An assumption implicit in the emerging professional tradition was that demand by unpopular clients for defense would go unanswered in the open market unless there was also an appeal to a higher duty. Recognition of this higher duty, even prior to its general acceptance by the profession, has given rise to some of the finest moments in Western legal history, moments such as Sir Edward Coke's defense against the excesses of the Star Chamber and the Crown,[18] John Adams's defense of the British soldiers accused of murder in the Boston Massacre,[19] and Charles Evans Hughes's representation, on behalf of the Association of the Bar of the City of New York, of the five Socialist legislators who were refused their seats in the New York Assembly in 1920 at the height of the postwar anti-Red hysteria.[20]

Notwithstanding these examples of response to a higher calling, there was no early universal statement by the organized bar regarding its public responsibilities. Although early views of a lawyer's responsibility to represent all who sought representation did include reference to the unpopular cause or client, they failed to include any recognition of a duty to

17. Curiously, however, concern for the indigent criminal defendant did not arise at the same time. Supplements to the price model for distributing necessary legal services came later.

18. C. Bowen, *The Lion and the Throne: The Life and Times of Sir Edward Coke* 315 (1956).

19. P. Smith, 1 *The Life of John Adams* 114 et seq. (1962).

20. Martin, *supra* note 11, at 206–12. The story of the action on this matter, which resulted in a deep split and bitter acrimony within the Association, is worth reading.

The Lawyer, the Public, and Professional Responsibility

represent those who lacked the lawyer's price. To a great extent the legal profession was reflecting the broader community where, before the beginning of the twentieth century, little formal attention was directed to the needs of the poor. The poor were dismissed as "paupers," morally stigmatized,[21] dependent on charity, and always with us.

But there appears to be a more specific reason why the legal profession did not develop a response to the poor as a group. The lawyers' ethos, before the emergence of the minimum-fee schedule, allowed for differential pricing—or at least was assumed to allow for it. This supposedly had the effect of meeting the needs of the nonmoneyed, nonpropertied individuals in the community, and did not require the development of any concept of group needs.

The emergence of a minimum-fee concept,[22] along with growing community attention to "the poor," forced the profession to consciously doubt the assumption that all in the community had access to counsel.[23] Paradoxically, although logically, it was when the bar acted more like a trade association than a profession that it was forced for the first time to formally take cognizance of the problem of making services available to some by means other than a market model for distribution of these services. By adopting a minimum-fee

21. See D. Matza, "Poverty and Disrepute," *Contemporary Social Problems* 610 (R. Merton and R. Nisbet eds., 1966).

22. See B. Christensen, *Lawyers for People of Moderate Means: Some Problems of Availability of Legal Services* 56–58 (Chicago: American Bar Foundation, 1970) for discussion of the theory underlying minimum-fee schedules.

23. See J. Hurst, *The Growth of American Law: The Lawmakers* 328 (1950), where he observes that most nonpoor white Americans could get counsel prior to 1850 and the rural poor could obtain counsel after 1850, but the urban poor were less and less able to obtain it. For the black American the problem still persists.

It may be, as one of our colleagues at the American Bar Foundation, Dorothy Maddi, suggests, that there is a more direct causal connection between the minimum-fee concept and community attention to the poor. She suggests that several major institutions and resources seemed at the same time to be formalizing structure and access and that a broader conception of poverty resulted from defining as poor those without means of access to a wide range of community resources.

schedule—by fixing a formal price of entry—the legal profession defined a group which could not afford services. If attention had not been paid to those who could not afford minimum fees, the bar would have been open to community charges and to self-admission that law and justice were for the rich and not the poor. The paradox is that the poor became more clearly objects of concern for the bar out of the bar's indifference to the poor in setting minimum fees in the first place.

As a term applied to professional work done for clients— as distinct from nonprofessional civic effort or effort addressed to professional standards—*pro bono* was first used to characterize work done for indigents. Moreover, the first professional discussions about supplementing the processes of gaining access to the law forum and of obtaining the services of a lawyer centered, as they still do, on the problems of the indigents. We are referring, of course, to the background and emergence of the legal aid movement.[24] Although there was legal aid work in New York as early as 1876, Emery Brownell, in *Legal Aid in the United States,* locates the real beginning of the legal aid movement in the years following World War I and in the publication in 1919 of Reginald Heber Smith's *Justice and the Poor.* There were only forty-one Legal Aid organizations in the United States in 1916;[25] the following year, at the first conference of state and local bar associations, a resolution was adopted urging bar associations to foster the formation and "efficient administration of Legal Aid societies for *legal relief work* for the *worthy poor* with the active and sympathetic cooperation of such associations."[26] [Emphasis supplied.] By

24. See R. Smith, *Justice and the Poor* (1924), and E. Brownell, *Legal Aid in the United States* (1951), for a history and description of the legal aid movement.

25. Brownell, *id.* at 11.

26. J. Bradway and R. Smith, "Growth of Legal Aid Work in the United States," 1936 U.S. Dept. Lab. Bull. No. 607, p. 166. Note the critical phrases "legal relief work" and "worthy poor." They describe the central charitable spirit of the effort, and implicitly describe the status of *pro bono* conceptions of professional effort. At the time *pro bono* and charity were viewed as one and the same. See notes 3 and 21 *supra.*

The Lawyer, the Public, and Professional Responsibility

1922 the American Bar Association had recommended that every state and local bar association appoint "a Standing Committee on Legal Aid Work."[27]

While early legal aid work focused some attention on the question of professional responsibility for equalizing access to the legal process, the subject by no means entered either the thoughts or the conscience of the entire profession. This is evident from only one fact: The delivered effort of organized legal aid work in the United States did not reach significant levels.[28] Even the possibility of reaching meaningful levels of effort had to await the creation of the Legal Services Program of the Office of Economic Opportunity in 1965.

Limitations seemed to be present from the start and can be best understood in terms of the outlook of the bar toward legal aid work. Charity, not professional duty, characterized the effort. *Pro bono* work and charity seemed synonymous. Legal aid work was something that was outside of professional pursuits—in fact, as organized, it was done by others, by staff lawyers considered marginal by the bar generally.

Most members of the bar saw Legal Aid Societies as deserving support but did not think that, in the absence of Legal Aid Societies, they themselves would have to perform the function of the Legal Aid Societies. It was a nice thing for the Legal Aid Societies to do, but not a necessary thing for the bar. Legal aid may in fact have been born, in part, of the practitioner's apathy toward the noneconomic aspects of the legal profession. The bar's indifference to legal aid work was underscored by the accommodations that were reached between the organized bar and the emerging legal aid movement. Ethical questions, such as solicitation of business[29] and of practicing in a

27. 47 *A.B.A. Rep.* 402 (1922).
28. By delivered effort we mean services received by, or benefiting, clients. See Brownell, *Legal Aid in the United States, Supplement* (1961), and J. Carlin, J. Howard, and S. Messinger, *Civil Justice and the Poor: Issues for Sociological Research* (1967).
29. *ABA Canons of Professional Ethics* No. 27.

corporate form,[30] were continually being raised by the bar as obstacles to legal aid work, until the limits and standards of legal aid operations were set in such a way as to avoid competing with the bar.

There were exceptions, of course, to the limited view of legal aid work as charity. Reginald Heber Smith, in his prescient book *Justice and the Poor*, urged a broader, more duty-centered view. He said:

> There is a direct relationship between legal aid organizations and the members of the bar, both as individual attorneys and as a collective body. Out of this relationship there spring reciprocal obligations. . . . While the responsibilities are bilateral, the performance is still very much one-sided. . . . [T]he lawyers are only dimly aware that *they owe a debt to legal aid work,* and as yet they have not taken the part which may fairly be expected of them. . . .[31] [Emphasis supplied.]
>
> [I]n all their work, [legal aid societies] are relieving the bar of a heavy burden by performng for the bar its *legal and ethical obligation* to see that no one shall suffer injustices through inability, because of poverty, to obtain needed legal advice and assistance. *Each case which a legal aid organization undertakes puts the bar in debt to it, for in the conduct of that case, it is doing the work of the bar for the bar.*[32] [Emphasis supplied.]

For Smith, legal aid work—rendering legal assistance to the poor—was a professional duty and not a charitable option. But, as already noted, there is little or no indication that the bar as a whole heeded his call. This is not to say that individual lawyers did not contribute money to legal aid or, as a matter of charity, render assistance to "deserving poor" on a no-fee or a reduced-fee basis; they did. It is simply to say that the bar as a whole did not assume this responsibility. There was no substantial effort within the organized segment of the profession

30. *ABA Canons of Professional Ethics* No. 35.
31. Smith, *supra* note 24, at 243.
32. *Id.* at 246.

20

to deliver services. Moreover, there is little evidence that the need for such services was even perceived.

While the token efforts to deliver legal assistance to the poor did not capture the attention or enthusiasm of the bar as a whole, a special segment of the problem area did seem to command growing attention: the problem of the indigent criminal defendant. Representation of defendants was seen to be both a necessity and a duty, even while the language and effort surrounding civil problems reflected attitudes ranging from indifference to charity. The growth of individual and bar effort to deliver legal services to the indigent defendant can be seen as necessarily extending the meaning of the term *pro bono*. It began to remove *pro bono* works from the realms of charity and to flavor them with an element of professional duty. To be sure, a charitable outlook still prevailed, but now it was charity tinged with duty or, for the more dedicated, it was duty tinged with charity.

Several factors seem to explain why perception of a professional duty to defend the poor in criminal cases preceded any comparable perception about the civil problems of the poor. First, criminal issues have always been more visible and more immediate. Also, since a very small percentage of the bar made its living on criminal defense, extending the notion of professional responsibility to include free legal counsel in that area would bring little threat to the economic self-interest of the bar as a whole. Most significant, perhaps, was the awareness that the Sixth Amendment of the United States Constitution provides that a person accused of a crime shall be entitled to the assistance of counsel.[33] This amendment treats the right of counsel as an essential ingredient for the equitable provision of due process. Although the issue involved would appear to be constitutionally clear-cut, judicial interpretation did not immediately extend this basic right to those who could

---

33. U.S. Const. amendment VI reads: "In all criminal prosecutions, the accused shall enjoy the right . . . to have the assistance of counsel for his defence."

not afford counsel. In 1932 the right to counsel was interpreted as applicable to the indigent defendant in state capital cases.[34] In 1938 it was extended to indigents in all federal felony cases,[35] and, finally, in 1963 it was extended by *Gideon v. Wainwright* to indigents in all state felonies.[36]

While judicial development was occurring, there was substantial legislative initiative as well. Even before *Powell v. Alabama* obligated states to do so, many jurisdictions had made statutory provision for supplying counsel to indigent defendants in capital cases, some provided for counsel in noncapital cases, and a few provided for counsel in misdemeanor cases. For the most part, however, legislative efforts to supply counsel for indigent defendants in noncapital cases occurred after the *Gideon v. Wainwright* decision in 1963. What legislative actions were taken received at least part of their impetus from pressures exerted by the organized bar in support of the public defender movement.[37] Bar activity in this area far exceeded support for the legal aid movement, which it paralleled in time and underlying conception. Nonetheless, inadequacies of the public defender system necessitated supplementation by the assignment of counsel—mostly from volunteer panels. Volunteers were not always easy to find. Somehow the perception of the accused's right to counsel and the system's dependence on the actual presence of counsel for the accused occurred ahead of any view that the bar had a duty to provide counsel for defendants who could not pay. The public defender, to be sure, was viewed by the bar as a surrogate for the bar's discharge of professional responsibility more than was his civil counterpart, the legal aid attorney. But the courts, both trial and appellate, found that cases awaiting assignment of

34. Powell v. Alabama, 287 U.S. 45 (1932).
35. Johnson v. Zerbst, 304 U.S. 458 (1938).
36. 372 U.S. 391 (1963).
37. See 62 *A.B.A. Rep.* 714, 718 (1937) for the conclusion of the 1937 Committee on Legal Aid Work that every "man accused of serious crime is absolutely entitled to counsel and . . . if he is too poor to employ one society must furnish him one."

counsel required judicial effort to locate counsel. And when counsel was found, he was likely to be from among the relatively few members of the bar who had made themselves available for assignment.

Two points here provide insight for a general understanding of the slowness with which the bar moved from the limited *pro bono* concept of professional duty to the broader public interest concept. First, notwithstanding ever clearer statements of the rights of the accused, the courts failed to articulate, by word or by deed, a corollary duty of the profession. Assignment of counsel frequently relied on voluntarism. Compelled assignment was used only as a last resort.[38] Hence, the existence of public defenders and voluntary panels possibly obscured for the profession the full realization of a duty to supply counsel in criminal cases. Duty, even, can look like a dispensation of grace if the correct symbols are used. Second, except for a small group of lawyers who made up the criminal bar in the large cities, thoughts and actions about due process and a criminal justice system were reserved for the judges and for the very young. Perhaps for the individual defense attorney allocation of energies was a matter of professional interest, commitment, and short-run career pursuits. But with criminal defense efforts limited to volunteers and with the central economic pivot of modern law practice becoming more tightly secured to a corporate client base, the profession as a whole was not forced to deal with the issue of criminal law and procedure.

This tendency to deflect criminal defense of indigents to young volunteer attorneys may reflect in microcosm the basic public interest dilemma. Law school curriculum has traditionally included constitutional law courses and criminal procedure courses, both of which touch on the right-to-counsel problem. The student is easily able to relate the right to counsel to issues of the integrity of the judicial process, to presumptions of innocence, to the relationship of individuals to the

38. We will return to the issue of compulsion vs. voluntarism in Chapters 2, 3, and 6.

state, and to a framework of limitations on state action. Moreover, he is able to relate these matters to a view of his role in the process. He is just beginning the process of being socialized into the legal profession. Later, as a young lawyer—either on his own or as an associate in a large firm—he may make the time to translate into action his conception of professional role. He can volunteer to defend an accused indigent or to appeal the conviction of an indigent defendant. He sees himself performing an important social role.

Institutionally, the major law firms have long had a permissive attitude about their associates taking "one or two indigent defense cases," and the partners in the firms are "interested" in the process. But as a lawyer progresses further in a firm, the competition—dollar competition—for his time becomes greater and the nonprofit aspects of his profession are relegated to an extracurricular status. Many of the older lawyers we spoke with during the course of this study said that although they used to take criminal case assignments they did not anymore, but that the younger lawyers in their offices were still taking assignments, carrying out firm "traditions" in this regard.

In summary, *pro bono* activity on behalf of indigent criminal defendants has the following characteristics: (1) It is conceptualized as a necessary adjunct to the criminal justice system; (2) it is organized, albeit at minimum levels—volunteer panels of young lawyers are made available for assignment; (3) it represents a tradition passed on from the young to the young and with clear institutional support among members of the private bar; and (4) unlike its civil assistance counterparts, at least some element of perceived duty is attached to it.

In a limited way *pro bono publico* work came of age with the development of the right of indigents to free counsel. Here the profession for the first time truly merged public interest and professional duty. Further, the representation of indigent criminal defendants, when added to the efforts of the legal aid movement, contributed substantially to the institutionalization

The Lawyer, the Public, and Professional Responsibility

of a nonprice supplementary distribution of services. The description of these efforts, however, continued to be in terms of *pro bono*. When the term *pro bono* has been used in reference to professional duties—serving clients—it has been most often limited to the defense of indigents.

Throughout the entire development of the *pro bono* concept the term "public interest law" was notably absent. As used today it connotes a substantially broader vision of a lawyer's professional duties. But it has not been used to describe work done by the private bar until quite recently. There are two main reasons for this. First, the level of professional services delivered on a nonfee basis was quite low, and second, there was a prevailing and unarticulated assumption that professional pursuit and public interest were synonymous. The laissez faire view that representation of client interest automatically led to just and proper rules for society as a whole was an extension of the Social Darwinism prevalent in the United States in the late nineteenth and early twentieth centuries.[39] Certainly no harm to the public could be seen to result from such a view unless people and interests not having access to the system were seen as important. And lawyers, like other professional groups during this period, were complacent.[40]

Once the people and interests not being represented forced the legal institutions to see them and abandon a laissez faire complacency, they sought intercession not from private practitioners but from the government. As the evils of urban poverty and congestion, unhealthy working conditions, child labor, and economic concentration of business were exposed, the emerging social welfare and progressive movements followed the Populists' path and sought legislative solutions to these problems. Moreover, they sought not merely legislation which would give new remedies to private parties but also— and this is important—legislation that allowed for the creation

39. See R. Hofstadter, *Social Darwinism in American Thought 1860–1915* (1944).
40. R. Hofstadter, *The Age of Reform* 148–64 (1955).

of governmental agencies with substantial corrective and regulative powers. The era of governmental regulation and governmental dispensation of powers dawned; its arrival had a serious impact on the legal profession. The prime effect was an intensification of the division of the bar. There were private practitioners serving clients—and there were government lawyers serving the public. A number of lawyers turned to public service.[41]

The split of the bar into private and public bars continued; the branches separated most pronouncedly during the New Deal and the twenty years following. The bifurcation was not limited to a division in functions alone but was accompanied by a division in professional responsibilities and skills as well. The public bar was charged with special responsibility for guarding the public interest. As the public sector received this charge, the private bar was further removed from obligation— not that the private bar had accepted the obligation in the first place. As a result, the private segment of the legal profession was further isolated from participation in identifying and resolving important social, economic, and political issues.

The lawyer's role in a democratic society had been viewed as central by de Tocqueville in the 1830s.[42] Certainly in the Revolutionary period the role of lawyers in community dialogue and community decision making was highly visible. By the end of the nineteenth century, however, the profession had lost much of its central moral and intellectual position and become an ancillary service industry for emerging and expanding business enterprise. Those professional instincts toward moral and social leadership which survived into the twentieth century were substantially—seemingly permanently—curbed

41. Henry Stimson claimed that when he turned to federal service as a U.S. attorney his "first feeling was that I had gotten out of the dark places where I had been wandering all my life, and got out where I could see the stars and get my bearings once more. . . . I have felt that I could get a good deal closer to the problems of life than I ever did before, and felt that the work was a good deal more worth while." *Id.* at 163.

42. A. de Tocqueville, 1 *Democracy in America* 278 (Bradley edition, 1945).

for the bar by its split into public and private sectors. Concern for policy became the domain of the public sector.

As we mentioned earlier, different skills and techniques were employed by each sector of the bar. The private sector had and still retains an almost holy—and possibly inaccurate—view of its method of operation. The training and socialization of lawyers has, since at least 1870, concentrated on process over content.[43] The skills and techniques employed are intimately connected with the operation of the adversary system. As the adversary procedure proved increasingly inadequate for identifying and resolving broad social conflict, there was a shift toward making rules and, consequently, policy in the legislature rather than in the courts. The private bar, however, did not consciously shift from the common law techniques; it continued to pursue process ahead of policy. The public sector, on the other hand, was given an opposite set of priorities; policy discussion and decision were to come ahead of concern for techniques. Nevertheless, the public sector developed and employed new techniques—including investigations, hearings, policy statements, and legislative drafting—to achieve new goals.

This is not to say that members of the private bar did not acquire these new skills and techniques. They did, and they used them for their business clients. They, too, used lobbying, legislative drafting, negotiating, public relations, arbitration, and the manipulation of political, economic, and social symbols. The point is subtle: The private bar's acquisition of these skills and techniques went unnoticed, perhaps even by the

43. The case method of teaching, introduced by Langdell at Harvard, while contributing greatly to the acquisition of professional status—an institutionalized skill base—is a commitment to process over substance. Its universal adoption may have had much to do with rigidifying skill and technique with the result that the profession could not adapt to changing social need and demand or to changing mechanisms of conflict resolution and avoidance. See P. Stolz, "Clinical Experience in American Legal Education: Why Has It Failed?" *Clinical Education and the Law School of the Future* (E. Kitch ed., 1970), and R. Nader, "Law Schools and the Law Firms," *New Republic,* October 11, 1969, p. 20.

practitioners. The religious insistence upon the centrality of the common law method had hidden private lawyers' capacity to deal with contemporary social, economic, and political issues. The common law method allowed for the disowning of result. The method was the message.[44]

Although the emergence of the public bar further obscured from the profession as a whole a sense of responsibility to the public, on the positive side it had much to do with focusing attention and stimulating dialogue on public interest issues. Further, the discussions which both preceded and followed the emergence of a public bar served to indicate more precisely what it was that the private bar had *not* been doing. Voices from without as well as within the profession took part in these discussions.

In 1888 Lord Bryce had commented on the general decline in the public influence of the American bar.[45] He attributed this decline mainly to the inability or unwillingness of the bar to deal with the political and social issues of the time.[46] Bryce

44. See A. Fortas, *supra* note 5, at 1002, where he appears chagrined at the emergence of the conscience- or policy-laden private lawyer. One wonders if he would show similar mystification at these qualities in the public lawyer. Contrast his views with those of Mr. Justice Brennan in "The Responsibilities of the Legal Profession," *The Path of the Law from 1967* (A. Sutherland ed., 1968), at 97, where Justice Brennan states:

Let us consider first what is still by far the most prevalent form of full-time public-service activity engaged in by lawyers: employment by the government. To an excessive degree, the paths of government service and private practice are now distinct and, in the vast majority of lawyers' careers, mutually exclusive. There can be no doubt, I think, that shuttling between government service and private practice should be encouraged. It is good for the lawyer to have his vision broadened and his judgment enriched by direct participation in the concerns of government and close contact with the public-interest considerations that, in private practice, are too often submerged. It is good for the government to have infusions of talent, fresh points of view and familiarity with private business and other aspects of national life with which career government officials necessarily tend to lose touch.

45. Lord Bryce, *The American Commonwealth* 306–307, 671–76 (Macmillan edition, 1917).

46. *Id.* at 673–76. This is merely another way of talking about the diminished importance of the rule of precedent—common law—and the emerging importance of a legislative approach.

found the Americans more conservative than their English brethren and than they, themselves, had been before. He noted that, while English lawyers took a leading role in seeking law reforms, American lawyers did not.[47] In other words, Bryce found that American lawyers simply did not address themselves to the public interest questions underlying the operation of the legal system.

Louis D. Brandeis, in 1905, further observed that the bar's overwhelming concern for the private interests of its large corporate clients had resulted in a retreat from both its independent position and its concern with questions of the public interest.[48] As the century progressed, it became increasingly clear that the perceptions of Bryce and Brandeis were accurate and that the bar was representing private interests far more adequately than public interests.[49] In discussing this, Brandeis said:

> It is true that at the present time the lawyer does not hold that position with the people that he held seventy-five or indeed fifty years ago; but the reason is not lack of opportunity. It is this: Instead of holding a position of independence between the wealthy and the people, prepared

47. Id. at 671.
48. L. Brandeis, *Business—a Profession* 318, 321 (1914). Brandeis, in this address delivered in October 1912, credits Bryce with the economic cooption argument. He quotes him as saying:
> Lawyers are now to a greater extent than formerly businessmen, a part of the great organized system of industrial and financial enterprise. They are less than formerly the students of a particular kind of learning, the practitioners of a particular art. And they do not seem to be so much of a distinct professional class. . . .
> But I am bound to add that some judicious American observers hold that the last thirty years have witnessed a certain decadence in the Bar of the great cities. They say that the growth of the enormously rich and powerful corporations willing to pay vast sums for questionable services has seduced the virtue of some counsel whose eminence makes their example important.

49. In 1908, at their twentieth class reunion Henry L. Stimson told his Yale classmates: "It has always seemed to me, in the law from what I have seen of it, that wherever the public interest has come into conflict with private interests, private interest was more adequately represented than the public interest." Hofstadter, *supra* note 40, at 163.

to curb the excesses of either, able lawyers have, to a large extent, allowed themselves to become adjuncts of great corporations and have neglected their obligation to use their powers for the protection of the people. We hear much of the "corporation lawyer," and far too little of the "people's lawyer." The great opportunity of the American bar is and will be to stand again as it did in the past, ready to protect also the interests of the people. . . .

For nearly a generation the leaders of the bar with few exceptions have not only failed to take part in any constructive legislation designed to solve in the interest of the people our great social, economic and industrial problems, they have failed likewise to oppose legislation prompted by selfish interests. They have often gone further in disregard of public interest. They have at times advocated, as lawyers, measures which as citizens they could not approve. . . . *They have erroneously assumed that the rule of ethics to be applied to a lawyer's advocacy is the same where he acts for private interests against the public as it is in litigation between private individuals.*[50] [Emphasis supplied.]

Here and elsewhere Brandeis raised the crucial issue of whether the narrow vision of professional ethical standards prevented fuller service to the public interest. Brandeis's comment suggested that the standard of ethics called for in representation that affects or may affect public interest should be different from that adhered to by lawyers where the dispute is between two private parties.[51] Yet the lawyers adhered to a view that the adversary system was a satisfactory model for the resolution of broader social conflict—at least it was the only one private lawyers cared to contemplate. These ethical

50. Brandeis, *supra note* 48, at 321 and 323. The late Mr. Justice Brandeis, too, seems to voice opposition to the simpler adversary model of lawyer responsibility advanced by Abe Fortas. Contrast these views with those of Fortas cited in note 5, *supra.*

51. Also, H. F. Stone, "The Public Influence of the Bar," 48 *Harv. L. Rev.* 1, 10 (1934) (Copyright 1934 by The Harvard Law Review Association), in an article criticizing the bar for failing to live up to its calling, for failing even to pursue the public interest, and for its captivity by business enterprise, observed: "Our canons of ethics for the most part are generalizations designed for an earlier era."

The Lawyer, the Public, and Professional Responsibility

standards contained the assumption that private-party law *was* public law.

Brandeis was the spokesman for the dissident members of the bar in the early twentieth century. He was dissatisfied with the results caused by a bar oriented toward business enterprise. For that matter, Brandeis would have remained unhappy as long as the bar did not address itself primarily to questions of public interest. Brandeis raised questions that are central to any study of public interest law: Can the issues of professionalism and public interest ever be separated? Is it possible to define the profession of law in a functional way without resting that definition on the public interest functions of the law?

The public interest content of present dialogue and effort was presaged fifty years ago by the Brandeis suggestions: The issue of public interest cannot be addressed without, at the same time, addressing the nature of the profession itself and the nature of the professional organization. Those who criticized the bar for its lagging attention to the public interest produced a basis for the reexamination of professional role. Brandeis was the boldest of these critics. He suggested that even the legal profession's special client group—business— should be viewed as one of the professions.[52] He applied three criteria to a profession:

> *First.* A profession is an occupation for which the necessary preliminary training is intellectual in character, involving knowledge and to some extent learning, as distinguished from mere skill.
> *Second.* It is an occupation which is pursued largely for others and not merely for one's self.
> *Third.* It is an occupation in which the amount of financial return is not the accepted measure of success.[53]

52. See L. Brandeis, *supra note 48,* at 1–12. A. A. Berle and G. Means, twenty years later, in *The Modern Corporation and Private Property* (1932), suggested that business-enterprise managers have policy responsibilities which arise out of their duty to several competing groups: the shareholders, the workers, the customers, and the community. This observation in reality extended Brandeis's suggestion that an analysis of business as profession was applicable.
53. Brandeis, *id.* at 2.

The Profession and the Public: Historical Antecedents

He believed business, as well as the bar, could and should fulfill these criteria. And, as professions, both groups required a set of self-limiting rules, rules arising out of a recognition of the public interest aspects of their respective callings or occupations.

The plea to business to adopt a self-regulating professional model and, indirectly, the plea to the legal profession to take a more rigorous view of its own behavior are neither casual nor gratuitous. They spring from the same basic philosophy that led to protective legislation, to regulatory agencies, and, ultimately, to a public bar. Where the public is affected, a duty is owed.

Brandeis's analysis suggests a public utility approach to the practice of law. When the term "public interest" is applied today to new forms of lawyer activities or newly recognized responsibilities, it seems indeed to spring from the same sources as did earlier judicial extensions of the public utility concept. The classic American case in which such an extension is spelled out is *Munn v. Illinois*.[54] There the United States Supreme Court upheld the constitutionality of the Interstate Commerce Act against the assertion that rate regulation (of grain elevators) was a confiscation of private property. In extending long-held common law principles, the Court said:

> This brings us to inquire as to the principles upon which this power of regulation rests, in order that we may determine what is within and what without its operative effect. Looking, then, to the common law, from whence came the right which the Constitution protects, *we find that when private property is "affected with a public interest, it ceases to be juris privati only."* This was said by Lord Chief Justice Hale more than two hundred years ago . . . and has been accepted without objection as an essential element in the law of property ever since. *Property does become clothed with a public interest when used in a manner to make it of public consequence, and affect the community at large. When, therefore, one devotes his property*

54. 94 U.S. 113 (1876).

> to a use in which the public has an interest, he, in effect,
> grants to the public an interest in that use, and must sub-
> mit to be controlled by the public for the common good,
> to the extent of the interest he has thus created. He may
> withdraw his grant by discontinuing the use; but so long as
> he maintains the use, he must submit to the control.[55] [Em-
> phasis supplied.]

The Brandeis critique of professional role suggests an extension of this "public utility" concept to callings as well as to
capital goods.[56] When one's property is used in such a way that
it affects the community, the community has a right to an
interest and a say in that use. Similarly, when the carrying out
of one's occupation or calling directly affects the welfare of
the community, the interests and needs of the public must be
of central concern. The point becomes even bolder when we
focus on legal practitioners, for we are dealing then with a
calling which is a profession, both by common recognition and
by self-proclamation. And a profession is, by definition, "pursued largely for others."

Furthermore, crucial qualities intrinsic to the legal profession lead it to have a greater impact on the public interest
and hence a greater involvement with the public interest than
do other professions. Indeed, it is difficult to define the legal
profession without acknowledging its public interest base.
Even those urging a traditional adversary model assume that if
the legal process is functioning correctly—and, axiomatically,
the legal profession—then the public interest is being served
and the existing or impending conflicts in the community are
being resolved—or at least being raised and structured in such
a way that they are capable of peaceful resolution. The purpose of the legal function, then, is realized only to the extent

55. 94 U.S. 113, 125–26 (1876). Mr. Justice Harlan, dissenting in the
Civil Rights Cases, 109 U.S. 3 (1883), discusses the utility concept extensively,
as does Mr. Justice Brandeis in a later extension of regulatory power. New
State Ice Company v. Liebman, 285 U.S. 262 (1932).

56. Ironically, the history of regulation stems from recognition and
regulation of calling during the guild days in England (1623). See the Statute
of Monopolies, 21 Jas. 1, c. 3.

that it accurately defines the public interest, i.e., in such a way that the definition itself does not produce new conflicts or intensify existing conflicts. It follows that the profession, too, assumes its proper role in society only to the extent that the legal system is effectively moderating community conflicts.

Implicitly, supervision by the state of minimum standards for admission to the bar and grant by the state of a monopoly license to represent parties and interests in court and to advise individuals, groups, and organizations about their relative positions with respect to the law are recognitions by the state that concern for the public interest must be central to the practice of law. It may well be that the education required by the state, the skills considered necessary by the state, and the limitations imposed on lawyers' behavior by the state are themselves so misguided that the grant of the monopoly license has given leverage to serve private and self-interest to the detriment of the public interest.[57] The fact remains, however, that licensing —a monopoly on the right to practice law—involves a recognition of the public interest character of the legal profession.

Brandeis's impact went beyond suggesting to the legal profession the centrality of questions of public interest, and even beyond attempting to identify the discrepancy between professional activity and public need. Brandeis was also an active agent. He had urged the advent of "the people's lawyer."[58] And, in the early decades of the twentieth century, that is what he tried to be; there was an active role he believed a

57. The form of the licensing is pertinent in this regard. It is administered by the judiciary. Lawyers are admitted to practice before the courts. That was the scope of the original grants. The state legislatures, prodded by the organized bar, supplemented this grant and forbid others to advise the public with respect to their legal rights. This securing of the role of solicitor was, by 1914, enlarged into the extended concept of unauthorized practice of law, whereby roles in certain kinds of transactions—not necessarily professional roles—were engrafted onto the license. See K. Llewellyn, "The Bar's Troubles, and Poultices—and Cures?" 5 Law & Contemp. Prob. 104 (1938).

58. Brandeis in the early 1900s had been and still was a preeminent corporate counsel in Boston. Perhaps his acute sense of public responsibility derived from his observation that policy was made by the powerful in the absence of outside or self-limitation and from his view that policies changed as either or both of these elements were added.

lawyer should perform.[59] Brandeis was the first modern "public interest lawyer," not only in his style but also in his search for more relevant tools and skills. He occupied for his day—in a lonelier way—the niche occupied by Ralph Nader today. He relied primarily on the "big case" approach. This approach, to him, was not simply an enlarged or extended model of the one-to-one private adversary situation. He saw it as an opportunity to publicly identify and articulate broad social issues and interests not theretofore even identified. By introducing the big case approach Brandeis was able to see to it that the decision makers—the courts, the legislatures, and the people—had the pertinent data before them.[60] The big case to him was an opportunity to debate policy. He saw the marshaling of a broad spectrum of social and economic data—the underlying facts—as central. The "Brandeis brief" made its way into history.[61] In *Muller v. Oregon*,[62] for example, which involved maximum working hours legislation, Brandeis devoted only two pages to traditional legal argument, and over one hundred pages to underlying social and economic facts and their analysis.

Implicit in Brandeis's action was an assertion—found also in his speeches and his later opinions as a Justice—that the individual lawyer and the collective bar have an obligation to temper and redirect their representation of private interests.

59. A. Mason, *Brandeis—a Free Man's Life* 254–81 (1946).

60. This outlook is fundamental to Brandeis's view of legal function. See his discussion in Associated Press v. International News Service, 248 U.S. 215, 248 (1918), where, as a dissenting Justice, Brandeis felt it was erroneous to treat the issue of claimed news piracy as a simple dispute between two private business organizations. He felt, rather, that broad interests in free speech, access to information, and consideration of economic concentration required a legislative approach. He decried the Court's creation of "Common Law Property" for one of the parties—Associated Press—*in vacuo* as a judicial response to private petition.

61. The similarity of Nader to Brandeis can be seen. Investigation and the presentation of new data is central. Because of differing lawyering strategies and different contemporary styles—and perhaps trust—only the immediate forum and audience sought are different. Nader finds less sense in making even a nominal presentation to a court.

62. 208 U.S. 412 (1908). See also Mason, *supra* note 59, at 248.

The bar has an obligation to attempt to locate the point at which private interest ends and considerations of public interest begin. Not to do so would result in the conversion of law practice from a profession to a service trade. Brandeis saw clearly that the profession in his day had already moved in this direction—away from exercising responsibility to the public and toward rationalizing and securing private interests. Lawyers had been pulled into the strong and expanding web of business.[63] Brandeis did not believe that the bar discharged its public responsibility by delegating the task to the public lawyer. He believed the private bar could become viable again. To him, professionalism and public interest were one. The bar could be both private and responsible. Brandeis was an optimist. In his days as an active lawyer, however, there was no general sense of resignation about the professional viability of the private bar. That came later—on the eve of and in the early days of the New Deal. It was this later dismay that accelerated the trend toward a bar bifurcated into private and public segments.

By the early 1930s the abuses carried out by business in

63. Brandeis was not alone in this view. Woodrow Wilson, in "The Lawyer and the Community," 35 A.B.A. Rep. 419, 424–26 (1910), said before he was President of the United States:

A new type of lawyers has been created; and that new type has come to be the prevailing type. Lawyers have been sucked into the maelstrom of the new business system of the country. . . .

And so society has lost something, or is losing it—something which it is very serious to lose in an age of law, when society depends more than ever before upon the law-giver and the courts for its structural steel, the harmony and coordination of its parts, its convenience, its permanency, and its facility. In gaining new functions, in being drawn into modern business instead of standing outside of it, in becoming identified with particular interests instead of holding aloof and impartially advising all interests, the lawyer has lost his old function, is looked askance at in politics, must disavow special engagements if he would have his counsel heeded in matters of common concern. Society has suffered a corresponding loss —at least American society has. It has lost its one-time feeling for law as the basis of its peace, its progress, its prosperity. Lawyers are not now regarded as the mediators of progress. Society was always ready to be prejudiced against them; now it finds its prejudice confirmed.

The Lawyer, the Public, and Professional Responsibility

the free-wheeling market of the 1920s were evident. So, too, was the role played in these abuses by the corporation lawyer. While there were few cases in which the actual dishonesty of lawyers was proved, instances of active manipulation by lawyers on behalf of the narrow interests of the enterprise client were abundant, visible, and unaccompanied by a sense of paradise lost. It was as if the public did not exist. Enterprise degeneracy and unquestioning lawyer "loyalty" to the client reached stages reminiscent of the 1860s. Again powerful voices sounded the alarm. They were a reminder of the voices of men like Evarts, Strong, and Tilden, who in 1870 called for professional responsibility and for stewardship in the public interest,[64] but this time the call was sounded in the midst of massive economic failure and growing social and political ferment.

Harlan Fiske Stone, addressing law school educators and law students in 1934, made the following eloquent plea:

> The rise of big business has produced an inevitable specialization of the Bar. The successful lawyer of our day more often than not is the proprietor or general manager of a new type of factory, whose legal product is increasingly the result of mass production methods. More and more the amount of his income is the measure of professional success. More and more he must look for his rewards to the material satisfactions derived from profits as from a successfully conducted business, rather than to the intangible and indubitably more durable satisfactions which are to be found in a professional service more consciously directed toward the advancement of the public interest. Steadily the best skill and capacity of the profession has been drawn into the exacting and highly specialized service of business and finance. At its best the changed system has brought to the command of the business world loyalty and a superb proficiency and technical skill. At its worst it has made the learned profession of an earlier day the obsequious servant of business and tainted it with the morals and manners of the market place in its most anti-social manifestations. In any case we must concede that it has given us a Bar whose leaders, like its rank and file, are on the whole less likely to

64. Martin, *supra* note 11, at 3–39.

be well rounded professional men than their predecessors, whose energy and talent for public service and for bringing the law into harmony with changed conditions have been largely absorbed in the advancement of the interests of clients.[65]

Around the same time, Adolf A. Berle described the modern legal profession for the *Encyclopedia of Social Sciences* in the following way:

> In both [England and the United States] the legal profession in addition to exercising its historic monopoly over control of the machinery of the courts and over the giving of private counsel to parties with respect to their legal rights became virtually an intellectual jobber and contractor in business matters. . . .
>
> The law firm became virtually an annex to some group of financial promoters, manipulators or industrialists; and such firms have dominated the organized profession, although they have contributed little of thought, less of philosophy and nothing at all of responsibility or idealism. What they have contributed, however, is the creation of a legal framework for the new economic system, built largely around the modern corporation, the division of ownership of industrial property from control and the increasing concentration of economic power in the industrial east in the hands of a few individuals.[66]

Berle observed that the corporation law firms of his time dominated the profession and set the style for the way that law was practiced. They attracted most, if not all, of the bright young lawyers. If a lawyer wanted to do something for the public he was "forced to turn to his books and become a scholar or to turn to public life and go on the bench or into political office."[67] However, this last, according to Berle, was not always as final as it might appear on the surface:

65. H. F. Stone, *supra* note 51, at 6–7.
66. A. A. Berle, "Modern Legal Profession," 9 *Enc. of Soc. Sci.* 340, 341 (Copyright 1933) by The Macmillan Company).
  67. *Id.*

> The forces of financial concentration needed political influ-
> ence quite as much as they did legal ability; and the lawyer
> who was successful in public life was all the more valuable
> to them. The common result was that after a relatively brief
> period of public office the lawyer returned to his profession
> with enhanced reputation and became a more effective
> servant of the evolving industrial scheme. The lawyer as
> statesman or public officer too readily yielded to the temp-
> tations of the lawyer as practitioner and interpreted or
> served the business groups instead of furnishing a states-
> manlike leadership. He conceived of himself as a techni-
> cian rather than an originator of policy.[68]

Berle added two elements. The public lawyer was subject
to cooption by private interests. And policy-making skills became engrafted to a lawyer's set of neutral techniques. The
lawyer with public role exposure added nonadversary skills to
the arsenal of techniques he was willing to array for his corporate client. He, as Berle suggests, deployed these skills as a
"technician" rather than as a statesman or an originator of
policy.

Harold Laski during that same period referred to the corporation lawyer as "the legal strategist of high finance."[69] Everywhere, critical evaluation returned the same verdict: The bar
was too heavily oriented toward the problems of business.
Expression of concern for the public interest, much less action
for it, was absent. By the mid-1930s the total bar effort directed
toward public needs was still meager: a little legal aid work,
some defense of indigent defendants, and some direct *pro
bono* work for the "deserving poor." But at the same time the
general indicators of the kinds of tasks lawyers should be performing for the common good were clear. Economic policy
had failed and needed reshaping. More particularly, the "ir-
resoluble conflict" between management and labor had to be
solved. Those aspects of the worker's life which contradicted
our view of a just society—dangerous working conditions,

68. *Id.*
69. H. Laski, "The Decline of the Professions," *Harper's Magazine*,
November 1935, p. 676.

inadequate wages and living conditions, unequal access to jobs had to be faced. The same conditions which had mobilized Brandeis to action a generation before were still rife, and in the 1930s the lack of their resolution was threatening the very fabric of our society.

To meet these tasks, interest in deployment of the public interest lawyer revived. The need for lawyers who would address themselves to policy discussion and decision was re-affirmed—lawyers who could use the techniques of social, economic, and political problem identification, lobbying, legislative drafting, administration, and public relations toward solving, settling, or mitigating broad and acute social conflict. A new breed of lawyers did emerge at that time, but they served almost exclusively in the federal government. The concept of the public interest lawyer was realized, but strictly as a public sector phenomenon.

The Douglases, Cochrans, Cohens, Franks, and a literal multitude of young lawyers took their places in the prolifer-ating agencies such as AAA, NRA, SEC, and NLRB. The alpha-bet-agency lawyers and the executive-branch lawyers replaced the public prosecutors as the dominant public-sector lawyers. They were a highly visible force in the public-policy debates and, in addition to their advocacy skills, they brought with them, or developed, additional skills: amassing large quan-tities of pertinent data for consideration by legislative and administrative bodies; drafting legislation and regulations; lobbying; and counseling rule and opinion makers. All these skills had also become developed in the private sector, but were rarely acknowledged or identified there.

Now such skills were to be deployed for what was defined as the public interest. These lawyers and the agencies they represented dominated policy debate for the next thirty years. The process of bifurcation, moreover, was complete: Public interest issues were dealt with in the public sector; private in-terests in the private sector. Private interests, however, con-tinued to play a dominant role in the shaping of public policy,

The Lawyer, the Public, and Professional Responsibility

a role which in curious ways was aided by the bifurcation of the bar. The public bar was serving the public, but was in daily contact with the private interests that it sought to regulate. An understanding by business and its legal representatives of the power of the government led to a redirection of their effort. For them government became the adversary. And the absence of clearly defined public interest groups allowed business-government dealings to lead to policy which frequently served only private business interests, by default if not by design. Private enterprise, paradoxically, came to have a larger voice in public policy by the pretense of and through the excuse of protecting its interests from the excesses of government.

Moreover, the process led, as Charles Reich has suggested, to an independent institutional existence for government.[70] Big Government had arrived. It had internal bureaucratic needs independent of the needs of any group outside of Government. A condition was fast being reached where Big Government was being represented by the public lawyer and Big Business was being represented by the private lawyer. The people were notably absent. This condition led Robert T. Swaine, an eminent Wall Street lawyer, to observe in 1949:

> Big Business, Big Labor and Big Government are all here to stay. But in the gigantic concentrated power of their aggregate collectivism there is real danger that they may be leading us along the road to state collectivism. If we believe that such an end would be a tragedy, and that individual freedom of opportunity in a system of private enterprise should be maintained, it behooves all of us who render "specialized service to business and finance" to seek such solutions of the legal problems of our clients as are compatible with changing social concepts and as will avoid the abuses of economic power to which our profession too often contributed in past decades. Deterred neither by self-complacence nor by the slanders of pseudo-reformers, we must strive, not alone for improving standards of practice, but as well for improving law, better adapted to the needs

70. C. Reich, *The Greening of America* (1970).

The Profession and the Public: Historical Antecedents

> of the times and better administered, and by the same token we must continue to challenge laws we believe anti-social and administration we believe arbitrary, never forgetting that the ultimate objective of our profession is that complete justice shall not only be granted to, but shall be enforced against, all members of society, rich and poor alike.[71]

The issue was formulated: Who spoke for the unrepresented and identified the "enemy"? The legal needs of the people were not being met by the profession—neither by the public nor by the private bars. Few stepped forward in the 1950s to either suggest or fill this need.[72]

But the 1960s brought new community attention to the issues of poverty and social injustice[73]—and once again brought the legal profession's failure into sharp focus. One part of this past failure was most glaringly evident—the failure to democratize the means of access to the legal system. With the advent of the Office of Economic Opportunity (OEO) Legal Services Program in 1965, substantial organized professional attention was finally paid to the question of how to deliver legal services to the poor in a broad-based nonprice manner. The limitations of the past legal aid voluntarism were recognized. This recognition was forced on the bar, in part, by increasingly vocal and persistent demands for specific legal service, and also by demands for access to the broader legal and political processes.

The American Bar Association played a central role in the efforts to bring legal services into the comprehensive war on poverty.[74] It was the ABA, in fact, which initiated the move to

---

71. R. Swaine, "Impact of Big Business on the Profession: An Answer to Critics of the Modern Bar," 35 *A.B.A.J.* 89, 171 (1949).

72. The efforts of law reform organizations like the American Law Institute or the Commissioners on Uniform State Laws, heeding the needs of consumers and debtors, for example, were exceptions rather than the rule.

73. See M. Harrington, *The Other America: Poverty in the United States* (1962).

74. See 1 CCH *Poverty L. Rep.* ¶6020, for the background of the OEO Legal Services Program. Also in 1965, the Federal Defender Act, 18 U.S.C.A. §3006A (1969), was passed. It extended the scope of both the assigned coun-

add a legal service component to the Office of Economic Opportunity.

The OEO Legal Services Program has had profound and paradoxical side effects on the profession as a whole. On the surface it has appeared to shift the burden for extending legal services to the poor from the private sector of the profession to the public sector. The deeper and more lasting effect, however, has involved the private sector of the profession in the operation more fully than it ever had been in the older Legal Aid model. The private sector of the legal profession was involved in the birth, the control, and the direction of the OEO Legal Services Programs. While the new public lawyer was funded principally by the federal government, OEO Guidelines compelled him to operate for the most part through existing and expanded bar and Legal Aid structures. The operations of Legal Services Programs were local. Some funds were derived locally. But, more important, the actual direction of the programs involved the local bar—either in its organized or its *ad hoc* form. The character of the programs was consequently influenced by the private bar. The Legal Services Program lawyer looked less like an agency lawyer than like a private lawyer with a public charge.

Further, the opening of new career opportunities, and the community ethic which grew up around them, revealed a new kind of lawyer, the short-term service lawyer. As his nonlegal counterparts, the peace corps volunteer and the military draftee, did not see themselves, nor did the community see them, as being permanently out of the private sector of the job market, neither did the Legal Services Program lawyer see himself, nor was he seen, as being permanently out of the private sector of the legal profession. The interchange between public and private service was thus facilitated.[75] Moreover,

---

sel and the public defender systems—federal funds were made available to pay assigned counsel and support defender projects in federal courts.

75. For comments on the interchange process, see Brennan, *supra* note 44, at 101.

even though he was being paid by Government, the new Legal Services Program lawyer continued to think of himself as a non-Government lawyer.

The OEO programs and lawyers contributed to the underscoring of a second major failure of the private bar—the failure to address policy issues. (The first major failure, of course, consisted of not adequately supplementing the price model for distribution of legal services to those who needed them.) One ingredient of the OEO program that distinguished it from the traditional Legal Aid approach was its overall commitment to law reform. This element was not only stated in the program guidelines.[76] but was also pushed as a program imperative by the funding and evaluating authorities. While this part of the OEO program met the greatest amount of resistance from the private bar, it nevertheless involved significant numbers of private lawyers in the persons of program board members. They became heavily involved in discussion and decisions regarding test cases, legislative campaigns, and the other paraphernalia of a law reform approach. The suggestion here is not that the law reform mode was the dominant mode for the OEO

---

76. The OEO Guidelines read:

First: To make funds available to implement efforts initiated and designed by local communities to provide the advice and advocacy of lawyers for people in poverty.

Second: To accumulate empirical knowledge to find the most effective method to bring the aid of the law and the assistance of lawyers to the economically disadvantaged people of this nation. O.E.O. will encourage and support experiment and innovation in legal services proposals to find the best method.

Third: To sponsor education and research in the areas of procedural and substantive law which affect the causes and problems of poverty.

Fourth: To acquaint the whole practicing bar with its essential role in combating poverty and provide the resources to meet the response of lawyers to be involved in the War on Poverty.

Fifth: To finance programs to teach the poor and those who work with the poor to recognize problems which can be resolved best by the law and lawyers. The poor do not always know when their problems are legal problems and they may be unable, reluctant, or unwilling to seek the aid of a lawyer.

1 CCH Poverty L. Rep., ¶6010.

programs; their service dockets made—and continue to make —persistent demands which placed a limit on law reform efforts. The important point is that the mere existence of the law reform docket created a verbal currency of public interest questions—a currency exchanged between the private and public sectors of the legal profession.[77]

The law reform approach of the OEO Legal Services Programs, and to some extent even the service cases, served to clarify another issue for both the bar and the community as a whole. Simply put, government became identified as an active enemy on some occasions and at least a passive adversary on most occasions. Even though governmental programs were relied on as a source of money and services for poor communities and individuals, government in its role as social reformer had lost its New Deal look or myth of monolithic beneficence. Governmental programs were seen as causing, as well as resolving, social conflicts. In addition, since these programs were seen to involve the distribution of rights, the breakdown of program administration came to be viewed as new injuries—actionable wrongs.[78] The new breed of lawyers, and the bar generally, were learning what the corporation lawyer had been acting on for years: Government as a limiter and as a dispenser of rights is an adversary. To some in legal services, as formerly to some in the corporate community, government was not just an enemy—it was *the* enemy. The paradox is deep. The conflict in role and loyalty is apparent.

The experience in the 1960s with public lawyers as poverty lawyers seems to underscore the inadequacy of a model that

77. There is a parallel to the ACLU and NAACP boards over the years as distinct from Legal Aid Society boards. Not that the latter did not make policy. They did each time they set eligibility standards—financial and subject and character eligibility. But there the board members made policy by default, by not discussing implications. In the law reform mode, board decision making was made active.

78. A changing view of Government, which shifts from seeing Government as social reformer to seeing it as a principal distributor of wealth, is brilliantly expounded by C. Reich in "The New Property," 73 *Yale L.J.* 733, 735 (1964).

calls for public lawyers to act as people's lawyers. That model seems to break down when the charge is to represent the interests of a segment of the population—in this instance, the poverty segment. The legal service program lawyer now shares with the private lawyer a fundamental characteristic: Each has an identifiable set of client interests to represent. No longer is mere access to the legal process the charge. But, unlike his corporate law counterpart, the legal service program lawyer has explicitly stated that he is concerned with public policy. This may be his single most significant contribution to the modern legal profession. He has become a kind of corporate counsel for the poor, and, because of a sense of mission, or because of a sense of professional pride, or perhaps because he is equalizing the combat, he holds up his head and announces: "I am the people's lawyer. Let us talk policy." And thus he provides one clear signal that the historical division into public and private bar is disappearing—if not in name at least in function and style.

By the mid-1960s the private bar was faced with the demands of groups which had either not been represented before or had traditionally been part of the "public" that the government bar purportedly represented. The legal profession as a whole—the public, private, and new-style OEO lawyers—was unable to meet current demand for services. Nor could comfort be taken in even the remote possibility that demand could be met, because the nature of the unresolved conflicts in the community and the intensity of the community temper suggested that the need for representation of neglected interests was seen to be different from articulated demand. The legal profession could well ask if it had been performing the function required of it: the structuring of community conflict so that it was capable of peaceful resolution. It could well doubt the adequacy of any of the traditional answers.

PART TWO

The Forms and Present Levels of Public Interest Response

Introduction

Our study examined the new forms of public interest response engaged in by the private bar. We were not concerned with cataloguing public interest effort, because it was our impression that the total of these efforts was as yet a small percentage of the total enterprise of the private bar. Rather, our intent was to study the public interest phenomenon by identifying and examining the various types of professional response to the needs of the public, in particular and in general. While we discuss our methodology elsewhere,[1] it is necessary for the reader, at this point, to understand our operational definitions of "public interest response" and "private bar" and some of the difficulties inherent in those definitions.

As a starting point in defining "public interest response" we chose self-definition—that which was called public interest work by the participants. There were obvious difficulties with such an approach. For example, one respondent in a large firm

1. For a discussion of the methodology used, see Appendix.

speculated that his exclusive work in the field of municipal bonds qualified as "public interest" work, because it produced the necessary capital for public works and projects.[2] Difficulties notwithstanding, we were forced to include self-definition as a part of our operating definition. Too much would have been lost by ignoring it, since self-definition of public interest work describes a perception of self in relation to the community. It also involves a self-definition of professional role. And this view of self in relation to both the community and one's own profession was far too central to our objectives to discard. The limitations of self-definition, however, meant that we would have to apply an external definition as well.

Any external definition of a "public interest response" must encompass at least one of two elements: (1) efforts to extend access to the legal processes to individuals or groups lacking the means to bring their injuries or interests into the legal system; or (2) broad policy or investigative approaches designed to identify social injury or particular abuses in advance of or in cooperation with individual or group identification of these wrongs. The former would include legal aid work, the extension of services for the "unpopular" case, and any other effort which involves extending services to meet or respond to articulated demand. The latter would include those efforts which precede articulated demand for service, or which frequently substitute for such demand. Thus we perceived two modes of public interest response—passive and service-oriented on the one hand, and active, reforming, and investigative on the other.[3]

The passive or service model of public interest response tended to be relatively specific and was easy for us to verify.

2. Unless there is a strong intellectual reason for attribution, names will be omitted, and assigned code numbers for respondents will be given. The respondent here is R53.
3. The two modes parallel the two basic approaches to lawmaking—the common law and code approaches. The common law approach is passive and assumes that the ills of society will make themselves known soon enough; the code approach represents an attempt to locate problems in advance.

The investigative or active approach, however, posed subtle problems. For if we attempted to determine which policy efforts qualified as "public interest" and which did not, would we not be substituting our judgment of public priorities for that of the respondents? The most we could do was add our "sense" of public policy as a weak verification of the self-defined activity of others.

When the lawyer becomes a policy planner, he may be engaging in his finest moment. But it is also his most frightening, because he leaves the familiar precinct of responding to a specific plea. He must rely on his own judgment. So, too, with us, the researchers. Without articulated demand, and without an opportunity to test our guidelines, we decided to take our own subjective standards into account. Perhaps two subjective standards—theirs and ours—would comprise a better index.

Our definition of "public interest response," then, is that which includes both efforts to democratize participation in the legal processes and policy efforts addressed to the overall good of the community.

Before deciding on an operational definition, we had to consider the alternative, an ideal definition of "public interest": policy resulting from the sum total of all interests in the community—possibly all of them actually private interests—which are balanced for the common good. In an ideal society the U.S. Congress or other rule makers, as ideal legislative bodies, would be public interest responders, weighing all interests before promulgating a balanced rule. The ideal rests on an assumption that all interests are equally represented before the decider or rule maker. This assumption, however, breaks down in the real world where the problem is: How can all the interests of the community be so represented that the goal of full airing may be reached? The method for obtaining a full or equalized presentation of competing sides in a conflict, whether they be people or ideas, is the central problem for our legal institutions. It is the central focus of a "public interest response."

The Lawyer, the Public, and Professional Responsibility

An operational definition, therefore, lies closer to the real world than does an ideal definition. A public interest response must always be considered, in some sense, as compensatory or remedial in an imperfect system.

The term "private bar," when simply defined, is *all of the professional enterprise of the legal profession that is not carried on by the public or government bar.* This definition, however, proves inadequate for our concerns. Since we were looking at new forms of public interest response, new techniques and skills, and new directions of effort, we saw we might have to extend previous definitions of what constituted a professional in the field of law.[4] Quite obviously we were concerned with the phenomenon of the public interest law firm—with unorthodox forms such as the Center for the Study of Responsive Law, Businessmen for the Public Interest, and the Washington Research Project. Our definition clearly had to cover such operations without getting into the parochial question of whether the participants were "men of the cloth." We therefore agreed that, if operations were manned by law-school-trained persons, whether or not those persons possessed the relevant license for the locale of their activity, we would consider the operations responses of the private bar.

The breadth of our definition of the private bar, however, seemed at first to raise some logical problems. If the lawyer-director of a public interest law firm was included, what about house counsel for corporations, or even businessmen with law degrees? Logically, they also should be included, although they seemed to lack a quality possessed by others—an ability to reach out to the public (in the case of the practicing lawyer) or to address questions of public concern (in the case of the research or public relations-oriented lawyer). Further consideration of our extended definition, however, convinced us that the law-trained executive and the house counsel possessed

4. On analysis, it turned out that what was needed was not a new definition of professional effort but simply a reassertion of the classic or traditional definition involving service ahead of gain. This, however, might be "new" for the profession as organized today.

the credentials for inclusion in our operating definition. Their inclusion lends balance to our analytic framework but actually matters little since efforts on behalf of the public from those segments of the bar are not, for the most part, visible. There is no question in our minds, however, that the enterprise employee-lawyers, along with their brethren, the corporation lawyers, do, by their actions and their decisions, profoundly affect public policy, whether or not they explicitly deal with the public interest issues.

The study, as we have said, is about new forms. This in itself posed problems. One of our principal difficulties lay in discriminating between that which was in fact new and that which merely appeared to be new. Because of differing individual and institutional attention to matters of public concern, because institutions always speak through their most active participants, because of the historical continuity of at least some level of professional response or reaction to public need and public interest,[5] and because of ambiguities arising out of attendant rhetoric, it was not easy to tell what was really new. We frequently tasted old wine in new bottles as well as new wine in old bottles. What, then, are the main elements of distinction? Discovering some of these elements is a necessary preliminary to a consideration of the forms themselves. At the same time it must be remembered that the older forms of response still represent a significant part of the bar's total delivered response to public needs and demands. The distinction between the old and the new can be found in differing perceptions of professional roles and skills, differing personal and institutional life styles, and differing degrees of formal address. The intensity of external crisis and demand upon the legal system is also a factor which shapes the newer responses and redirects the more traditional ones.

As already noted, there has been in the past some percep-

5. The legal profession, even in its stages of indifference, has been capable of attracting a relatively high proportion of idealists. Therefore it has always been capable of some public interest response, notwithstanding prevailing modes of professional socialization.

tion of the need to offer the services of lawyers on a basis other than price demand in the market. And, in response, there has always been some level of activity by the private bar. It has, for the most part, taken the form of voluntary effort by individual lawyers. Services have been rendered directly to clients unable to pay a full fee, who have come to the individual lawyers,[6] or services have been offered to the public, indirectly, through intermediate agencies, such as the Legal Aid Societies, the American Civil Liberties Union (ACLU), or the National Association for the Advancement of Colored People (NAACP). In some instances the lawyers have joined together for the combined offering of their services on voluntary panels such as those from which trial and appeals appointments are made in criminal cases involving indigents. Beyond that, the lawyer *qua* citizen has been active in a variety of civic enterprises, including charity and not-for-profit corporation boards. With the exception of formal public service rendered in legislative or governmental agency work, these were the traditional career or service options available in the past to the individual lawyer.

Such private activity has depended principally on the *voluntary* efforts of individual lawyers. The individual chose his activity according to his view of professional role of "duty" and his perception of need. He was for the most part unaided by an institutional definition of what constituted the lawyer's public responsibility. There were pockets of institutional definition, to be sure. Organizations like Legal Aid implicitly defined lawyer responsibility. So, too did ACLU, NAACP, the ABA, and the National Lawyers Guild. Needless to say, their definitions varied.

The dominant mode of the older response to need for legal services was simply to meet articulated demand. Services rendered were supplemental to the price model but very much

6. In a study recently completed by the American Bar Foundation, a survey of 1,496 persons in poverty indicated that 75 percent of the problems which these people took to lawyers were taken to members of the private bar rather than to a free service program.

in the same genre—one-to-one service to individual clients requesting service. To the extent that lawyers rendered the service on a basis isolated from the overall needs of the client, little attention was paid to the fact that the client belonged to a certain interest group and that his needs could be evaluated and responded to beyond his immediate description of immediate legal symptoms.[7] Even the organizations dealing explicitly with public need reflected this narrow perspective. The Legal Aid Societies and the panels for the defense of indigents accused of crimes took—or were "assigned"—their clients as they came. They did not seek out their clients nor did they look for typical overall problems which needed group or societal resolution. Organizations like the ACLU and the NAACP, which now look like forerunners of the public interest law firm, reflected, in their earlier styles, a traditional conception. Although potential litigation was viewed broadly by such organizations—i.e., it was placed in its situational context—for the most part, the mode of response was reflexive rather than strategic. The *amicus curiae* posture dominated. Situations rather than clients came to them. The posture of those organizations was similar to that of Legal Aid except that the focus was on a specialized segment of articulated demand—clients who raised constitutional issues, clients in "situations." Little effort was expended on locating problems or in setting priorities. The ACLU and others waited for the telephone to ring.

One major point of departure for the newer forms of professional response, then, relates to perception of need and the manner of meeting that need. The newer forms of response see that legal need is something more than that which is articulated. This departure is similar to that implied in the "law reform" charge given to the local OEO Legal Services Program lawyers; they were charged with being lawyers for the poor. In Brandeis's terms they were invited to become "lawyers for the

7. See F. R. Marks, *The Legal Needs of the Poor: A Critical Analysis,* Legal Services for the Poor series (Chicago: American Bar Foundation, 1971).

situation" and not merely advocates for the immediate client and his immediately articulated needs. The types of public interest response which we examined reflect this charge in varying degrees. Even where the traditional service approach is adopted as a model for rendering legal assistance to under-represented groups, such as the poor, the Indian, or the consumer,[8] the newer public interest lawyer has a broader charge than such an approach would indicate. He, like the Legal Services Program lawyer, is faced with a conflict between reform and service. He is learning to listen better for both the immediate and the deeper aspects of a problem. He more frequently asks questions about the further implications of the case he is handling and the meaning of his efforts. Whereas the traditional public interest forms of response allowed for the separation of effort from policy, the newer forms—even at their most mundane level—do not seem to allow for the same separation. It may be that the change has taken place more in the persons of the new breed of lawyers than in the institutions themselves. Either way, the change showed up in the operations we examined. A broader view of need was reflected there, a broader range of response. And the new style is permeating even the older forms. The ACLU and Legal Aid lawyers look more policy-oriented than they once did.

The second major point of departure between past and present styles relates to voice. The past was dominated by isolated individual response. The responsibility of the entire profession to the public was defined solely by the lawyers who were actively engaged in public interest or *pro bono* responses. The institutional response closest to a public interest response was that of laissez faire, a policy of permissiveness. In particular, law firms rarely encouraged public interest work; for the most part it was tolerated if not discouraged. Furthermore, the law firms did not seek an institutional voice in public interest work. On the far side of their permissiveness was a set of verbalized negatives which reflected anxieties about such

8. The categories are not mutually exclusive.

things as diversion of law firm time, diversion from the affairs of "paying clients,"[9] involvement in controversy, or general image. On the near side there was no sound. There may have been monetary contributions from the firm to the Legal Aid Society, but firms gave as a matter of charity and not out of a sense of duty. Individuals put their reputations and earning power on the line in policy debates. Firms did not.

In this regard, recent trends appear in bold relief. At the level of rhetoric, at least, there is now a quest by the law firms for an institutional voice. This is important because it raises the question of whether a law firm has an institutional meaning separate and apart from the sum total of the attorneys in the firm. It may be that in the law firm's quest for an institutional voice the character of the law firm will be affected. This will depend on whether the quest is hindered or furthered by the rhetoric. It will also depend on how well the new kinds of clients and issues are integrated into the daily life of these firms. In the past the character of law firms has been identified with the specific clients or type of clients the firms represented—firms have been known by the companies that keep them. One of the crucial questions raised in this study is whether the new endeavors of the respondent law firms will affect definitions of professional role and responsibility and whether the law firm will or can be seen in a different light by its lawyers, its clients, and the community. In any event, the quest itself is a major point of departure from the past.

The third major point of departure from the past involves issues of formality and organization of effort. There is a close relation between this point and the other two points of departure—perception of need and manner of response and the search for institutional voice—but it rests more directly on questions of voluntarism, professional autonomy, and the nature of professional organization. It involves questions of

9. The language was usually draped with mystic references to loyalty to clients rather than stated in terms of depletion of the firm's inventory of billable hours.

The Lawyer, the Public, and Professional Responsibility

professional life style and divisions of loyalty and effort as well. The newer forms or the revisions of older forms have developed a formal structure around the central assumption (tacit for the most part) that lawyers as lawyers *owe a duty* to society at large. Formalization of effort signals a departure from the view that a lawyer's professional life is one thing and that his personal commitments, including the delivery of professional skills for the good of the public, are another. This view is evident in the division our respondents made between the lawyer's "own time" and "firm time." The view may still be with us, as we shall presently see, but the language and institutional supports for the distinction between "own time" and "firm time" seem to be disappearing. This clearly sets apart the past and the present.

The world of the private practice of law is not monolithic, nor is the world of the law firms. Sole practitioners account for over one-half of the membership of the practicing bar.[10] But they are not a part of our study. This is not to say that their public interest work is not important. From what little we know it appears to be an important part of total bar effort on behalf of the public. Most of the sole practitioner's public interest effort, however, is informal. The sole practitioner is just what the term implies: The way in which he conducts his business, accepts or rejects clients, styles his practice, senses his professional identity, commits himself to personal and public interests, and uses his time lies always within the ambit of his choice. There is no requirement that the sole practitioner adopt a policy. He, in fact, makes policy about professional responsibility through the series of small decisions he makes each time he takes or does not take a matter and each time he presents a bill. Personal autonomy and professional style are

10. In 1970, 36.6 percent of all persons admitted to practice were sole practitioners. However, inasmuch as only 72.7 percent of all license holders were then in fact practicing—the rest being in private employment, in government, or retired—sole practitioners represented over one-half of the membership of the private "practicing bar." *The 1971 Lawyer Statistical Report,* table 5 (Chicago: American Bar Foundation, 1971).

almost one and the same for the sole practitioner."¹¹ Sole practitioners have delivered services on behalf of public interest in
the past, occasionally in the grand manner but more often in a
marginal manner. The sole practitioner, even the marginal
practitioner, has the facility to charge below suggested minimum fees, and often, because of the nature of his practice, he
is forced to. He also extends services on a contingent-fee basis.
In these ways the sole practitioner reaches significant segments
of the population who articulate demand for services but do
not have the means to pay full freight. In this way the sole
practitioner democratizes access to the legal processes. The
percentage of lawyers practicing alone and the greater frequency of their contact with those who are seen as under-
represented indicates that any present or future public interest
response of the private bar will rest in part with the character
and style of the sole practitioner. So, too, will it depend on
external definitions of professional role and responsibility,
which in turn, and again in some degree, will be affected by
the sole practitioner. For the most part, however, the way that
lawyers practice law together and the things they say to each
other through the media of law firms and bar associations are
more crucial.

The styles of law firms in the handling of both their external and their internal affairs are quite dissimilar. Size alone
is an important determining factor: Firm size varies from two
lawyers to over 150. Nevertheless, general observations can
be made about how lawyers practicing together handle their
commitments to one another, to the firm, to society at large,
and to themselves. Further (of direct bearing here), observations can be made about the role that the "establishment law
firms" play as culture bearers. The role is inescapable because

---

11. We do not mean to suggest that the sole practitioner is the sole
master of his professional identity. External definition of professional status,
external limitations on his behavior—as in the form of ethical standards,
whether enforced or not—and economic reality are major shaping forces.
For an excellent study of the sole practitioner, at least in an urban area, see
J. Carlin, *Lawyers On Their Own* (1962).

of the direct and indirect effects that such firms have on definitions of professional function, on professional ethics and standards, and on legal economics such as salary scales and fee schedules. The direct effects are achieved by operation in and influence on such formal organizations as the bar associations. Through competition for resources (lawyers) and customers (clients), the establishment firms also affect the very structure of the marketplace. The indirect effects are achieved by the fact that the stature, recognized excellence of skill, and levels of success of these firms serve as models for all others in the profession, whether already practicing or aspiring to practice. Therefore from the beginning of our study, change in formal structure within the large establishment firms occupied much of our attention. We were interested in the larger establishment firms because formalized and announced public interest responses were more prevalent there.[12]

In the past, that time which a young associate or a young partner in a large establishment firm devoted to an indigent prisoner case, an ACLU matter, or even a bar association committee was strictly his "own time." This was the dominant ethic; it existed even if a firm had a permissive policy toward *pro bono* work. A composite statement of the older ethic would read: "If a man wants to play tennis, or collect stamps, or represent an indigent defendant, or serve on a bar association committee on his own time, that is his business." The distinction was clear: There was the firm's time, and there was free time. True, there was not much free time. One need only exchange reminiscences with the law school graduates of the 1930s, 1940s, and 1950s to be regaled by tales of weekends lost, night secretarial and clerical crews, and the every-evening

12. The number of lawyers in a firm is not the sole criterion we use in our definition of a large establishment firm. The economic strength of a firm's clients and the size of its billings can also be meaningful. Our operational definition is satisfied if the firm possesses sufficient resources to compete effectively in national markets for lawyer talent and clients. This criterion may also be relevant to a firm's ability to publicly and formally dedicate a portion of its resources to public interest efforts.

dinner-break gatherings of the establishment lawyer in his native habitat.[13] If a young lawyer wanted to spend a busman's holiday doing legal work in the public interest, it was indeed his business, poor devil, and in the absence of an explicit policy permitting outside legal work it was also his risk.[14]

There was a subtle assumption underlying such an attitude: *Pro bono* work was not part of a young lawyer's professional obligation nor of his professional identity. It was an avocation. Moreover, this ethos was still prevailing for senior partners who had gone through the same socialization process and had spent years serving the clients and the firm. Their view of or justification for their own *pro bono* activities, which in terms of professional status were risk-free, was that these activities, either directly or indirectly, benefited the firm.

The inclusion in an establishment firm's formal structure of such things as allowing for public interest time, handling public interest matters as the firm's business, or providing for a separate public interest department is a signal that a break in tradition has occurred or is in the process of occurring. There exists now in many firms either a remittance of some professional time to the individual lawyers in the firm or a retention of some professional autonomy by the lawyers entering the firm. In this there is not only the implication that some of the lawyer's time is his own but also that some of his *professional* time is his own. A paradox may be seen here: This kind of formal structure indicates that what the individual lawyer sees as his professional duty is accepted by the firm as a proper professional pursuit; however, the formal structure itself may

---

13. The senior author here can attest to the verity of the cited bench marks, having in 1952 emerged from law school into the pace of a Chicago establishment firm where one was told that life could be worse—in New York. The ethos is captured by author-lawyer Louis Auchincloss in *The Great World and Timothy Colt* (1956).

14. The fact that the risk was taken during "free time" is of no consequence. It is a comment on the extension of institutional influence beyond the office door. One is reminded of the tale of Sewell Avery, who, as President of Montgomery Ward, fired a top executive who, vacationing with him, was late for breakfast.

be a subtle, and not necessarily deliberate, step toward re-acquisition of complete jurisdiction over the professional life of the individual lawyer.

The changing ethos is perhaps best underscored by an item in the *Wall Street Journal* on May 20, 1970, reporting the presence of Wall Street lawyers en masse in Washington, D.C., to protest the Administration's policies in Southeast Asia. The lawyers, 1,000 of them, traveled notoriously and openly on a working day. The *Journal* said:

> Today's trek to the capital is an outgrowth, the lawyers say, of their concern about the effect of the widening war on "our institutions." Some observers say, however, that it's simply one more sign of a growing tendency toward activism in social issues on the part of the New York legal establishment. . . .
>
> Many lawyers have always been active in politics on an individual basis, of course, and most firms have long permitted their men to spend working hours on such causes as community chests and acting as public defenders for indigents. But now an increasing number of big firms are arranging to devote significant portions of their energies to public service activities that are far less conventional. They range, for instance, from civil liberties defense work to efforts to challenge the management policies of General Motors and other big corporations.[15]

The explicit announcement by law firms of policy—even of a laissez faire policy—and the formalization of public interest work seems to us to have played a role in the phenomenon reported.

The formal attention paid by firms introduced an element of supervision over public interest work, sometimes explicit and sometimes merely felt. What had heretofore been casual, albeit skilled, for the lawyer in a firm was now plugged into a well established set of expectancies about skill, finished and polished product, and punctuality. By formalizing public interest effort the law firm adopted a sense of responsibility for

15. Wall Street Journal, May 20, 1970, at 1, col. 1.

it. This, too, was a marked departure from the past. What had been voluntary for the individual lawyer from start to finish had now lost its purely voluntary nature. The partners in firms sometimes supervised the work done for firms—in or out of the office—by the firm's lawyers. The standards of the firms were always involved.

In the chapters of Part II we will first look at the new forms in existing law firms: the public interest partner and committee, the public interest department or section, and the branch office. We will then examine the new functions of the volunteer agencies which, because of increased public interest activity by law firms, now perform a brokerage function for public interest issues and work. It will be a view of new agencies and old agencies with new scope. We will next examine a new and different type of organization, the public interest law firm. And, finally, we will look at the new efforts of the organized bar and the new types of lawyer associations. The view in Parts II and III is based on the data gathered during our study.

As our study progressed, one crucial question began to recur in many forms: Could we deal with the innovative responses of the private bar to public interest needs without dealing with the central issue of the overall professional responsibility of the private bar? Our answer was that we could not. The themes of vocation versus avocation and of the painful pulls on the individual lawyers toward "reputation" on the one hand and a sense of duty and public responsibility on the other were far too central to be ignored. The way that the bar as a whole addresses or attempts to address public interest issues is a direct reflection of attitudes about professional role. Ultimately, the meaning and scope of the "new" effort and the success of such effort will turn on this. The new forms may be only surrogates for the entire bar in this respect.

The emerging public interest response, then, may be as descriptive of professional disease as it is of professional health. Before moving on to an examination and analysis of

64

the new forms, we might consider an alternative statement which echoes the theme of this central dilemma. It was pronounced by Walt Kelly, the originator of Pogo:

> Resolve then, that on this very ground, with small flags waving and tinny blasts on tiny trumpets, we shall meet the enemy, and not only may he be ours, he may be us.[16]

16. Walt Kelly, *The Pogo Papers,* foreword.

cHApTER 2

ThE PrivATE LAw FiRM:
ThE PublIc INTEREST PARTNER
OR CoMMiTTEE

Among the larger established law firms the most frequently
adopted form for addressing public interest work or nonfee
matters is the designation of the "public interest" partner or
committee.[1] The ultimate meaning of formally designating
such a partner or committee depends on several factors: the
way the firm has customarily organized its acceptance and
supervision of regular fee-generating business, the type and
extent of past and present public interest work engaged in by
the firm or by the individual lawyers in the firm, the firm's
tradition about public interest work, and the individual and
collective styles of key partners and associates in the firm.
While the variations among public interest partners or committees are almost as numerous as the law firms having a conscious public interest response, the approaches can be classified for our purposes into three basic kinds: (1) firms that have
merely regularized their approval of nonfirm legal work (*the*

1. Other designations are: public service committee, community
service committee, *pro bono* partner.

auditors); (2) firms that, in addition to approving nonfirm work, have a procedure for taking on public interest matters as work of the firm (the integrators); (3) firms that participate in a single ongoing public interest project (the program approach). Although our classification differentiates between certain aspects of the address of firms to public interest work, there are elements and problems in the partner and committee approach that are common to all.

There is no intrinsic meaning in the selection of a public interest partner beyond initially identifying the policy of the firm with issues of public responsibility. Unlike the branch office or special department approaches, the designation of a public interest partner or committee does not in itself reflect an automatic commitment of dollars, manpower resources, or even moral imperative. In the short run, what follows such designation seems to be dependent on the individual character of each firm. The level of commitment and the ensuing performance are idiosyncratic. In the long run, however, the mere act of formally designating a public interest partner may have overall institutional implications for the way law is practiced. At the very least, a firm's designation of a public interest partner or committee is a statement by the firm that public responsibility is a proper subject for professional address. Even if viewed as ancillary to the business of practicing law (the business of earning a living) indeed, even if viewed as charity, a firm's attention to these matters carries with it the potential of involving partners and associates alike in dialogues about events, matters, goals, and priorities not theretofore considered part of the firm's business.

The process of structuring the firm's approach to public interest work can operate to distribute to more people work previously done by isolated individuals, or it can have the reverse effect of not distributing the work but of relieving the tensions of those who have not and do not respond to public needs by allowing them to say that now their firm is doing something. To enlarge upon our previous point: The ultimate meaning of a firm's designation of a public interest partner or committee will reflect each firm's initial and revised expectations about such work. One thing is clear for all firms—the designation of a public interest partner or committee invariably ends the *ad hoc* procedures previously used for such matters by the firms.

Firms which have a long tradition of public service work have formalized their approach as a concession to new demands and to their own changed perception about the role of the lawyer and the law firm in such work. We interviewed a partner of a firm which has had such a tradition of public service work, and he recognized that there were new inputs:

> In recent years there is more consciousness of an obligation of a lawyer of a firm to give legal means to the poor and to society.[2]

This particular firm had recently designated a public service committee to emphasize the firm's ethic and to offer "assurances" to law student interviewees and young lawyers in the firm who wanted to participate in public interest work.

The Auditors

The auditors do not seek to identify public interest work as firm work. They operate closer to the traditional model that public interest work is the separate affair of the individual lawyer. But they now see it as a separate affair that, because of demand from outside and increased activity by their lawyers, appears to have consequences for the firms. The adoption of a public interest style by the auditors does two things, apparently contradictory: It indirectly sanctions such work as professional work, even though it is still considered nonfirm work, and it brings to bear a modicum of control over that with which the firm had previously not wanted to involve itself.

Traditionally, associates in large law firms have felt it

---

2. Unless there is a strong intellectual reason for attribution, names will be omitted, and assigned code numbers for respondents will be given. The respondent here is R35.

necessary to receive approval from a partner before embarking on a nonfirm matter of public interest which would necessitate the use of legal skills. Those associates usually knew which partners were more likely to approve such projects; they also knew, approval aside, from which partners they needed clearance. Time records were rarely kept, and the relevant files invariably rested in drawers marked "personal." In short, the "firm" did not know of the activities of these lawyers. Such anonymity ended with the advent of the public interest committee or partner.

The public interest partner or committee in the auditor firms functions primarily to avert conflicts of interest. As the amount of the nonpaying activity of lawyers in these firms increases, the need to scrutinize more methodically the "intake" for such work becomes obvious. *Ad hoc* procedures are bound to break down. One partner cited us an incident in which one of the firm attorneys was "fairly deep into" a case before a conflict situation was discovered.[3] This embarrassing situation led to the designation of a public interest partner responsible for checking "nonfirm" work for possible conflicts with firm or client interests. The public interest partner, of course, has either to be aware of all of the work in the office, paying and nonpaying, or devise a procedure for letting all of the partners and associates in the firm know what is being done.

The regularization of intake may lead to other controls. Once the firm is aware of what its associates are doing it can ask: How much time is being spent? Many auditor firms have asked that all work—firm and nonfirm alike—be reported on time sheets. For example:

> We want to find out where our lawyers' time is being devoted to public service and how much money and out-of-pocket disbursements we are generating.[4]

3. R47
4. R13

The potential exists for limiting or inhibiting a public interest response. Auditors are still basically using a laissez faire approach, which, considering the accompanying formal approval of nonfirm work and timekeeping procedures, is a mixed message at best. Lawyers in firms seek guidance, which only sometimes are they able to estimate from attitudes in the firm. The guidelines are never clear:

> There is no hard and fast rule [about public interest work]—
> how much time you can spend and when you can spend it,
> other than a general rule which we have been able to live
> by so far: "So long as you are able to carry your share of
> the day-to-day workload, do what you want. And if you
> can pace it to where you have to take a week off to do *pro
> bono* work, and still cover your other tracks, that's fine.[5]

Some firms are seeking information to aid them in thoughts about more formal involvement in public interest affairs. Others keep time records and screen intake, but are simply watching and waiting before making additional moves. We feel that all we talked with were sincere about finding an answer, and saw no evidence that they were trying consciously to diminish the public interest response of the young lawyers. Most of the auditor firms were indeed sensitive about interfering with or seeming to interfere with the professional autonomy of their lawyers.

The ambiguity of this approach remains confusing for the individual lawyer. A firm styles the work "professional" but labels it "nonfirm work." The responsibility for finding the work is the lawyer's. But he knows he is subject to scrutiny about the nature of the work, the time spent, and, unavoidably, the level of skill he brings to the work. Further, he is left to figure out for himself how much regular firm work he will deliver for the salary he receives. Even when his public interest work is "approved," a young professional, caught in the ethos of a law factory, can develop considerable guilt about diverted

5. R47

time. We classified six firms as auditor firms—two in San Francisco, two in New York, one in Los Angeles, and one in Philadelphia. By and large the character of work taken by associates in these firms remained about the same after the designation of a firm committee or partner as before. Formal approval frequently only confirms an understanding of that which was always understood to be "approved" work. For some firms this can mean working for American Civil Liberties Union. For others it means appeals on behalf of indigents accused of crimes.

The Integrators

The firms we have classified as integrators have public interest or public service committees and have adopted procedures and policies *encouraging* the intake of matters under the aegis of the firm. This fact may be hidden from the outside world; briefs are not always signed in the name of the firm, and public interest clients and others dealing with individual lawyers in the firm may not understand that the firm itself is involved. But the anonymity of the firm does not change what the lawyers in the firm think or feel about it when the firm is indeed involved and communicates the degree of involvement to its lawyers. Those firms which have an integrated posture toward public interest work have clearly distinguished between that work and bar association work or other personal activities of their lawyers—a distinction not made by the auditors. The integrator approach is brought about by the attitudes and statements of key partners. Formal designation of a committee is usually accompanied by a greater degree of commitment and a clearer set of signals to the lawyers in the firm than we observed in the auditor firms.

The public interest partner or committee member in auditor firms is often simply a passive reactor to offered public interest cases; he refers the matters to interested associates. He rarely seeks cases. The partner in the integrator firms, on the other hand, actively seeks public interest cases or encourages others to do so, because it is something that the firm *should* be doing. The integrator partner in fact reaches out. He often seeks contact and association with those in the community who are likely sources for public interest cases and clients. He seeks to tie in to a network of case senders.

As we have indicated, the active approach to public interest work has as much to do with whether such work is treated as firm work as does the formal designation given a matter, or the way that files are maintained once the matter is in the office. In the past, firms may have represented charities, such as hospitals, as "firm" obligations—assigning file numbers and billing numbers, and directing partners and associates to do the work. Now some of these same firms engraft a sense of professional responsibility onto public interest matters, without necessarily limiting such effort to charity causes. The view that public interest work is firm work usually results in more active firm management of such work, e.g., the assignment of lawyers to it and supervision of the work.

We classify three large urban law firms in our study as "integrators." They are trying to incorporate their conception of public interest work into the daily management of the firm. When a partner from one of these firms was asked if he noticed a shift in the attitude of the firm's lawyers toward public service work he responded:

> There has been a noticeable shift to the extent that instead of having a permissive policy as in most of the big law firms, the associates and partners are actively encouraged to involve themselves in activities of the community. And those are the words [that] we use in the policy statement in our firm, that we have distributed to everybody, and that we put in our description that we send to the law schools.[6]

Wilmer, Cutler & Pickering in Washington, D.C., has formed a committee which consists of those partners and associates who concern themselves with the public interest work done in the firm. The committee's first duty is to protect

6. R61

the firm from conflict of interest problems. However, the committee also decides whether individual cases are really public interest material and whether the firm should charge full fee, a reduced fee, or no fee at all.

The Wilmer, Cutler & Pickering committee concerns itself with two kinds of situations: those matters or projects that individual attorneys wish to have "approved," and those matters with no definite sponsor. The committee is free to assign nonsponsored work to the appropriate department of the firm or to a lawyer in the firm who has relevant expertise.

The firm of O'Melveny & Meyers in Los Angeles has a committee structure similar to that of Wilmer, Cutler & Pickering. There is, however, no emphasis on handling matters by department. Six committee members (three partners and three associates) handle the intake and management of public interest work.

The O'Melveny firm appears to have three types of public interest approach. The first is typified by the representation of a large and sophisticated public interest client: The firm is general counsel for the local (Los Angeles) Urban Coalition. (The client, it should be noted, is itself a body representing the public interest.) This ongoing relationship is not constantly examined and "approved" by the committee but is, in fact, handled as are other major clients.

The second approach has the committee members acting as middlemen between those in the community with public interest matters in need of attention and lawyers in the firm who might be interested in doing such work as volunteers. The firm has ongoing but informal relationships with such organizations as the Western Center on Law and Poverty, an OEO backup center. When a case arises from one of these sources, the committee sends a memo asking for volunteers. In some cases it is necessary for a partner to supervise the work. The cases are handled as "firm business"; they are given their own files and at least the tacit blessing of the firm.

The committee is also charged with approving the nonfirm

public interest legal work of the firm's individual lawyers. This includes instances where the matter or case is not handled entirely within the firm (e.g., work on ACLU briefs) and instances where cases could be filed in the name of an outside attorney or organization. At the time we talked with the O'Melveny firm a few associates were working on Selective Service appeals. These associates were allowed to do such work but were on their own. This was true, too, for political activity.

The firm of Gibson, Dunn & Crutcher of Los Angeles has a committee which puts the firm's official approval on public interest matters. The committee conveys the impression that the work taken will be considered the firm's work, but they leave the primary responsibility for developing a public interest docket to selected or self-selected lawyers, who are encouraged to draw public interest work into the firm.

For the integrators the voice of the firm is strong, even where the operating styles are loose. The firm as a whole uses the term "we" when referring to its public interest cases. This indicates an approach which tends to draw more of the firm's lawyers into public interest work. The lawyers in the firm compete with each other on occasion for available public interest work already in the firm and also over who can bring the most exciting cases into the firm. Active lawyers in these firms are viewed with pride by the members of the firms and are used as symbols in any discussion of the firms' efforts. This attitude can be contrasted with the attitude of the auditors, who tend to isolate the public interest activities of their lawyers.

Even in the integrator firms there is a tendency to let "someone else" do the public interest work. The nonresponders, however, have a sense of satisfaction that the work is being done by a visible and related surrogate. This tendency and sense of satisfaction were observable also in the other forms of response—the branch office, the department, and released time.

The Lawyer, the Public, and Professional Responsibility

One of the most striking results of the integrator committee is the accessibility of public interest work to the lawyers
in a firm. Because of the communication network, the young
associate may find as well as produce public interest work.
But he is not necessarily left with the burden of doing both. He
can get his work from or send it to other lawyers in the firm.
Indeed, he will be assisted in this process. Although public
interest work may not have the same status in an integrator
firm as do traditional matters, it does have its own quality of
respectability. Public interest work can become an intrafirm
currency in acquiring the respect of fellow lawyers and their
aid and support for a particular job. And the associate in the
integrator firms is given at least a thin insulation which protects
him from reprisals from partners unsympathetic to public interest work; the work, after all, "comes through the firm."

The supervision of public interest work is basic to the way
the integrator firms operate. Even if this supervision is benign
or nondirective (because the matters involved are considered
"firm" work), its presence is felt. Where assignments are made
or partners coordinate the work of associates, the supervision
is clearer, of course. In addition, the lawyer in the integrator
firm knows that the firm always expects him to do a craftsman-
like job. He may also understand that the firm sees his public
interest work as a part of his overall training as a lawyer. (Even
the lawyer in the auditor firm, working on his own, has some
sense that his legal skills are involved and that he is expected
to do a good job. However, for these lawyers this sense of
understanding is not accompanied—as it is in the integrator
firms—by explicit or implicit supervision.)

The Program Approach
This category consists of firms in which a committee or partner
has approved or developed a single project as a public interest
response. Invariably such projects or programs provide staff
for a legal aid or legal service program office one night a week

or one night a month.[7] The work involved is then brought downtown and done at the office. Here the firms have adapted a traditional form of individual volunteer effort. They have simply organized the volunteers and moved from an individual to a firm effort. They sometimes do more. Some firms supervise as well as organize—a partner may reassign a case from one lawyer, who may have conducted the initial interview with the client, to another lawyer better qualified to handle it.

The program approach differs from the integrator approach in its single-mindedness. The firm has indicated and approved a specific public interest response. Although none of the firms we visited admitted to preempting the individual lawyer's public interest work, this form of response does seem to have a built-in chilling effect on individual public interest endeavors. The firm in effect is saying, "Don't do your thing. Do ours." The chilling effect, of course, does not take place if a firm's program is only one part of a broader response by the firm. However, firms taking this approach are usually content with their single-shot program.

Associates in these firms (as in integrator firms) who volunteer for the public interest program are somewhat protected from the reactions of partners who would not approve of the work if it were done on an individual basis or who might try in more obvious ways to intrude on their lawyers' volunteer time. When a partner participates or supervises, the associates are better protected. This can be seen from the experience of one New York firm:

A public interest partner explained that virtually no member of his firm wanted to participate in a specific project until the partner scheduled the participation of individual lawyers and supervised their work. At the time of the study, twenty-eight of the forty lawyers in the firm were participating in the project. Yet the partner readily admitted that the overall time

7. Examples: Young lawyers from San Francisco firms staff a Neighborhood Legal Assistance Program office on Saturday mornings; in New York, some firms cover a Legal Aid office one night a week or one night every two weeks.

committed to the program was not extensive.[8] He explained that in the early stages of the program he had not been as concerned about the overall time spent as he was about getting the project institutionalized. As a result, the overall time commitment had been kept at a relatively low level to appease some of the partners, and the *pro bono* partner was prepared, when necessary, to shift the program's work around so as to free the volunteer associates for work on regular clients' matters.[9]

A program is in reality a part-time branch office, and is rent-free, flexible, and easily terminated. Moreover, intake decisions are made with relative ease; the program managers are able to avoid the tough intake problems which plague other public interest committees and partners.

In all law firms engaged in public interest work, decisions about what matters to take and not to take are what separate myth from reality. It is at the intake stage that public interest partners or committees find out if their title is a shadow or is accompanied by commitment on the part of the firm. It is here they may face dissonance from partners: "Why *this* matter?" "How did we get this case?" "Can we control the situation?" and "Can't we do something else with these allocated resources?"[10] We do not suggest that the dialogue is frivolous. On the contrary, it makes very clear that it is one thing for a law firm to make an abstract commitment to public interest work and a vastly different and more complex exercise to decide specifically *what* work will be done. Making this decision, in the early stages of the public interest phenomenon, has

8. Total time committed was 183 hours for the first three months of the program. This averages a little over two hours a month for those lawyers who participated in the program.

9. R12

10. From our interviews with partners and associates alike, we heard more than fifty explicit statements of questions raised at the intake stage. They helped to spot not only the sensitivity of the intake stage but also the complex way that differing partner views are brought into play.

occupied a disproportionate amount of the allocated energies of public interest partners and committees.

The sensitivity of the public interest partner's or committee's intake task can be better understood when one realizes that the designation of the partner or committee was made, primarily, to satisfy one or two constituencies—the law students being sought by the firms[11] and the younger associates already in the firm—whereas the intake procedures must satisfy a wider range of constituencies. The competing views of partners must be adjusted; if a firm is to be maintained, all must be "satisfied" to some extent. The possibility, if not the reality, of response from the firm's regular clients must also be considered. So, too, must the firm's sense of responsibility to these clients and their interests. The client constituency may not actually be present during intake considerations, but they are represented by the partners, who speak for their interests. Additionally, there is the felt constituency of the legal profession; the partners' feelings about the "proper" uses of professional skills and "proper" professional life styles are involved.

Overall we saw a degree of circumspection and agonizing over public interest intake which betrayed the rhetoric of firms ("We have always allowed our lawyers to do this anyway") and the "ease" suggested by the more or less informal styles of handling everyday public interest caseload. In part, this circumspection results from awareness by managers that the formalization of a firm's style for handling these matters has obliterated former distinctions between firm and nonfirm work, that the act of designating, itself, is tantamount to certification of this vast unknown area as a proper object of law firm address. Even a minimal commitment of a public interest partner or committee gives the practice of law a dimension to which the firm partners are not accustomed. Caution follows. Perhaps the strangeness of the encounter most dramatically highlights the abdication of professional responsibility in the

11. The dominant reason given for designating a public interest partner or committee was "the law students." The reasons are dealt with in Chapter 8.

The Lawyer, the Public, and Professional Responsibility

past. Generally, the older partners had not developed a public style, nor had the firms developed a visible tradition of public service.[12] Public interest and public service matters were relegated to an extramural or avocational status. For the most part, then, even an attempt to formulate an approach to public interest work is new. Uncertainty, ambivalence, past habit, and obvious distress dictate the observed caution. Further, uncertainty and caution continue to exist well after there has been a decision to take a matter on as a "firm matter."

"Handling a matter as a firm" has a variety of meanings, and reflects varying levels of involvement. In some firms it simply means that secretaries, paper, and filing services are available to lawyers who take public interest matters on their own, and that the lawyers are free to work on these matters during working hours.[13] In these firms the public service partner has the principal function of *permitting* the matters to be discharged *as though* they were regular firm matters. He can tell the lawyer involved that there will be no direct penalties for working on a matter, that the firm, in fact, encourages his work "so long as he discharges his obligations to the firm's clients." It is up to the lawyer to interpret the limits and the double messages for himself. The firm has no external identification with a matter, and little or no internal identification beyond institutional permissiveness.

In other instances individual lawyers are encouraged to use their own names rather than the firm's name for external identification but to "by all means" consider the matter a matter for the firm and to draw on *all* of the firm's professional and ancillary services. In firms which operate in this way, and in the aforementioned ones, there is a tacit assumption that *pro bono* or public interest matters come to individual lawyers and

12. There are, of course, exceptions. Firms like Covington & Burling, Washington, D.C., were repeatedly cited to us as having a history and tradition of public service. This tradition was claimed by many, but only rarely did a law firm cite other firms as possessing a public interest or public service élan.

13. R49, R64.

not to the firm, and that the exercise of taking the matter on as a firm is principally supportive in nature. Somehow the public interest client never comes to be regarded as a "client" in the same sense as the firm's retainers or other regular clients. And this tends to be so in firms like these even when a matter has been addressed to the firm's attention from a source like the Lawyers' Committee on Civil Rights Under Law (LCCRUL). Acceptance of the case, quick assignment to a lawyer, and an attitude that the case belongs to the assigned lawyer still tend to undermine the client's status as a "regular client."

In yet other instances firms which have a public interest partner or committee insist on a parity of treatment between accepted public interest clients and regular clients.[14] These firms have a stronger sense of commitment. They seem more willing to use their names on pleadings or briefs[15] or letters about public interest matters. They are willing to be publicly identified for specific matters as well as the general gesture. For the more involved firms there is generally more supervision of work product. Some firms require the assignment of a senior partner or a supervising partner to any public interest or *pro bono* matter just as would be done for any other matter in the office.[16] (These firms also often require intrafirm consultation rather than simply invite it.)[17] Supervision frequently blends with active coordination. Attempts are made to match the expertise within the law office to the requirements of a given public interest matter; sometimes a matter is shifted from the lawyer who initiated it to an experienced trial man or to an experienced adviser.[18] In rare instances a firm's supervision has

14. R12, R47, R60.

15. Use of a firm's name is not always an indicator of commitment. The use of either a lawyer's name or a firm's name for paying matters for regular clients is frequently a regular function of a firm's style, as well as of local or jurisdictional rules and general local styles of practice.

16. R57, R62. Too often, however, a supervising partner's name is merely placed on the file. Some firms substitute the appearance of supervision for the reality of supervision.

17. R28, R63.

18. R12.

led to bringing in outside counsel or to trading matters with another firm.[19]

The public interest partner or committee then is not always merely reactive. In some firms we have seen evidence of positive planning toward a more active or more extensive involvement. The attitude behind this approach was typical of those we classified as the integrators and was accompanied by a high degree of supervision and coordination. It seemed to be part of the quest for total commitment.

In these instances the public interest partner or members of the committee are actively seeking or are already involved in a community network about matters that require legal vocalizing or clients who need representation. A partner may indeed be on the board of the LCCRUL, the ACLU, Community Law Offices, or the local OEO Legal Services Program. The public interest partner or committee member may seek a public interest docket or a specific project capable of absorbing the energies of a large number of the firm's lawyers. Such a project is usually in the form of the "big case," a challenge felt by lawyers in large firms to be uniquely suited to the talents, predispositions, and organizational realities of the large firm.[20]

The quest for activity and involvement is not always directed outward. Sometimes the public interest partner or the members of the public interest committee act as a catalyst for their firm's involvement; they have the job of selling their partners and colleagues. Many public interest partners or committee members were appointed to their positions in the first place precisely because they had added their voices and expressions of conscience to the growing external pressures for

19. These procedures can be used to avoid conflict of interest situations. Rather than being flatly told, "We won't handle the matter," the public interest client can be treated as the regular paying client would be and told, "We will find you other counsel."

20. See E. Smigel, *The Wall Street Lawyer: Professional Organizational Man?* 225 (1964). The seduction of this view is so total that we witnessed substantial frustration by partners and associates alike when their public service energies found them on the line, doing the job of representing poverty clients in what seemed to be only mundane day-to-day matters.

involvement.[21] Even after their appointments they continue missionary work among colleagues in an attempt to convert gesture into delivered effort. Paradoxically, the missionary work is not expended solely on the older members of the firm. Effort has been required to get the younger lawyers to volunteer their time. Successful missionary work is sometimes reflected in a firm's project, e.g., the twenty-eight lawyers out of forty in a firm who signed up to man a legal service office. Or the effort might result in the acceptance of a case involving police abuses,[22] de facto segregation,[23] or another piece of litigation or representation thought to be suitable for large-scale, multi-lawyer involvement.

Ultimately, the meaning attached to the public interest partner or committee depends vitally on the personalities of the lawyers selected to do the job, as well as on the pressures from, and the personalities of, the larger constituency that led to the designation of the form in the first instance. The creation of such a form can be either a positive or a negative step. A cautious and conservative firm, which feels that it has been coerced into a public interest posture, may very well use a coordinating partner or committee as a device for overseeing and controlling energies deployed on other than regular business, lest the diversion of these energies get too far out of hand. As new and increased demands are made, even those firms that have a more hospitable view, and some tradition, of public service come to view the device of the coordinating partner or committee as a means of clocking the time spent in that service. In this way they are able to make more enlightened moderating or extending decisions.[24]

For some firms, designating the public interest partner or committee is a temporizing move. These firms feel the need to allocate resources and effort to public interest work and have the will to do so but do not know which way to turn. As we

21. R12, R60.
22. R40.
23. R62.
24. R13, R62, R65.

have already pointed out, the partner or committee form is the simplest commitment. All options about the expenditure of dollars and manpower are still open. So, too, are noneconomic costs such as the risk of losing prestige and credibility not only among the firm's regular clients but also in the community at large—the ultimate source of public interest matters and clientele. Risks like these can be accepted slowly as cases and matters are taken. Meanwhile, the temporizing firms use the time to study the options available for major commitment, such as opening a branch office, forming a full-scale department, adopting an ongoing public interest project or client, or arranging for the systematic release of the firm's lawyers to such endeavors. An explicit policy choice sometimes becomes unnecessary, because the intervening process of accepting or seeking individual matters may produce a level and balance of public interest work satisfactory to a firm's members and associates.

The public interest partner or committee form of commitment can also be a dead end. Because of the relatively low costs of maintaining these forms, the public service partner or committee may be used, consciously or otherwise, as a place to ride out the storm, a place in which to take refuge while the demands for involving the legal community in contemporary problems subside in the law schools and the community alike.

We feel that the level of commitment to public interest work is revealed by the extent of partner or committee involvement and supervision. When there is little or no supervision, delivery of services can be erratic; it depends on volunteers from the firm, who receive no *real* encouragement. Time spent and quality of service vary greatly.

If public interest work is considered by members of a firm, and by the lawyer working on a matter, to be a part of the firm's work and if involvement in and supervision of this work is extensive enough, there is a standard of quality, an expected level of professional competence. The lawyers always feel that judgments will be made about their nonfee work as well as their fee work. The firm realizes that it too can be judged for such work—by clients, by the community, and by its lawyers. It seems to be committed to professionalism no matter what the undertaking.

The emphasis in this discussion has been on the large firm's coordinating partner or committee. It should be noted here that some of the most effective public interest work and some of the most direct delivery of legal services for meeting both articulated and inchoate demand has been done by the middle-size firms (such as Munger, Tolles, Hills & Rickershauser in Los Angeles) and small firms. Because of their own organizational and professional flexibility, smaller firms most closely resemble in their operating style the coordinating committee form we have just examined. These firms operate more or less as a committee of the whole.

In sum, there is nothing that the designation of a public interest partner or public interest committee by large firms can tell us beyond the recognition of a felt need to change at least some internal symbols. The designation can reflect energy or apathy, commitment or rhetoric, growth of a sense of professional responsibility or attempts to draw limits. It necessarily involves a risk to the firm that either attorneys within the firm or potential clients will utilize it as a forum for testing the reality of the firm's commitment. Conversely, it is a device by which the firm can test its lawyers for the levels of their commitment. The existence of a coordinating partner or committee can be seen as introducing a whole range of possible policy decisions. In turn, the operation of such a committee or partner can be seen as reflecting policy decisions already reached—explicitly or implicitly—as well as the personalities of the coordinating partners in particular and the firm in general.

Since this form is the most simple and neutral response to public interest need and demand, little can be inferred as to a general attitude or outlook of the firms employing it. Each firm must be looked at separately for its idiosyncratic outlook or response. One thing can be seen generally among the adopting

The Lawyer, the Public, and Professional Responsibility

firms: The label of professional indifference has been removed. Insulation from the demands of the times no longer exists; theoretically, at least, these firms are open for a business broader than that of simply responding to the needs of their traditional and sustaining clients.

chapter 3

The Private Law Firm: The Public Interest Department or Section

The public interest department or section is like the public interest partner or committee in many ways. Its options for screening or structuring intake, for auditing and controlling the levels of those efforts of the firm which are devoted to nonfee or public interest work, and for managing, supervising, and coordinating delivered effort are much the same. The options, however, become more important in the department form because the department (or section) represents a purposeful and substantial level of commitment—dollar and manpower. It has an element of permanency and continuity. And, as a seemingly permanent part of the law firm, the department interacts with both the internal world of the firm and the external world of the community. The public interest department, accordingly, can become a regular part of the law firm's address to the practice of law. It is perhaps this potential that has discouraged many firms; very few firms have adopted a department approach.

The public interest departments we observed have at least

85

one lawyer assigned full time or nearly full time to the task of responding to the new demands for legal service and for professional involvement on other than a price basis. The salaries or draws of the lawyers assigned, the costs of office space and secretarial services, and an aliquot share of overhead expenses are the minimal commitments that the firms make to the department. No direct economic return on the investment is expected.[1] The selection of the department form and the distribution of economic rewards to lawyers assigned to the department is, in and of itself, an attempt to bring the new style of work and the new client group into some parity with the way that the firm has always addressed its regular work and its retaining clients. The firms adopting the public interest department have all had a similar, departmentalized approach for handling regular client work. The designation of a public interest department, then, can be seen as a profound step. Public service matters and public interest clients begin to be systematically approached in much the same way as are tax, probate, and other matters. Even where a partner is the sole full-time lawyer assigned to the public interest department, the regularized and, theoretically, the equal status of the department enables him to assemble—with some authority—a team for the accomplishment of a specific major piece of public interest business. Too, the regularized status of this work enables the manager of the public interest department to make explicit or implicit demands on the specialized talents of partners or associates within the firm, seeking advice or consultation, and to share or assign work on a given matter. This is certainly the way that tax, antitrust, corporate, and other regular matters have always been handled. Lawyers frequently operate in more than one of a firm's major departments; the public interest department is now included. Many lawyers may be active in this department on some basis, but few will be permanent members. This is one of the unique items that a

1. Hill & Barlow in Boston is an exception to this statement about anticipated return. This firm's approach is discussed later in this chapter.

large, well-organized firm, in fact, markets: a structured organization with versatile skills capable of meeting *any* kind of demand for services, capable—overnight—of assembling and bringing to bear a vast array of resources and skills. Pepper, Hamilton & Scheetz, a Philadelphia firm, has fifteen lawyers who have worked in, received assignments from, and are considered "part of" its department of urban legal problems—a department principally addressed to poverty problems. All have responsibilities in other departments as well. But they can be easily and repeatedly brought together for the execution of a given matter.

The strength within a firm of the symbolic meaning of a public interest department can best be understood by considering the young associate in the team-assembly or lawyer-assignment process. An associate in a large firm may be perfectly willing and even eager to work on a public interest matter, but he has to consider whether his diverse commitments within the firm will enable him to do so. Even if he so decides, he has the painful job of allocating his time so that he is able to meet the work demands of matters for regular clients. The dilemma is generally present for the young associate even when the firm, in hiring him, has assured him that he will be able to work on public interest matters or that he will be "encouraged" to work on such matters. The dilemma of the double message inherent in his situation will also face the young associate if the firm has a public interest partner or committee. The young associate can limit his work to matters that extend the applications of his skills, curtail further work, or feel his way along.

He is "assigned" to a public interest department in much the same way he would be assigned to any other department in the firm, either on a rotation basis or for a single matter. In either event, by virtue of the regularized status of the public interest undertaking, he has some insulation from the pressures of those who attend to the regular business of the firm. Paradoxically, he may have more insulation from the "getting ahead" game than do the partners or associates permanently assigned. Moreover, since all of the public interest departments we observed were directed by partners,[2] the protection is formal as well as practical. A partner active in his firm's public interest department explained in a rather interesting statement the attitude of the department toward parity of cases and in terms of what we call the insulating effect:

> It is the objective of this department to treat poverty cases coming into the firm as firm matters, with the same credit to associates working on them as would be received for working on client matters.[3]

The statement is interesting because the partner by not modifying "client matters" with the word "other" does not give "the same credit" to poverty work; it reflects the hold of the traditional dichotomy. We often observed during our study a commitment toward the achievement of some parity but, at the same time, the existence of a psychological distinction between fee and new type or nonfee work. The habits acquired in the days when *pro bono* work was avocational remain. They will disappear slowly, perhaps never, if the realities of rewards for and approach to broader professional responsibility do not match rhetoric. Until that time, the most an associate can hope for is insulation from discredit, not credit itself.[4]

Partners direct on a full-time basis the public interest departments of two Washington, D.C., firms, Arnold & Porter and Hogan & Hartson. Both departments were new in 1970. Arnold & Porter plans to rotate partners annually to head its

2. Further, all these departments except one were directed by a partner devoting full or major time to the department. The exception was Foley, Hogue & Eliot in Boston, where the full-time director of the department was a senior associate. However, a public interest partner supervised the department and lent his prestige and status to "assignments."

3. Unless there is a strong intellectual reason for attribution, names will be omitted, and assigned code numbers for respondents will be given. The respondent here is R15.

4. Another partner (R31), who directs a public interest department, more accurately refers to the effect as a "shield" for associates.

department. The partner in charge (Bruce Montgomery during 1970) may call on any partner or associate of the firm for up to 15 percent of that lawyer's time. The 15 percent is a limit, not an allocation or tithe. The public service partner decides how much of the lawyers' time will be used; as of mid-1970 the caseload for the department had not required anything near 15 percent of the firm's total enterprise. Describing the philosophy behind the 15 percent limit, Montgomery stated:

> There are people who don't want to even contribute 85 percent of their time to commercial practice, and I think it's wise of them to recognize it early and get out.

The statement correctly spots the persisting primary goal of the firm and the built-in tension between this goal and a public interest orientation. As law is now practiced and as long as the levels of reward for doing a community's work remain low, the lawyer entering the field has a restricted set of career and role choices that affect the question of where and how he will practice his profession. In view of the unresolved tensions, the 15 percent limit may be realistic. Any firm that has a separate public interest department and keeps time records can have a fairly accurate view of the proportions of time and energy devoted to the new efforts.

Hogan & Hartson approaches public interest work in a way similar to that of Arnold & Porter, but its public interest department looks more regularized. A permanent partner, especially brought in from outside the firm, was charged in advance with the task of developing policy guidelines for the establishment of the department and for its operation. A senior associate was also permanently assigned to the department full time, and junior associates come to the department temporarily as part of the firm's regular policy of rotating new associates to all of the departments in the firm. The background of Hogan and Hartson's partner seems to characterize that firm's approach. The partner, John Ferren, came from Harvard Law School, where he had developed a clinical program and studies in the area of urban and poverty problems.[5] This selection of a knowledgeable man indicates recognition of a fact which again and again in the course of our study was made evident: The existence of a firm's good intentions does not in itself produce either an understanding of or a sensitivity to urban and poverty problems or clients having these problems. The firm of Hogan & Hartson, by its selection of a directing partner with experience, has moved public interest work a step further away from avocation. Not only has it regularized the approach to public interest, it has professionalized it. Hill & Barlow in Boston appears to have gone further in this direction. That firm has attempted to make the process of consciously doing the public's business pay—they are attempting to "do well" by "doing good."

Foley, Hoag & Eliot of Boston, with a part-time partner and a full-time associate, uses a department approach. Rather than rely on work coming in casually or simply coordinate the public interest matters that various lawyers in the firm acquire on their own, the firm makes a conscious attempt to develop the image that the *firm* takes public interest matters.

In none of the firms with public interest departments is there an attempt to preempt the field from lawyers in the firm who generate their own public interest cases or projects. The firms do, however, seek to coordinate and follow up the work generated by the individual lawyers. The firms' dockets of public interest matters are something more than newsletter listings; they perform the function of drawing in or coordinating the work of the firms' lawyers.

The permanent nature of the commitment of firms with public interest departments and the integration of the department into the firm places a different emphasis on the words "taking a matter as a firm matter." It also alters the dynamics of the intake, the coordination, and the audit and control functions. An established public interest department needs to

5. Prior to that Ferren had been an associate in one of the largest law firms in Chicago.

justify its existence. The partner in charge of it will usually take an active stance with his partners in seeking to overrule their objections to cases that he wants to take. He tries to predict their objects. After all, he is assembling a docket that will not only keep the department occupied but will also develop an image—an external character—for both the department and the firm. This does not mean that the other lawyers in firms with a public interest partner or committee are not also frequently active in advocating the taking of a given matter or client. They are. But they are not sustaining a going department. The public interest department seems to stimulate internal planning and internal avocacy. It, like the other forms, has conflict of interest problems, but the department partner will actively try to limit partner objections to real rather than imagined conflicts. The department partner does more than merely present matters for intake screening; he attempts to educate and sensitize his partners to the kinds of cases that he wants to take—the kinds of cases he wants the department and the firm to be identified with. He will be sensitized, of course, to the firm's views of "conflict of interest" and image. Intake is an orchestrated process, and the department partner attempts to perfect its art.[6] The ensuing dialogue within the firm has been cited to us as one of the positive results of the formalized approach to public interest law: Partners in private law firms are forced to consider problems not theretofore considered and to alter their more or less traditional views about what a law firm can or should do. In the process they must necessarily modify their views about the meaning and effect of the new type of work on their regular clients and regular caseload. A more formally structured dialogue, which more persistently points up the need to meet the demands of the department lawyer, or the community demands which he echoes, tests the substance of some of the partners' rote statements about role and conflict. Further, the firm develops an affirmative policy about areas of public interest concentration.

6. R31, and memo circulated by R22.

Such a policy makes the job of the department partner easier and seems to be a necessary guideline for the rest of the firm.

A case and project portfolio is a necessity for a partner directing a public interest department—and not simply because of the requirements of his department. The firm with a public interest department has placed at stake its reputation and credibility with the community. The department is highly visible; its effort and delivered service must match the announcement of its purpose. The firm looks to the department partner to deliver. He must actively seek cases—a function not always made easy by the conservative attitudes of establishment firms about the solicitation of business. He makes contact with community groups, the sources of potential business. For him the equivalent of country club solicitation may be on 14th Street in Washington or in Spanish Harlem in New York. He combs the list of the office's regular clients, too, to see if a large public interest project can be put together with client support—a housing project, for example. Most important, he plugs into a community network of public interest brokers— the public interest case and client finders, the market makers.[7] Because of the visibility of the department form, it is of little consequence if he does not find the network. The network will find him.[8] In either event, the brokers help him to avoid complaints from his more conservative partners about "chasing" business.[9] Further, by virtue of the prestige of the large firms with public interest departments, public interest clients such as the Urban Coalition and the Sierra Club (which often have an orientation as "establishment" as that of the firm they seek out) frequently come directly to the firm.

Keeping the department occupied is a minor problem compared to the problem of choosing between alternative types of clients, matters, and projects. Here the public interest department partner must make policy—or at least offer policy

7. The brokers are discussed in Chapter 5.
8. This statement was verified many times during our study.
9. R3.

to the members of the firm who make the choices. Theoretically, while the alternatives for deploying resources include such wide-ranging possibilities as sending manpower to supplement a legal service program, adding the brief-writing or counseling skills of lawyers to cases being handled elsewhere, directing representation of poverty clients in an everyday service mode (such as Legal Aid), taking or seeking a significant "reform" case, representing a community group, or playing a leadership role in an economic development matter, the large firm with a permanent department has few realistic choices. Part of the initial difficulty of the public interest partner's task is in recognizing the narrowness of actual choice. The firm's lawyers often want to make a big splash, and, as pointed out in the discussion about public service committees and partners, there is a natural predisposition in the large law firm toward "the big case." Sooner or later the public interest department partner will encounter frustration within the firm if he chooses to allocate the firm's energies to anything other than a "reform" model, that is, if he chooses to use lawyers to supplement an already existing service program. Although on-the-line legal service at neighborhood offices might be satisfactory to some of the lawyers in the firm, it hardly matches the overall expectancy about what the large firm as a whole should be doing. The expectancy rests on a broadly held view of the large firm. A public interest department lawyer, in support of his firm's choice of a reform approach, said:

> We have resisted appeals of the legal aid organization for full-time help as we are committed to the proposition that the large law firms are particularly suited to engage in efforts of highly sophisticated law reform test cases, in the drafting of proposed legislation, in the complex and dangerous litigation related to police-community relations, and in the organization and operation of self-help economic development organizations to such a degree that no other organization can so efficiently and effectively render service in these areas.[10]

10. R3.

In the public interest field this position is probably supported by the reality that individuals in the poverty community would rarely seek the services of a large firm directly unless a shingle were hung out in the ghetto.[11] Groups representing the poor will come directly to the firm once it has some credibility, but such groups, by their mere existence, evidence a step toward a generalized or reform model. It is not surprising, therefore, to find that all the firms that have tried to maintain a distinct identity for their public interest departments have developed an approach around a law reform core. John Ferren, the Hogan & Hartson public interest partner, has been attempting, however, to move more of the department's energies toward representation of individuals in poverty—toward a service model. He feels strongly that only by having such a caseload can the problems of the ghetto be understood, an understanding he regards as a necessary precondition to a reform approach.

Selecting a strategy of approach is not the only broad policy consideration for the firm with a public interest department. Areas of concentration have to be selected, too, or at least thought about, against the day when a case or project opportunity arises. This boils down to the questions: What interests will the firm represent or not represent? What clients? The predispositions of the lawyers will play a part in these selections. So too will the character of the firm's sustaining business. A firm representing a major polluter will be unlikely to choose environment as an area of concentration. Representation of municipal corporations would seem to negate concentration on suits against municipal bodies. On the other hand, a regular client group—such as real estate developers— may offer the possibility of a project. The reality and the conception of conflict of interest are clearly involved in the selection process and will be discussed elsewhere. The question we have to ask now is whether public interest clients or interests

11. See discussion of the branch office or the released-time forms in Chapter 4.

are balanced in the scale in the same way that a firm balances two competing private and paying interests. If style is affected each time a client is accepted, we can see that there may, through the operations of public interest departments, ultimately be some shift in the answer to this question. For now, it does not seem that the conflict is seen purely in terms of two clients; it is still seen in terms of clients versus things "we are free to do." And this may not always work one way. It may also be urged that a given public interest client may limit the firm's freedom to take certain traditional clients. By virtue of representing tenant unions, for example, one public interest department partner has expressed some doubt as to whether the firm should represent landlords.[12] He wants to maintain a credibility with tenant-group clients. The dimensions of the problem are complex. As we shall see in a separate discussion of clients, the policy approach may result more from the question "What interests do we see ourselves opposing?" than from "Whom shall we represent?" The first question is present even when a firm attempts to make itself available to public interest groups seeking representation on an ongoing basis. The answer will determine which groups are accepted and which are rejected.

The large law firm is uniquely suited to a retainer, or ongoing, relationship with its clients. The firm is accustomed to thinking about and acting for clients in a broader way than simply handling a single case or matter. This is particularly true of the Washington law firm; lobbying with Congress and administrative agencies is an evident part of its ongoing services. Advisory and counseling services are also an important part of the large firm's approach to its clientele. This richness and variety of services leads naturally to a search for group clients; the firms want public interest "retainers." As one public interest department lawyer said:

> The purpose of the department is to take on public interest representation on a nonfee or diminished fee basis. . . .

12. R22.

> essentially, to provide access to our firm to groups, princi-
> pally organized groups . . . which had in the past never
> really had access to a firm like ours.[13]

Once a strategy of approach is devised and a matching
caseload is taken (or, conversely, as a caseload affects the revision of strategy) the public interest department stands in a
different position with respect to assignment, coordination,
and supervision of work. When matters are originated by the
department, the partner in charge has the choice of making
assignments or accepting volunteers. If volunteers are taken
from among those of the firm's lawyers who are most en-
thusiastic about or most interested in the general or specific
problem, work will tend to be "assigned" in an uneven way.
Further, the strength of specialization is not as easily brought
to bear. Nor is the partner in charge meeting the challenge of
trying to accomplish in the firm as a whole a broader, more
balanced view of professional role and responsibility. On the
other hand, enthusiasts tend to do a better job and present
fewer supervisory problems. All the firms we visited have tried
to make assignments to people who have indicated at least a
willingness to handle a matter. Sometimes this involves "working on someone"—a specialist, for example. The effort is
somewhere between soliciting volunteers and drafting "volunteers." Public interest partners feel they can accomplish
their mission with reluctant lawyers by a general educational
approach and by trying to intrigue their quarry when the appropriate case encourages them to do so. All recognize that
the departments should be something more than umbrellas for
those who would in any case find a way of doing public interest
work. In the final analysis, it is commitment and effort on the
part of the firm which will validate the selection of a department approach. One lawyer stated:

> Ultimately, of course, fulfillment of our professional obliga-
> tion as individuals and as a firm will depend on what we

13. R26.

decide about the firm's institutional responsibility to support *pro bono* [efforts].[14]

The initial expectancy and operating experience of firms with public interest departments is deeply embedded in the notion that the work will not pay. This does not mean the firms will not and have not accepted fees for such work. They have—as an exception rather than as a rule. Several factors contribute to the centrality of ideas about eschewing, or at least not expecting, economic return. There is the past identification of good works with charity. There is the present reality that groups and interests needing representation cannot afford legal fees, at least not legal fees commensurate with the scope of their problems. There is the further reality that our society has not yet found ways of distributing the cost of needed legal service so that those supplying the service will not have to bear the entire burden. Too, there is the ever present spectre of ethical limitations. How can one seek some reward from doing good without running afoul of rules about solicitation or champerty, maintenance and barratry—without being charged with stirring up litigation and dispute? Fee avoidance is a facile way out, particularly in view of *NAACP v. Button*.[15] Also, not unrelated to notions of charity, but far more pervasive and personal, is the exercise of self-denial. One way of reassuring oneself that the public interest is being served by one's efforts is to remove the discomfort of reward. If a fee is attached, it may draw into question for the public interest lawyer whether something is worth doing at all. Further, by ducking the issue of a fee, the hard question of what constitutes "public interest" is avoided. A definition of "public in-

14. R22.

15. 371 U.S. 415 (1963). In *Button,* the Supreme Court, allowing solicitation of clients for law reform cases, draws a clear distinction between fee and nonfee work. One should also note that the District of Columbia Bar Association has recently changed its rules and allows a public interest law firm to advertise (In the matter of Advertising Conducted by Monroe H. Freedman and The Stern Community Law Firm, Opinion of the Committee on Legal Ethics and Grievance of the Bar Association of the District of Columbia). For a fuller discussion of this action see p. 166, *infra.*

terest" perhaps needs to be avoided by lawyers and clients in those situations where they themselves are actively selecting goals and priorities.[16] Where no fee is involved, the question is indirect or covert.[17]

One firm, Hill & Barlow, has ventured into murky waters by describing its new department as one which does the public's business and at the same time expects, and plans for, an economic return. The firm's department of urban and public law was established in the summer of 1969. An area of concentration—housing and land development and urban planning—that was, from the outset, likely to produce an economic return in the process of accomplishing public ends was chosen for and by the new department. This area's long history of public debate and legislative development has resulted in a system of subsidies for those seeking to accomplish public ends —i.e., an increase in the supply of quality low-cost housing units. Provision for adding lawyers' fees and other development costs to the federally insured mortgage base has produced anticipation of fee payment when a development entity is found or brought into being and when a development project is successfully accomplished. Hill & Barlow's new department has brought together and acquired skills in "zoning, urban planning, housing, administrative agency work, and [work for and in the creation of] non-profit organizations."[18] Organized around these skills, the department has been able to attract developers who are in the process of promoting low-income housing projects and to aid in the creation of development companies by community groups who want to develop housing for their constituencies. Hill & Barlow's department has made a profit. In addition to the new department, Hill &

16. As Edward H. Levi suggests in *An Introduction to Legal Reasoning* (1948), action is possible only because the actors refuse to wait for total clarification. Policy is debated and affected in the gap of ambiguity.

17. See discussion in Chapter 9.

18. This information—and that which follows—about Hill & Barlow's department was obtained from an interview with Carl Sapers, the partner in charge of the department.

Barlow has tried to develop a general consciousness about public interest work within each regular department.

Hill & Barlow's department has a rigid intake procedure. It refuses to be "the dumping ground" for every item that the rest of the firm wants to define as *pro bono* or public interest. The partner in charge of the department, Carl Sapers, explained that he and his people

> quickly disabused our partners of throwing to [the Department] trial cases of black guys accused of rape in Roxbury, or a young black entrepreneur who came into the firm and wanted corporate advice.

Sapers indicated that he and others thought these matters should be handled by the firm, but should be part of the ongoing professional responsibility of the firm's other departments—litigation, tax, corporate, and others. He explained that such matters should

> be handled in the appropriate department—if they are paying or nonpaying. Each department [should] take as much nonpaying work as it can tolerate; that's the department's business.

In its area of concentration the urban and public law department develops a network of clients and broad community interests which naturally leads to an acceptance of a great deal of free work, but free work related to the department's specialization.

The Hill & Barlow approach raises two issues simply and boldly: (1) the issue of economic return for doing the public's business, and (2) the issue of whether a firm's total public responsibility toward community clients and interests who cannot afford representation can ever be met in a single department. Hill & Barlow rejects a choice of strategies that seeks to include or exclude certain public interest responses. We will deal with the issue of economic burdens and incentives more extensively in a separate chapter.[19] Here, however, we raise the

19. Chapter 13.

The Lawyer, the Public, and Professional Responsibility

issue by posing the questions: "In the long run doesn't any piece of public business have to receive broader social support than simply that of a lawyer willing to accept the entire burden? Won't the public interest responders and the bar generally have to receive both social and political acceptance for their undertakings and part of their costs?" In the short run this may not be necessary. But in the long run the private bar will have to take on the task it has avoided in the past: leadership in the public debate about problems, priorities, and allocations—about which values should be sanctioned, which problems should be met, and which costs should be accepted. Hill & Barlow has not done this to any greater extent than have other firms. They have set up their department in an area for which the long history of the national debate on housing policy has already resolved some of the issues. These issues are not all resolved by any means; much leadership and wisdom are yet needed. But, relatively speaking, the area is in a matured field of public policy and therefore easily invites the attention of, and application by, the bar.

The second issue bears closer examination, for it presents the glaring weakness of the public interest department approach. It is the issue of whether a department that is predicated on a noneconomic base can be the total expression of a firm's public interest commitment. The unstated set of eligibility rules inherent in the strategy or caseload selections made by a public interest department excludes even nonpaying clients from being selected if they do not meet the eligibility criteria. Sophisticated and sensitive operation of a public service department may avert the gross excesses or distortions of this screening process. But because the firms with a public interest department have relegated to the department the task of defining the firm's public interest approach—even though isolated cases are acquired and handled by individual lawyers —the certification of matters worthy of public interest is left to individual or small-group preference and excludes an across-the-board sensitivity to matters which should, in the public's interest, be exposed and treated. In the long run, efficacy of effort will, of course, always depend on a high degree of individual prescience and skill. To gain this strength, Hill & Barlow seems to have coupled its choice of a department approach with a command that the rest of the firm remain sensitive and responsible.

In summary, the public interest department represents the clearest break with tradition that established law firms have undertaken to date. By virtue of the form's internal and external character, the law firm employing this form is committed to a course more likely than not to bring the firm into the arena of policy-planning—if for no other reason than to serve as a guideline for the development of a docket for its ongoing department. A law reform approach has been the usual mode for public interest departments. With this approach, the developed expertise and underlying philosophy seem to have the potential of leading involved firms into areas of law they have not theretofore embraced. New client groups emerge as a result. Theoretically, the form has as much flexibility as the looser form of the public interest partner or committee, but in practice this has not been the case. As a relatively permanent structure, a department seems to be more viable than a committee; because a firm consciously allocates its resources to a department, the department seems better able to withstand the pressures of producing fee-generating work on a regular basis than does a less formal arrangement. Further, it is visible from inside and from outside the firm as a structured level of commitment, a structure which, in the natural process, the department managers seek to preserve. On the other hand, the department may have a tendency to preempt the development of public interest work in other parts of the firm.

For the public interest department, voluntarism is still the underlying rule. But it is institutionalized voluntarism and for this reason has the potential, at least, of being viewed as a professional duty.

Even though the public interest department does not seem

The Lawyer, the Public, and Professional Responsibility

as new as the branch office or released-time programs, which we shall examine next, the department is more of a break with tradition. It represents—although perhaps only symbolically— an attempt to move beyond the *pro bono* culture. A branch office or released-time program, on the other hand, can be seen to rest more heavily on past modes of charitable support, of treating public interest work as something outside of and separate from the way that law is practiced in the firm. A department integrated into the firm has at least the potential of affecting to some degree the manner in which the law firm sees its role and offers its services. By its innovative manner of operation the public interest department increases opportunities for finding—for the firm itself and for the profession as a whole —approaches to problems that are capable of being institutionalized into the everyday practice of law and that, in turn, are capable of being supported by the community as a whole.

chapter 4

The Branch Office and Released-Time Approaches

A public interest department, as we have just seen, tends to organize along law reform lines. It searches for new client groups and new interests. In the process, the line between the unmet articulated demands by clients for legal service and the independent perception by lawyers of need for their services is blurred. New groups, acting as surrogates for individuals with injuries or seeking to achieve group goals, or groups organized in the hope of coalescing fragmented interests in the community—suggesting a sense of injury where none had been articulated—emerge as natural clients of public interest departments. The groups may present many facets of the poverty problem—welfare, housing and tenants' rights, police-community relations, crime and delinquency—but neither the service sought nor the service rendered can be described in traditional *pro bono* terms. Service to individuals with nothing more than self-identified injuries is for the most part avoided. When we examine the branch office and released-time programs, we find an opposite set of operating principles.

The Lawyer, the Public, and Professional Responsibility

Service is the primary model for the branch office and released-time forms. Firms with such forms have in essence extended traditional lines of support to persons in poverty who have requested legal services. These forms are sometimes innovative, but the approach, clearly in the form of extending services, is old. Firms with branch office or released-time strategies generally have directed their energies into a rejuvenation—or a structured expansion—of old-style legal aid voluntarism or into "ghetto office projects," a private outreach program.

We will look at two basic models here: (1) the branch office, which involves the staffing and operating of a ghetto office under a firm name or in a consortium of firms, and (2) participation—in varying degrees—in an already existing ghetto law office or outreach program.

Branch Offices

Two firms which we observed—Piper & Marbury in Baltimore, and Saul, Ewing, Remick & Saul in Philadelphia—operated their own "community" or branch offices. Many firms we visited had explicitly considered a community office approach but had rejected it—some at the eleventh hour. The negative points encountered by the rejecting firms at the planning stage were remarkably similar.[1] A major stumbling block has been the potential (and sometimes evidenced) hostility of both the lawyers already practicing in the particular community (the local lawyers) and the people in the community (the potential clients). The problem of community rejection of, or hostility toward, a branch of an establishment law office arises from lack of prior contact. The community is distrustful and alienated. The law firm is uncertain.[2] The law firm arriving in the ghetto is viewed as a colonial settler "bearing gifts into the

1. The firms interviewed that had rejected a branch office were located in Los Angeles (2), New York (1), Washington (2), Philadelphia (1), and Boston (1).
2. Both of the law firms we mention have been concerned about the safety of their lawyers in the branch office.

ghetto."[3] A partner in a Washington firm that eventually rejected the idea of a branch office reported on his informal poll of neighborhood lawyers:

> The reactions we got were mixed. There is a sizable group of black lawyers who did not like the idea at all. They said, "We can take care of this business and for those people who can't pay, there is the Neighborhood Legal Services operation."[4]

Similar reactions were expressed elsewhere. In Los Angeles, a group of firms, with the support of the Los Angeles County Bar Association, had planned a consortium office in Watts and had even taken steps toward the rental of selected office space when the black lawyers in the community formally opposed the move.[5]

Another major problem facing firms which are considering or establishing a branch office is the status in the firm of the lawyers who would staff the office. If the office is to be a full-time operation with a full-time staff,[6] would the lawyers in it receive the same consideration for advancement and, ultimately, partnership as the equivalent main office lawyers? Will their time in the branch office be considered disqualifying or as a leave of absence, or will it be treated as fully equivalent to work in the main office?[7] In the debate about branch office forms, partners explicitly expressed their doubts about work-

3. Unless there is a strong intellectual reason for attribution, names will be omitted, and assigned code numbers for respondents will be given. The respondent here is R31.

4. R31.

5. Most respondents in Los Angeles agree that advance discussion of this matter and joint planning with the black bar would have avoided or reduced this reaction. Most see this as a serious oversight.

6. R9 argued that community contact and credibility can be achieved only with a full-time office.

7. Of course, this problem of credit for public interest work toward advancement within the firm is encountered in the committee or department forms, too. The problem is more explicitly raised, however, by the existence of a branch office. The physical and functional apartness of the branch office quite obviously contributes to a more explicit dialogue about the status of the branch people within the firm. The separation also affects the psychological outlook of these "colonials."

ing full time in this type of work, and some also questioned whether a branch office should be the firm's *only* recognized public interest work.[8]

Piper & Marbury opened a branch office in a lower-income neighborhood in Baltimore in the autumn of 1969.[9] The office is a full-time office, open every day except Sunday. It was staffed by two associates when we visited it, neither of whom had been with the firm prior to his branch office debut. Peter Smith, the lawyer in charge of the branch office, was recruited from the OEO Legal Services Program in Washington and Edwin Villmoare was recruited directly from law school.

The status of these lawyers is unclear despite the firm's announcement that lawyers in the branch office will enjoy status equal to that of their colleagues in the main office. The reality of equal status might have been assured had a partner been placed in charge of the branch office. As it is, however, the two associate staff lawyers, although invited to use the resources of the main office and to engage in shared enterprise with the lawyers downtown, spend most of their professional lives in the ghetto—two miles away—without a built-in friend in court. It remains to be seen whether the staff lawyers of this office will acquire or maintain full status in the firm.

The physical plant of the branch office received extensive consideration: The style of office furnishings and the office location were debated. (The office furnishings chosen resemble those in the main office.) Because it has symbolic importance this seemingly small matter has troubled many. The managers of OEO Legal Services Programs have had many debates about pine board effect versus furnishings that conjure up images of the Inns of Court, the woolsack, and the Mace. Directors and board members of legal service programs have

8. R34.
9. Information on Piper & Marbury was obtained from an interview with Peter Smith and from the two National Legal Aid and Defender Association conferences.

disagreed about whether the symbol should give a feeling of "lawyer" or reach out and say to the client, "Yours."[10] The debate about furnishings among the partners of Piper & Marbury was bound to reflect, as it has with others, feelings about what it means to be a lawyer. These feelings, related to style as well as function, are central to this study. The tension between tradition and change is revealed in interesting ways.

The planning of office location touched on questions of lawyer safety, accessibility to a client group, and accessibility to the main office. The result was an office located on the respectable fringes of a low-income neighborhood, on a well-traveled street, and across from a major hospital. Direct mass transit between the downtown and branch office is available practically on a door-to-door basis. A direct telephone line through the firm's switchboard assures immediate communication between branch and downtown lawyers.

There is no formalized interchange between the branch office and the main office of Piper & Marbury with respect to work in progress. A firm committee directs the operation of the branch, and the lawyers in the branch can turn to it with their problems. Intake is supervised by the committee, but much of the day-to-day operation of the branch is autonomous. To facilitate communication, lawyers in the branch office visit the main office a few times a week. They are not, however, available for assignments to main office work. Lawyers in the main office may volunteer for, but are not assigned to, work in the branch. When they volunteer they must work through one of the branch staff attorneys; if they have special expertise, they may handle a segment of a problem downtown without supervision. Peter Smith indicated that the level of main office participation was low, both as to the number of volunteer lawyers involved and the quantity of work per-

10. The debate was replicated recently among producers at CBS. In midseries, a weekly program, "The Storefront Lawyers," changed its title to "Men at Law," and the "poverty lawyers" were moved from the barren facilities of a branch office to a swank large-firm setting.

formed. The principal reasons advanced by Smith for the low level of voluntary performance were: (1) the pressure of paying business and (2) the fact that "available time" was being spent on other public interest projects—the branch office had not preempted other *pro bono* work in the firm. Two ancillary reasons were also cited by Smith: (1) resistance to supervision —supervision which Smith defended as necessary to assure a "quality" job from lawyers not used to or sensitive to "poverty law," and (2) lack of supervisory time because of the press of branch office work. The two sets of explanations have cross-currents that lead to speculation about which reasons, if any, are the real ones. A possible ambiguity in the definition of Smith's role with respect to the use of volunteers leaves Smith in the same classic dilemma that confronts a staff lawyer in a volunteer agency. The choice facing Smith is whether to administer the wholesale delivery of volunteer hours or to spend his time handling cases. Failure to resolve this dilemma produces an uneasy and unmastered combination of the choices. As full-time professionals, paid to deliver legal services to the poor and allowed, although vaguely, to draw on volunteer help from the firm, it is natural for Smith and Villmoare to direct their energies toward a self-executing caseload. Both the nature of the caseload and Smith's criterion for selecting volunteers ("Can the staff attorneys do a good job?") indicate how the dilemma has been resolved by Smith.

Although Smith seeks to concentrate, at times, on court and administrative practices which affect a whole class of clients, when he describes the overall balance of the branch office docket he insists that it is not "test-case" oriented and not overly concentrated in any specific field. Rather, it has evolved into a general practice of law, with strong emphasis on the maintenance of a manageable caseload.[11]

Cases rejected by the branch office are referred to other

11. The following breakdown represents the acceptance and rejection rates in the various categories selected by the branch office during the first five months of Piper & Marbury's branch office operation:

firms, although there has been an ongoing debate between Piper & Marbury and the local bar association as to how this should be done. The bar association would like the branch office to use the Lawyer Referral Service for those clients they do not handle, whereas Piper & Marbury would rather refer clients to lawyers practicing in the vicinity of the branch office after giving due consideration to the areas of experience of each lawyer. At the time of the study, Piper & Marbury was continuing to use its own system of referral. The issue seems to be dormant rather than completely settled.

Piper & Marbury has not clashed with these neighborhood lawyers. Its referral policy and its frequent meetings with neighborhood people and attorneys who have contact with the local community may have helped to avoid conflict. This "problem" of local attitude, universally considered troublesome by firms contemplating a branch office, may also have been tempered by the small size and the nature of the neighborhood law practices in Baltimore.

The branch office of Saul, Ewing, Remick & Saul[12] in Philadelphia is quite different from the Piper & Marbury office. It is open only two nights a week[13] and is staffed entirely by volunteers from the main office. Very little supervision of the

Type of Case	Accepted	Rejected
Welfare	6	0
Housing	5	0
Consumer	6	2
Criminal	8	2
Domestic	3	3
Employment	2	1
Health	1	0
Economic Development	2	2
Miscellaneous	2	3

12. Called the Mantua Office by the firm's lawyers and on the firm's written materials. This is the name of the neighborhood in which this branch office is located.

13. The two associates we interviewed said that when they originally opened the office they did not wish to be "oversubscribed." As time went on, the two-nights-a-week policy was deemed an "appropriate" amount of work for the firm to handle through the Mantua Office.

branch work is done from downtown. After one year of operation every associate and a number of the partners had participated in the workload of this office.

The idea for the office came from associates within the firm. One of them, Winston Churchill, explained the genesis of the program:

> We kept thinking about what if we could get the firm to put an office in North Philadelphia or something, and the more we looked, the more it seemed absolutely impossible, because there were no formal ties with the community in any way. And then, by some stroke of luck, we ended up representing a community group out in West Philadelphia, called the Young Great Society, headed by Herman Rice. As time went on they encouraged us to try to establish an office in a neighborhood out there.[14]

The Young Great Society, a large, diversified, community development group and itself a public interest body, was accepted by the firm as a client before the Society was financially viable.[15] After a year and a half of this association, the firm was doing a "tremendous amount" of "straight downtown" legal work for the Young Great Society[16] in the firm's main office. Although this work is done at reduced rates, it involves "a great deal of money." As a result of the continuing and complex relationship, the ties between the firm, the community-group client, and the community in general have grown stronger:

14. The office was set up in a building owned by the Young Great Society. Rent was waived for a period of months in return for the law firm's renovation of the space to be used.

15. One of the associates related an incident in which other lawyers, who were close to the community, offered to handle some of the Society's legal work after the Society had been with the Saul firm for a number of months. Herman Rice reportedly rejected those offers, saying the Saul firm had handled Society work when all the other lawyers in the city would not, and it would keep the business.

16. During the Churchill interview, legal work for the Society's interests in housing projects, an architectural firm, and a black newspaper were mentioned.

> One feeds on the other. You have the neighborhood law office that makes the whole group organization feel good and you sort of tie to both of them.[17]

The docket of the community office contains a high percentage of criminal work,[18] in part because of the screening done by the Young Great Society and Herman Rice and in part because of community needs:

> There are people that come in there who obviously really had to scrape to get the money—just anything so that they don't have to be represented by the [Public] Defender.[19]

This type of caseload seems satisfactory to all parties involved. The people of the community, all of whom at least in theory have equal access to the office, have determined the heavily criminal caseload by their demands for this kind of service. And representation in criminal court is deemed by the partners in the firm to be a worthwhile public interest function—the law firm lawyers can address themselves to the general problems of criminal procedure while handling individual cases.

By virtue of its relations with the Young Great Society, Saul, Ewing, Remick & Saul has not merely institutionalized the operation of its branch office; it has extended the scope of its regular practice, meeting new-style client demand on a fee basis. In this respect, the core of the firm's outreach program resembles that of Hill & Barlow. Both firms represent clients who have business interests consistent with sanctioned or selected public interest goals. The Young Great Society has housing-development and black-capital business, the kind of business Hill & Barlow's department seeks. For the firm of Saul, Ewing, Remick & Saul, the client preceded the outlook. For others, the strategy may precede the clients. The result, however, is the same.

17. R16.
18. From February 1969 to February 1970 seventy criminal cases and forty-one civil cases were handled.
19. R16. A token fee is charged because "Herman Rice thought we should, and people in the firm felt better about it. We charge in accordance to what they can pay . . . it came out to less than $3.00 an hour the first year."

The Lawyer, the Public, and Professional Responsibility

Potential conflict between local lawyers and the people in the community on the one hand and the firm on the other is moderated, because the firm has a community-group client. The firm's presence in the ghetto is legitimized in the same way that some established law firms are legitimized in their worlds by being located in the home office building of one of their major clients.

The ghetto office, in an area called Mantua, and its work with the Young Great Society do not constitute all of the Saul firm's commitment to public interest work. The firm has, for example, an ongoing relationship with the Lawyers' Committee for Civil Rights Under Law, for whom it handles both projects and cases.[20]

Released Time and Block Deployment of Volunteers
In our discussion of the public interest partner or committee we indicated that one of the options available to a firm wanting to organize effort for, or at least to step beyond indifference to, public interest work is to designate a block of lawyers or lawyer hours to supplement already existing service outlets. This approach is the opposite of taking on a project, a "big case," or developing, in the office, a patterned approach for a series of cases in a given field of concentration, cases involving police brutality, criminal defense or appeal, or landlord-tenant relations. Offers for such service opportunities are continually being advanced to firms or their lawyers by the public interest brokers (discussed in the next chapter).

Programs through which members of a given law firm can staff an operating legal service program office at certain designated times are much more common than is the private branch office. Moreover, by virtue of these inputs from firms, the traditional styles of the service organizations are undergoing some change. Certain law firms have entered into an "of-

20. As a general matter, the reader should understand that singling out of a firm's approach to public interest work does not mean that the cited firm does not address public interest matters in other ways.

counsel" relationship with legal service programs or specific program offices. Other firms have released their associates to the Public Defender's office or to a legal service program. A relatively new approach is still in an experimental stage: a legal service office designed primarily for volunteers.

In New York, for example, groups of lawyers from certain large law firms have for years staffed legal service offices on specific nights. Firms in other cities have participated in similar programs. These programs, however, have rarely been administered by the firms nor have they been addressed to team effort. The model for participation in these programs was centered on the individual volunteer lawyer. He interviewed people who appeared at the legal aid office while he was there, took notes, and did the resulting legal work at home or at his office. A firm's adoption of a public interest approach of this sort has produced little more than a client file in the office and an understanding that volunteer lawyers may do such work on the firm's time with the firm's resources. The volunteer lawyer becomes truly a part of a team effort only if the adoption of public interest work includes supporting a program in which supervision and coordination of cases and skills replace the laissez faire tolerance of the past for individual volunteer effort.

Some law firms are now developing strategies that involve the deployment, supervision, and coordination of their lawyers as a unit as distinct from the efforts of individuals. The selection of a service outlet necessarily involves a choice of strategy. Service is considered more important than a law reform or big case deployment. Choice of service strategies, of course, may reflect the relative ease of coordinating and supervising effort through existing service outlets, the ease of setting maximum hours of deployed effort, and low visibility, which allows the firm to withdraw at any time.

The road is not always easy for the firms adopting a service outlet. The feeling of heroism which the individual volunteer may need to buoy his spirits during the tedium of handling routine public interest cases may be subtly flattened.

The Lawyer, the Public, and Professional Responsibility

With group enlistment the credit goes elsewhere. Also, the coercion to volunteer brings with it the risk that individual lawyers may not be ready to fill a service role; they may lack the maturity required to render routine effort of this sort. As one partner of a New York firm put it:

> It is our belief here that the lawyer serves as great a function in the representation of one underprivileged individual as a lawyer does in the representation of a broader number of individuals. I realize that may not be as exciting for the individual lawyer involved, and I would be less than frank if I did not tell you [that] we have had difficulty keeping our associates interested in the legal aid office for perhaps that reason.[21]

The firm, then, or the public interest partner, can be seen as taking on new roles for socializing younger lawyers to professional responsibility.

A firm can support a specialized segment of a legal service program's operation: for example, handle a specific kind of case for a legal service office. Or the firm may establish an of-counsel relationship with a neighborhood legal service office. This includes the handling of legal service program cases which may be beyond the skills or capacities of a neighborhood office.[22] These efforts are not in the individual service mode. They involve policy planning, the big case approach, and the law reform mode.

The released-time model is another approach. Associates work with public service agencies while their firms continue to pay their salaries. For fifteen years, a number of the larger Philadelphia firms have periodically released associates for a one-month period of work with the Public Defender office. One firm, Covington & Burling in Washington, with approximately 120 members, now has a program through which it

21. R12.
22. R13, R15. O'Melveny & Myers (see p. 72 *supra*) has an of-counsel relationship too—with an OEO backup center, the Western Center on Law and Poverty. This is probably the most versatile of the of-counsel relationships. Most of these relationships are with a single neighborhood office.

lends two of its associates to the Neighborhood Legal Services Program (NLSP) for six-month periods. Under this arrangement this local OEO program gets local contribution credit, in the form of the value of the donated hours, and benefits from an extended relationship with attorneys having a different long-run commitment and outlook.

Many other firms have considered released-time projects, but at the time of the study few of these projects were in operation. Hesitancy to release associates seems to arise from three major sources: (1) the idea that an associate would miss part of his "training" within the firm, (2) the idea that, although the program would allow a few associates to do this type of public interest work, such opportunities could not be offered to all the associates, and (3) the feeling of many associates that their positions in the firm might be jeopardized by their extended absences. In Philadelphia, the time spent on the Public Defender volunteer program is short enough and the tradition is old enough to make such fears inappropriate. However, the Covington & Burling program seems to face these challenges directly. At least one partner in that firm viewed the firm's public service program as beneficial to associates, because associates would be

> completely handling problems for the first time—on their own without having an older person to go to and say, "What do I do now?" I think this gives them greater confidence.[23]

This firm views the public interest experience as *part* of a lawyer's training. The released-time policy of Covington & Burling is not preemptive of other public interest work[24] or even other NLSP work. Associates, while working for NLSP, have access to the resources of the firm, and, at the time of the study, twenty-two lawyers in the office had participated in

23. Interview with three Covington & Burling partners.
24. Covington & Burling has long had a tradition as an "ACLU firm." Several of its lawyers have given their time to civil liberties and civil rights cases over long periods. The tradition has been attributed to past partners and to present individual partners, such as Charles Horsky.

The Lawyer, the Public, and Professional Responsibility

NLSP cases, which were usually derived by referral from the associate in the field—they were asked to lend a hand.[25]

To the extent that law firms are disposed to organize—or suffer the organization of—large blocks of released time and to supervise their volunteering lawyers' efforts, the role of the broker in locating suitable outlets for these efforts will become increasingly important—whether these be service opportunities or of-counsel opportunities or projects. We turn now to an examination of the brokers.

25. This is the ideal that Piper & Marbury hoped to attain, the feedback effect.

chapter 5

The Brokers: The Market Makers for Public Interest Law

Formal commitments by law firms to allocate part of their total resources—money, lawyer time, or prestige—to public interest work are not at this time enough to effect delivery of legal services to people or situations in need of those services. Delivery of legal services is not self-executing. Demand for services needs to be matched with supply. Until law firms have an institutional identity with their new constituencies so that demand for their services will be made directly to them, actual delivery of service by firms or by some of the individuals in firms[1] will have to be effected through go-betweens. These are the intermediaries or brokers, who make the market for public interest law. Firms opting for a released-time model have implicitly understood their need to rely on brokers and the brokerage function. So, too, have firms which encourage their lawyers to make their own arrangements, whether these ar-

1. Individuals in firms may have public interest credibility apart from their firms, which may be sufficient to produce direct demand for their individual services.

117

118

The Lawyer, the Public, and Professional Responsibility

rangements be working with the formal panels for the defense of indigents or spending an evening a week at Community Law Offices or a local OEO Legal Services Program office, or being available for case assignments from agencies like American Civil Liberties Union. Firms with a public interest department (and even those which have contemplated adopting such a model) have had to deal more explicitly with the problem of finding public interest cases and clients. In both the inter-office memoranda prepared during consideration of a public interest department or section[2] and in certain interviews,[3] we noticed that considerable attention had been paid to the question of where public interest cases come from and how a public interest docket is assembled. The need for case-finders was recognized, and notice was taken of the agencies in the community which performed this function. Little attention was paid, however, to the highly complex nature of the brokers and their functions and the many levels of problem solving and problem avoidance that the brokers offered.

In the first place, the law firms we observed, by relying on others to find cases or matters needing legal services, were able to avoid, at least in part, the painful process of making priority or rationing decisions. In fact, the brokers, as we shall see, often found either clients needing services or issues of community policy needing an advocate or counselor well in advance of commitment from law firms or lawyers and then played a vital role in obtaining from the lawyers or firms either a general commitment or commitment for a specific case or matter. The brokers, then, located both the buyers—clients and issues—and the sellers—the lawyers. This is truly market making.

Firms are particularly sensitive to the ethical constraints felt to be involved in actively seeking clients. Where specific

2. Five firms gave us access to interoffice memos dealing explicitly with the question of obtaining cases.
3. Unless there is a strong intellectual reason for attribution, names will be omitted, and assigned code numbers for respondents will be given. The respondents here are R4, R22, R34, R40, R45.

clients are signed up or where, in the case of affirmative or strategic litigation, they are sought, "chasing" is seen, by the firms, to be involved.[4]

The brokers just entering into operation, like the lawyers in law firms and like the managers of law firms entering public interest work for the first time, are faced with the priority dilemmas of choosing a problem area and awaiting or seeking client applicants in that area, or choosing a needy target population and hanging out a shingle in the hope of attracting part or all of that specific population's legal work. However, many of the brokers have been in operation for a considerable length of time. The Legal Aid Society, to the extent it has used volunteers, has been a broker, as has the ACLU with its extensive use of volunteers. Legal Aid, of course, is geared to a target population—the poor—while the ACLU operates in a problem, or policy, area. By virtue of their longevity, these organizations are similar with respect to the qualities they offer to that part of the established bar desiring to allocate services in the public interest. They offer continuity; they also offer an established constituency. The newer brokers, on the other hand, offer a contrasting benefit. They have clients and issues available, too. But the clients and issues they work with reflect that these brokers have made more contemporary, and perhaps more pertinent, priority choices among populations and issues. Possibly they may also have new techniques and more active modes of operation. Their target decisions are easier to comprehend in the present social, political, and legal context. They may also be more explicit about their client choices and the reasons for their choices.

Brokerage functions are rarely fulfilled by an agency

4. We will discuss separately the apprehension of law firms about ethical constraints on seeking clients as nominal parties for affirmative litigation. It is sufficient to say that much of it is misapprehension—an ignoring of the principles of NAACP v. Button, 371 U.S. 415 (1963). One firm, with a public interest section, has even had a partners' meeting on whether it is proper for lawyers in the firm involved in a constitutional class action to engage in the process of assembling a class (R37).

The Lawyer, the Public, and Professional Responsibility

which is a broker and nothing more. The brokers may be public interest law firms, new-style bar groups such as the Council of New York Law Associates or the Chicago Council of Lawyers, or welfare or other single-purpose law or nonlaw agencies. Most frequently the brokerage function is tied to the decision of a single-purpose agency to use or seek volunteers. The use of volunteers is generally ancillary to the agency's central purpose. The lawyer referral model has no direct counterpart in the public interest field. Even agencies like the Lawyers' Committee for Civil Rights Under Law (LCCRUL), which was principally and explicitly formed to stimulate lawyer commitment to public interest or *pro bono* work, are far more than mere service bureaus. Because they cannot be divorced from the explicit or implicit public-policy choices they have made, they do not resemble lawyer referral operations. The brokers, in other words, are not neutral; they are policy laden. This fact is important because law firms, by choosing the intermediate agencies they will work with, or by allowing themselves to be available to these agencies for general effort or for the duration of a single case, are making policy and priority choices. By being explicitly identified with policy, then, the brokers are doing more than bringing together cases, clients, and lawyers. They are also providing an orderly market for the policy choices of individuals and firms. They are, in other words, also policy brokers.

The brokerage operation is not always wholly separate from the law firms which are seeking to deliver legal services in the public interest. The firms may have participated in the efforts to set up third-party entities which perform the marketing and brokerage functions. The Community Law Offices, an agency discussed below, is a creature of the firms and of the lawyers who operate through it. So, too, are the local chapters of LCCRUL partly creatures of that part of the law firm world which ultimately uses their brokerage functions. When law firms in the past participated with the bar association in creating panels of volunteer lawyers for criminal defense or appeal work for indigents, they, too, were setting up a brokerage out-let, although the courts managed the market.

Lawyers and law firms having direct contact with the public or with issues may even act as brokers for each other. This is particularly true where conflict of interest makes it impossible for one lawyer or firm to handle a case—the client may be referred to someone else.[5] The principal brokering agencies serve the new public interest law firms as well as the traditional ones. Cases, information, and policy dialogue are traded across jurisdictional and institutional lines and among the lawyers of "establishment law firms," the old and new community agencies, and even the public interest clients. A new network of exchange is emerging—a network based on a set of principles, loyalties, commitments, and experiences seemingly far removed from commercial law practice and economic incentives. The brokerage function is at the pivot of this new network. It is here that brokers provide their most important function—facilitating communication among all the entities operating in the public interest field. They find the cases, the clients, the issues, the lawyers and law agencies; they provide a set of policy alternatives and a forum for policy dialogue; and they make a market for exchanging or matching all of the aforementioned elements.

The following is a discussion of those new-style entities which we observed to have a central brokerage function or an incidental brokerage aspect.

Community Law Offices[6]

This organization's primary function is that of a broker—a

5. One respondent, R12, explained how this works: "It shouldn't be very hard to turn that particular case over to some other firm, and let us take back from that firm [another public interest case]."

6. The data regarding Community Law Offices (CLO) were gathered principally from the following sources: two interviews (one in June and one in September of 1970) with Stephen Kass, the director of CLO; from the transcripts of Kass's statements to the Atlanta meeting of NLADA, February 22, 1970, and NLADA's St. Louis meeting, August 9, 1970; and from the First Annual Report of the Community Law Offices.

clearinghouse for the delivery of volunteer legal services. It is an organization with a clear set of policy positions about who is to be served and how service is to be rendered. Community Law Offices (CLO) started formal operations from an office in East Harlem in June 1968. Prior to that time it was run as an informal experiment from a church in East Harlem. CLO has announced a dual objective:

(1) To provide legal services into a geographical area and to a population not previously served, and
(2) To explore methods by which the resources of the private bar might be brought to bear on the problems of the ghetto.[7]

The crucial role of volunteers was envisioned from the beginning; the essential staff role was to provide ways of delivering more effective volunteer services. CLO stated this central position in the following terms:

... CLO has sought to determine whether volunteer lawyers in private practice, working in conjunction with a small full-time professional staff, can make a significant contribution to providing legal services for the poor and, if so, how the time and talents of such lawyers can be utilized most effectively.[8]

This set of strategies most clearly distinguishes CLO from a traditional legal aid operation. Of course, similarities are present also: like Legal Aid, CLO is funded privately, principally from foundations,[9] and poverty clients are the focus of service eligibility. CLO is also formally affiliated with the Legal Aid Society of New York.

The differences between CLO and a traditional legal aid program, however, are far more revealing than the similarities —and far more pertinent to the brokerage function. First, recipients are defined both in terms of poverty and of neigh-

7. First Annual Report of Community Law Offices (for the year ended June 30, 1969), at 1.
8. Id.
9. Id. (Schedule of Grants, attached as Appendix to Report).

borhood. Second, the professional staff works to establish dual credibility—credibility with both customers and potential "sellers." Stephen Kass, CLO's director (on leave of absence from Debevoise, Plimpton, Lyons & Gates), is able to maintain an easy and comfortable working relationship between CLO and the lawyers in the large New York law firms. At the same time, he and his staff, with a high degree of visibility in their outreach office, are able to gain and maintain credibility with customers (the community). Third, CLO is relatively sophisticated about adjusting to the needs of both of its constituencies, clients and lawyers. It is aided in this respect by a board of trustees that has a majority of both lawyers and community members.[10] In more ways than one—in outreach, in community representation, and in experimental approach toward finding ways of making legal services more pertinent to a poverty population—the Community Law Offices resemble the OEO improvisations on a theme by Legal Aid. But with CLO the attempt is to deploy a private volunteer army rather than a cadre of publicly funded lawyers.

At the time of our study, CLO had a permanent staff of four lawyers and the ongoing participation of more than 200 volunteers from sixty New York City law firms. Sensitivity to client needs is amply demonstrated by the manner in which CLO has extended the scope of its operation. Criminal representation, for instance, was not included in the original plan for the program, because the director and trustees had doubts that the volunteers could supply the necessary expertise and experience. When it became apparent there was a serious community need for defense in criminal cases, a program for the representation of criminals was started. Now twenty-five volunteers and one staff attorney work on the criminal docket. As the result of a series of decisions concerning its caseload, CLO is now involved in "the general practice of law in East

10. The double majority is attained for CLO, as it has been for many OEO Legal Services Programs, by having neighborhood lawyers serve on the board in the dual capacity of "community member" and "lawyer."

Harlem, civil and criminal, individual and group, legislative drafting, and uncontested divorce."[11]

Sensitivity to the predominantly Spanish-speaking client group has been demonstrated in a number of other ways. There are minority-group lawyers on the staff, bilingual secretaries in the outer office, and a bilingual investigator-process server. Office hours are designed to facilitate optimal use by the community. Those who can pay an attorney are given the referral listing of two minority-group bar associations as well as the listing for the Association of the Bar of the City of New York. Educational programs for subjects like consumer and school matters have been instituted in the community.

The way in which CLO approaches and supports the sellers (the volunteer lawyers) reflects a similar sensitivity—to the professional needs and credibility of that group and to CLO's own professional credibility. Firms, as such, have not in the past been solicited by CLO for either direct monetary or direct manpower commitments. They have been solicited for broad moral support and for a position of either encouragement or permissiveness with respect to the release of their lawyers to CLO. Few firms in New York take on public interest work as firms—through either CLO or any other outlet—and the CLO approach takes this into account. Contact with lawyers and solicitation of their volunteer efforts is made directly with the individual lawyers—associates for the most part. This enhances the young volunteer lawyer's image of his professionally autonomous status. Doubtless, many of these lawyers have to work out with their firms their CLO arrangements, but CLO is not a party to this process. There was, at the time of our study, one exception to this general approach. A single firm did participate in CLO work as a firm. Twenty-eight of the firm's forty lawyers participated as a team, and the work was supervised by the public interest partner in the firm because he "wanted to be assured that the work would be handled just

11. Stephen Kass interview.

the way any firm matter is handled."[12] It is clear, however, that the attitudes of the firms of all the other volunteers are an important facilitating element in CLO's operations, even though the firms do not participate as firms. CLO has adopted a standard of staff support of and supervision over its volunteers—particularly where situations or cases are somewhat new to the volunteers—that is similar to the standard evidenced by the participating firms. It recognizes that the delivery of a skilled piece of work is part of both the establishment firm's ethic and the ethic of lawyers working for such firms. Staff work assures the same type of continuity of effort that the young lawyer receives from an older associate or partner in his or her firm. This is particularly important. It is the quality control, the excellence which, together with "prestige," makes up the source of the institutional pride that a young lawyer has in his firm.[13]

The other working arrangements also contribute to the volunteer lawyer's sense of autonomy. Appointments are made for the lawyer's CLO schedule, which he makes up a month in advance. He then takes a file—a matter—as "his" case and does whatever work is necessary to bring it to completion, reporting along the way, of course.[14] Duplicate files are kept, one at CLO and one by the lawyer.

Although some of the cases handled through CLO have law reform aspects, CLO does not have an affirmative law reform policy. Kass explains that the conscious choice of service work is one dictated by the dominant need to have a service relationship and a service credibility with the community. He thinks that, from the point of view of priorities as well as of

12. R12.

13. Regardless of whether one considers an establishment law firm an institution in a community sense (see Chapter 11), few will doubt that such firms reflect the existence of an institution when it comes to pride of craftsmanship.

14. Frequently, just as he would for a firm matter, the volunteer lawyer consults about "his" cases within his own firm. But note: Here he, and not the partner in charge, is the "finder." Sure, CLO is the real finder, but vis-à-vis his firm, it is the volunteer lawyer.

common sense, a broad policy approach to the issues of poverty has to await a professional relationship between the lawyers and the poverty clients that is *truly* real, that there must first be a substantive lawyer-client relationship. In essence, Kass is saying to his seller constituency: Come down to the ghetto—really come down—get acquainted, be professional, be bored with menial tasks if they come with the territory, and then, and only then, become a policy thinker or policy actor.[15]

After two years of the CLO "experiment," there are plans for both consolidation of position and growth. Kass realizes that foundation support is temporary by nature (firms have recently been asked to contribute money to the project). Another office, to be staffed by six to eight firms which have already given sizable support to CLO, is planned along the same guidelines as the first. If this goal is realized, these firms will be joint operators of a ghetto branch office.

Lawyers' Committee for Civil Rights Under Law[16]

This organization is similar to CLO in only one important respect—its primary function is brokerage. The LCCRUL makes an attempt to involve establishment lawyers in public interest work on a volunteer basis. Beyond that, however, in the areas of structure, policy goals, strategy, and operating techniques, CLO and LCCRUL are vastly different. To begin with, the Lawyers' Committee for Civil Rights Under Law is a national organization. Policy and format are national, but operations are local. For its present efforts (operating the Urban Areas

15. This issue, the sexiness of the cause and the stylish approach to public-policy issues versus the drudgery of doing the mundane job runs as a theme throughout the private bar's courtship of the public interest. It is, of course, the private bar's reprise of the free legal service chorus—service or reform? See F. R. Marks, *The Legal Needs of the Poor: A Critical Analysis*, Legal Services for the Poor series (Chicago: American Bar Foundation, 1971).

16. The data on LCCRUL was derived from interviews with three national committee members and with staff lawyers in Atlanta, Boston, Chicago, San Francisco, and Washington. In addition, several of our public interest respondents were on local boards of LCCRUL. Several reports and pieces of promotional literature were also made available to us.

Project since 1968), LCCRUL has established ongoing operations in thirteen major cities.[17] Prior to 1968, it was principally involved in sending volunteer lawyers from northern law firms to work as legal adjuncts to the civil rights movement in the South. The history of LCCRUL prior to 1968 is important here, because its formative years have had a lasting effect on its statement of mission, its credibility with its clientele, and its operating style.

In 1963, several acknowledged leaders of the private bar were summoned to the White House by President Kennedy and asked to find ways of providing legal counsel to civil rights workers in the South, who were unable to secure local counsel even for a price. The formation of the LCCRUL was their response, and the 1964 Mississippi Project was their immediate program. Students and a range of old and new civil rights and civil liberties groups were already in the Movement. The establishment bar now signed up. Its enlistment was to have profound immediate and long-range consequences in terms of the public interest focus of the private bar.

The Lawyers' Committee solicited large firms, not for money but for manpower—volunteers to go to Mississippi. Its brokerage function existed from the beginning. The base of the appeal was twofold: explicitly, that the legal system had a responsibility to peaceably assist or lead in the resolution of this acute social conflict and, implicitly, that the reputation and prestige of the legal profession was somehow at stake in the issue. The number of lawyers who went to Mississippi was relatively small, but, importantly, a significant segment of the bar not theretofore identified with social problems became, through this action, identified with an issue and with a cause. True, the lawyers involved and what they represented were at the conservative end of the Movement spectrum; their commitment was to making the system work. But they were there—

17. Atlanta, Baltimore, Boston, Chicago, Cleveland, District of Columbia, Indianapolis, Kansas City, New York City, Oakland, Philadelphia, San Francisco, and Seattle.

and with the blessing of the establishment bar. In a curious way they represented the conscience of the bar, or at least represented its quest for manhood and identity.

The importance of Mississippi Summer 1964 to the emergence of the public interest lawyer—the policy-committed lawyer—and to the bar as a whole cannot be overemphasized. We discuss elsewhere its contribution to a changing ethos.[18] It bears emphasis here, however, because it is directly germane to the credibility of the Lawyers' Committee and to an understanding of the loyalties and commitments of the lawyers involved. The Lawyers' Committee was an establishment version of the Abraham Lincoln Brigade. Mississippi was their Spain, and the returning lawyers had become not only changed men but folk heroes to some of their colleagues back on Wall Street, State Street, and LaSalle Street. Throughout our study, respondents identified themselves with pride as veterans of Mississippi 1964 or were so identified with reverence by others. More importantly, the leadership of these men in emerging public interest efforts has been significant.[19]

The Mississippi Project had all the elements of LCCRUL's present organizational character:

1. An identification of the bar with specific social problems.
2. The enlistment of volunteers, seeking support from the top of firms and troops from the bottom.
3. An overall commitment to making the legal system work—a view that the profession must take responsibility and provide leadership.

The general philosophy of the Committee is expressed on the cover of its 1969–1970 Annual Report:

The American promise is that we will MAKE THE SYSTEM WORK FOR EVERYONE. It is the high calling of lawyers to

18. See discussion in Chapter 8.
19. Perhaps if the public interest and the legal establishment in the future once again go their separate ways, the historical revisionists will impose a stigma on these veterans of Mississippi or invent phrases like "prematurely pro civil rights."

make certain that promise is kept, for unless the law can redress real grievances and serve as the instrument of re- form, men will look elsewhere for relief.[20]

In 1968, following the Kerner Commission Report, LCC- RUL launched its current Urban Areas Project with a large grant from the Ford Foundation. The format is the same as it was for Mississippi, except that appeals to volunteers come from established local operations. The broad purposes are stated:

> [The project] was based on the premise that the private bar has something unique and important to contribute *to im- proving* the *quality of life of the inner city poor,* that lawyers would recognize and discharge their responsibilty—as attor- neys and citizens—to provide this assistance; and that the victims of social and economic disenfranchisement would seek and accept their professional help.[21] [Emphasis sup- plied.]

The character of the voice behind the appeal to profes- sional responsibility is dramatically demonstrated by a glance at LCCRUL's national board of trustees.[22] Included among senior partners from the nation's leading law firms who serve on the board are one former United States Supreme Court Justice, twelve former top government officials,[23] and eight former presidents of the American Bar Association.

The local operations of LCCRUL were the result of appeals from the national organization to the leaders of local bars. Frequently, local bar leaders were already active in LCCRUL at the national level. Appeals were *not* made through the

20. Lawyers' Committee for Civil Rights Under Law, Annual Report (1969–1970), front cover.
21. Lawyers' Committee for Civil Rights Under Law, Annual Report (1968–1969), at 2.
22. Lawyers' Committee for Civil Rights Under Law, *supra* note 20, in- side back cover.
23. This number includes three former cabinet members and nine men whose positions required senatorial confirmation.

organized bar.[24] Communication was directed to prominent partners of large firms with an abundance of manpower and prestige reserves. Frequently, of course, the leaders of local firms were also active in the local bar association, and, generally, the organized bar was hospitable to a local operation of LCCRUL.[25] The fact remains, however, that the vitality of LCCRUL is independent of the organized bar.

The national organization has a staff director and several lawyers who run projects of national scope. Each local urban operation has a board of directors and at least one staff lawyer. The local boards are composed of lawyers from the largest and most prestigious firms in the city. These board members are linked to manpower pools—their firms. They can influence or direct "volunteers." They also have local policy-making potential. The functions of boards vary from city to city and range from deciding in which areas cases should be sought to deciding whether specific cases should be handled. Although a local board of directors is important in terms of the prestige and power that its members have within their firms, the staff counsel in one city considered it a necessary bureaucracy and tended to work around it whenever possible.[26] The most frequent local approach to obtaining counsel for any individual client, case, or matter is for a staff lawyer to get in touch with a specific contact partner in a cooperating firm. This partner may be a member of the local board or may have been predesignated as a result of prior missionary approaches or prior working relationships.

The LCCRUL approach differs from that of CLO in two important respects: Lawyers are solicited to volunteer for specific matters, clients, or cases; and they are solicited as a

24. There are two exceptions to this pattern: Cleveland, where the local bar association operates LCCRUL, and Los Angeles, where an operation has not taken hold and the Los Angeles County Bar Association is presently negotiating for such responsibility.

25. The San Francisco Bar Association, for example, provided quarters and services to LCCRUL.

26. R45.

firm unit or through a firm as individuals. The Lawyers' Committee stresses the involvement of firms as an important aspect of its brokerage function. It bargains through the strength of its constituents' prestige and support. This strategy lends itself to ultimate financial soundness, for, as we shall presently see, moral and professional commitment easily lead to a self-taxing concept. The approach to firms varies somewhat, depending on the nature of the client, case, or matter that requires placing. Sometimes, for large projects, cross-firm teams are assembled, but in most instances a firm's identity is maintained. Law firms, of course, do not do the work; their lawyers do. And the work is not always, or even predominantly, done by the contact partners; most frequently it is done by identifiable groups or cadres of public interest-oriented lawyers within the firms. The Lawyers' Committee staff lawyer needs to be sensitive to how the assignment process works within the cooperating firms and also to how the work will be supervised and how and when the work will be delivered. As in CLO, the LCCRUL staff lawyer is a critical element, even though the LCCRUL staff does not supervise delivered product in the same way. The staff has had to develop a sophisticated view of its volunteers' potential. It has had to separate rhetoric from commitment, to sense what turns some people on and some people off, and to meet the needs and demands of the private bar. The Lawyers' Committee is more appealing to the romantic side of its lawyer-constituency group than is the CLO. Both organizations take cognizance of the skill base of their lawyers, but LCCRUL, with some justification, feels that the large law firms and their lawyers are psychologically and organizationally more geared to the "big case" than to the service model. Along the same lines, there seems to be an intuitive feeling that, as an added incentive for the younger lawyer who will do the work, the "big case" offers release from the tedium of writing office memoranda or dealing with subparts of problems.

The approach of the Lawyers' Committee to law firms

rather than lawyers fits the realities of law firm needs quite well. As we see throughout this study, it suits a firm to be able to say to prospective young lawyers—and to themselves—that the firm supports and is "part of" the Lawyers' Committee. A staff lawyer for the Lawyers' Committee, who was used to help recruit law students for constituent firms, said:

> I've been used more as a recruiting device this summer than I ever expected. The firms are proud of their association with the Lawyers' Committee and they want you to go [and] speak to potential associates. . . . They see it economically![27]

The usual procedure for the handling of a specific case in a given firm is for the work to be funneled, through a partner, to willing associates. Some partners remain actively involved in the work. One staff attorney described it as mutually advantageous to firms and to the Lawyers' Committee for partners to be members of the Committee's board of directors. In this way the partners become actively involved. A staff lawyer explained:

> As the year went along, every so often we'd do something which would spark the interest of one of the members [of the Board of Directors] and he'd work hard with us on that project and continue working hard thereafter. I think, as time goes on, more desires will get sparked and caught onto the Committee. [We have] four or five groups [within firms], but next year we'll have four to five more.[28]

The most notable exception to the policy of approaching the firm through the contact partner has been in Atlanta. Most firms in Atlanta have no set policies about public interest work. In fact, files on Lawyers' Committee cases are kept by the Committee and by the volunteers but not by the firms.[29] However, when one compares Lawyers' Committee work in Atlanta to that in other cities, one finds this lack of set policy has not discouraged interest in public interest work. The Law-

27. R45.
28. R45.
29. R39, R40, R41.

yers' Committee operation in Atlanta is impressive both in terms of volunteer hours and the substance of its caseload. The caseload has included a school desegregation case, a suit against the police department, and a suit to enjoin discriminatory real estate practices (blockbusting).[30] The tradition among Atlanta firms has been one of neutrality—not to interfere with the nonfirm activities of its members and not to identify the firm with these activities.[31]

In one sense, such traditions have been the strength of the Atlanta Committee. The individual professional, barring an obvious conflict of interest, is responsible for deciding whether he will do such work. He must work out any concomitant policy problems with his firm. David Crosland, director of the Atlanta Committee, has, in light of this policy, developed direct working relations with volunteers, and has been able to organize projects with volunteers from a number of different firms. In this way Crosland operates as does CLO's Stephen Kass.

The makers of LCCRUL's national policy, influenced by the predilections of local staff lawyers, seem to have developed a strategy for attracting clients and issues which capitalizes on the predisposition of the volunteer lawyer for the big or exciting case. As distinct from the service model of CLO, the Lawyers' Committee with its law reform approach and as a broker seeking clients seeks a different kind of client and a different type of case. This approach started in Mississippi. There is an attempt to locate issue-bearing matters —an affirmative litigation model is used. Because of foundation support, the Lawyers' Committee per se cannot emphasize legislative resolution. This does not necessarily prevent a cooperating firm or lawyer from developing a legislative approach to a matter. The case or client mix of the Lawyers' Committee docket has concentrated on problems of civil rights, indigency, and urban affairs generally. Because of its

30. R40.
31. R41.

identification with these issues and because of its visibility, the Lawyers' Committee has been able to attract a wide range of "buyers" of legal services—the public interest clients. It has credibility directly with the clients and indirectly with the community of welfare, civic, and other voluntary organizations. Its brokerage function of attracting clients can be seen to be located in and crucial to a network of case and client finders and referrers.

Depending on staff sensitivities, many of the LCCRUL local operations have gone beyond waiting for clients or issues to develop. They have programmed priorities and projects and searched for issues, bringing them to a stage where they can be packaged for legal representation. In Chicago, the Juvenile Court was studied. In San Francisco, a study panel including many persons in the city government has been brought into being to examine the city's penal system. These activities may help the Committee's brokerage function by locating rather specific areas of client injury for lawyers to work on; at the same time the Committee is representing a broad client group in what it conceives to be a more effective manner. Those involved in the brokerage of litigation also commonly see their positions at these two levels. Richard Morris of the San Francisco Lawyers' Committee described the birth of the penal study:

> We began to assess complaints that we got and determined that a set of reforms should be sought; most of them had been studied. We came to the conclusion that there is no point in talking about piecemeal law reform.

The staff attorneys for each Urban Areas Project have the task of deciding what has public interest priority, based on their relations to the community, the desires of their constituent firms, and their own desires. The Lawyers' Committee as a whole has had an organizational bias against "piecemeal" reform cases. The local groups attempt to develop a balanced docket for both of their constituencies, lawyers and clients. One staff attorney explained how he had developed a relationship with a consumer organization but, after a period of time, was doing work in this area only when contacted, because he had difficulty locating volunteer attorneys for such cases.[32]

When the Lawyers' Committee first undertook the Urban Areas Project, it suggested to local groups that they work on economic development for blacks to develop capital in the ghetto. Community development organizations were matched with law firms, which acted as general counsel. Banks were formed; manufacturing companies were started; and housing developments were built. More recently, LCCRUL has de-emphasized this work because of conflicts with people in the communities (brought about by the shifting views of the prob-lems involved) and conflicts with the black bar.

In 1969, LCCRUL's Report indicated that LCCRUL antici-pated brokering the delivery of an estimated 23,000 hours of volunteer time from lawyers for an estimated 850–900 projects, cases, and matters.[33] This large number may be made even more significant by considering the nature and quality of the matters handled, but in terms of the law firm constituencies of LCCRUL (the number of potentially available lawyers in the supporting firms) it amounts to an annual allocation of about five hours per lawyer.[34] This is hardly a massive redirection of lawyer effort. Two observations are in order: The Lawyers' Committee seems to be gaining ground from year to year; and, more importantly, the Committee's immediate significance can be measured only in terms of whatever credibility the bar has, through the Committee, with the clients and their com-munities and also in terms of whatever exposure to and result-ing understanding of these client groups the Committee has given the bar. The Lawyers' Committee may have brokered policy, understanding, and professional responsibility to a far greater degree than it has brokered lawyer hours.

32. R40.

33. Lawyers' Committee for Civil Rights Under Law, *supra* note 21, at 11.

34. Using the conservative base of 1,200 billing hours a year for each lawyer, the lawyer effort delivered through LCCRUL is 0.4 percent of avail-able time of supporting firms.

The Lawyer, the Public, and Professional Responsibility

The Committee has also brokered social policy commitment from the bar in ways other than by providing legal services. In particular it may have indirectly introduced a self-taxing concept into the lawyer's lexicon of professional responsibility. To be sure, firms have contributed to legal aid in the past, but there is little evidence that this has been viewed as anything but charity. It has not been fully related to professional duty. The self-taxing concept of LCCRUL arose from necessity.

The Ford Foundation grant, which started the Urban Areas Project, was one of limited duration. In the second year of the project, a portion of the operating expenses was sought from participating firms. At the time of our interviews it was anticipated that full operating expenses would have to be raised locally, and solicitations for per capita contributions were being planned. Necessity gave rise to the self-taxing concept. Richard Morris of the San Francisco Lawyers' Committee was quite explicit about the evolution of the concept:

> At the end of the year [second year] we had 45 firms make firm contributions . . . a kind of *per capita tax to practice law.* Everybody really understood that, [although] we didn't say it that bluntly. This year we are. This year we are upping ante double. [Emphasis supplied.]

In this way, the operating expenses and salary for staff personnel are obtained so that nonfee work can continue to be injected into traditional private practice. One staff attorney described the process as "Pay us, and we'll change you."[35]

During the period of our study, only the Urban Areas Project in Atlanta was having serious difficulty raising law firm contributions.[36] The private firms in Boston, like those in Atlanta, have had a tradition of not supporting legal service organizations monetarily.[37] But the tradition was broken by the

35. R51.
36. R40.
37. Y2. "Y" numbers indicate interviews made available to us by the *Yale Law Journal* (see Appendix, p. 300).
We feel this tradition of not supporting legal service organizations

Lawyers' Committee, and the firms that participate in the project have taxed themselves $50 for each lawyer in the firm.

The brokerage value of LCCRUL to the law firms that have formally committed a portion of their efforts to public interest work cannot be understated. It was frequently summed up for us by lawyers this way: They are our chasers. This position is held—and valid—for two reasons: (1) Firms entering the arena need time to develop a public interest portfolio because they have no credibility with the public interest client groups, and (2) they have some rather rigid ideas about soliciting even no-fee clients.

The Free Legal Service Programs and Older Public Interest Forms

These organizations, many of them in existence for some time, supply the new public interest energies of the private bar with an outlet. That is why they are of interest to us here. To the extent that they accept volunteer services from the private bar, or to the extent that they develop a programmatic approach with the newer public interest organizations, they are making a market. They are performing a brokerage function. But they do not exist for, nor were they formed for, the purpose of calling upon or directing volunteer energies. Their brokerage functions are secondary to their main purpose of providing legal service through staff personnel. Even though some of the older organizations are relatively sophisticated about the use of volunteers and rely heavily on volunteers, their brokerage functions are still secondary.

When the Legal Aid offices and OEO Legal Services Programs utilize volunteer services at their established free legal service offices, they are performing for those volunteers a function similar to the one CLO performs. As the world of the law

---

monetarily was adopted by firms in Boston because they recognized this old style of contributing to legal aid or other charities as being unrelated to professional duty—as copping out. For LCCRUL the monetary contribution was *in addition to* serving.

firm increases its formal commitments to *pro bono* and public interest work, these existing service programs become increasingly important market outlets. The legal service programs have established an identity as a resource for the indigent person who believes he requires legal service. Many of these programs have an established clientele. The persistent demands for service made of the free legal service programs are not being met by present staff, nor is it anticipated that even a substantial increase in staff could begin to meet the demand. Further, articulated demand for service is increased as resources are extended. It is also clear that eligibility rules have operated to suppress part of the real demand.

A law firm has a number of options in this area: It can release lawyers to a legal service office, as Covington & Burling has done; it can, as a firm, operate a specific office of a legal service program as a Boston law firm has done; or it can become, again as a firm, associated with a legal service program or one of its offices in an of-counsel relationship, as a Philadelphia firm has done. In each case the firm is utilizing the brokerage function of a program in the same way—it is plugging into an established market. The market-making function of the legal service programs is also important for the informal law firm forms of public interest work and for the isolated volunteer inputs of private lawyers. A lawyer in a firm who is allowed to do his own thing may choose this path of relatively little resistance and report for service at a program office on a particular evening of the week or month. Sometimes this arrangement is made through yet another brokerage operation, as is the case with young lawyers in San Francisco who volunteer hours to the various offices of the San Francisco Neighborhood Legal Assistance Foundation through a panel supervised by the Barristers Club, the branch of the San Francisco Bar Association for those under thirty-six years of age.

The levels which the established legal service programs reach when seeking, using, supervising, and coordinating the activities of volunteers vary from city to city, program to program, and office to office. When firms are sought and the service model is in use, the fact of the firm's presence is of little consequence except as it contributes to the prestige and the supervision of the work of the lawyers on the line.

Criminal defense and appeals programs for indigents have similarly provided established market outlets for the public service activities of volunteers. Variations of these programs include the autonomous efforts of individual volunteers, signing up for Bar Association committee pools, and subpanels assembled within law firms.

When the legal service programs use volunteers in the law reform mode (planning strategy or affirmative litigation) they clearly depart from the traditional model. This is true, too, when professional skill is employed off the line—not directly in connection with clients seeking service from these programs. The of-counsel arrangements are in this mode. The law firm is acting as a backup group for the professional staff of these agencies. When service is rendered for a particular case or on an *ad hoc* basis, the nature of the brokering function more closely resembles the LCCRUL approach than it does the CLO approach. Several legal service programs have brokered in this way, calling upon a firm, a group of lawyers, or individual lawyers to handle a particular case or matter. Frequently, it is a big case—a test case—requiring extended services. California Indian Legal Services Program (OEO), for example, has on occasion assigned specific cases or specific tribal problems to large California law firms.[38] So too has the Western Center on Law and Poverty.[39]

The older single-purpose agencies, such as ACLU and NAACP, have, to the extent that they have deployed volunteers, also provided a secondary brokerage function similar to

38. David Getches, a former Indian Legal Services Program staff member, is now directing the Native American Fund, a privately funded program, where he is seeking to use law firms more extensively on an "assignment" basis. As of this writing he has not been too successful. See discussion in Chapter 6.

39. R64.

the primary brokerage function of the Lawyers' Committee. Both are in the policy-oriented market, and both seek volunteers for specific matters only. Unlike LCCRUL, however, these organizations have rarely sought the services or commitment of law firms. They direct their search for lawyers to the individual lawyer, whether he be a partner, associate, or sole practitioner. Like the Lawyers' Committee they provide an extremely important outlet for lawyers who want to commit time to public interest work. They, too, have an established or potential clientele. They may even have a clearer set of policy and program statements than has LCCRUL, something which can be of benefit if the lawyers in question are having difficulties determining their priorities for commitment. If the volunteers are predisposed to work in a designated area, they find a ready market for their services; the cases and matters have already been chased.[40]

In the law reform or policy area, the question of whether volunteers are sought as firms or as individuals is more crucial than it is in the service area. The matters handled tend to have a higher degree of visibility. It has been felt, in the past, that firms would not want to associate their names with such matters—and indeed many have not. Some firms may have been willing to let their associates work on controversial civil liberties or civil rights cases but have asked the associates not to sign even their own names to pleadings or briefs—to operate in the blind. Perhaps the style of commitment and identification introduced by the Lawyers' Committee and seemingly accepted by some firms will result in changes in the brokerage styles of the older organizations using volunteer lawyers for specific matters. The emerging ethic of treating the outside volunteer work of individual lawyers in firms as "firm matters" is not without its problems, however. Unless autonomy over the decision to accept or reject is left with the individual, as it rarely is, decision making by the firm is brought into play, and the chances are increased that a controversial case or contro-

40. See NAACP v. Button, 371 U.S. 415 (1963).

versial client will be rejected or that factors limiting the scope of representation will be brought into play. And it seems that the more formal a firm's public interest approach, the greater the difficulty encountered by those organizations seeking volunteer assistance. A particularly striking example of this was cited to us. In Washington, D.C., the ACLU had a long, well-established working relationship with volunteer lawyers from a particular firm. Recently the firm formally adopted a policy of accepting public interest work as a firm, or at least identifying as "firm business" the public interest matters handled by its lawyers. Thereafter, the ACLU staff lawyer encountered the unavailability of those formerly willing lawyers when he was seeking help in interviewing former prisoners preparatory to a class action relating to abuses of prisoners. The firm's partners felt that, since a class action was contemplated, the act of interviewing could be construed as solicitation of business.[41]

For practical and psychological reasons, the older, established organizations provide an easy outlet for some law firms. There is a history and a tradition for working relations with these agencies. Even those who have not in the past had such working relations recognize the established identity of organizations like ACLU and Legal Aid. These organizations are a known quantity.

Council of New York Law Associates

This organization, formed by associates in large New York law firms,[42] provides a brokerage function which differs from the

41. R37. It has been suggested by some that this formal resistance will be of short duration and will diminish as partners in establishment law firms get the hang of the new world.

42. The Council of New York Law Associates is a misnomer. Partners now belong. N. Johnston, "The Council of New York Law Associates": What Is It? 25 Record of the Association of the Bar of the City of New York 312, 313 (1970): "We briefly indulged ourselves with the notion of offering an associate membership to partners, but finally, in the belief that all good things should be shared, we dropped all class distinctions; perhaps a dozen large-firm partners and another dozen sole practitioners have paid their dues." Most of our data on the Council came from this article, interviews

other agencies we have examined here. It is an informational clearinghouse. At the time of our study the Council had about 1,000 members from eighty New York City law firms—mostly Wall Street and Madison Avenue firms. The two main purposes of the Council are: (1) "to circulate information about public service work likely to interest an appreciable number of people," and (2) "to facilitate inter-firm contact, which, up until a few months ago, just did not exist."[43] The Council performs its brokerage function principally by publishing a newsletter which draws to the attention of its members public interest projects which can use volunteer legal assistance.[44]

Through its *Newsletter* and a card-sorting system of the members' interests and skills, the Council makes a market for public interest projects. Frequently a given project may use volunteers from many different firms:

> In general, the Council helps to shape and publicize any plausible project likely to interest any appreciable number of members. There is no institutional endorsement of any of these undertakings; our function is catalytic and communication.[45]

Within the loose guidelines of the Council any member may make announcements in the *Newsletter*. Announcements

---

with Neal Johnston and Paul Tractenberg, and from the regular issues of the Council's *Newsletter*.

43. R8.

44. The September 15, 1970, *Newsletter* included the following items: "Demonstration Observer Corps" (lawyers needed as observers for public demonstrations); "Drafting Environmental Planning Act" (lawyers needed to help redraft Environmental Planning Act for prefiling); "Returnable Container Ordinance" (lawyers needed to develop proposed city ordinance); "Bank Brokage Commission Reciprocity" (proposed research into ways banks allocate commissions); "Movement for a New Congress" (lawyers needed to develop sample briefs for cases involving students' right to absentee ballots); "New York Civil Liberties Union" (lawyers needed for prisoners' rights project either as interviewers or counsel for suits); "Legal Developments"; "Coming Attractions"; "Speakers Forum" [persons will will speak at council luncheons], "Theatre Party," "Winter Meeting in Curacao," "Basketball [Intra-Council League]," "Council Notes," and "Announcements."

45. N. Johnson, *supra* note 42, at 314.

are usually accompanied by the name and telephone number of the organization soliciting volunteers, so the Council is not involved in the actual organization or placement of volunteer effort.

The Council does not offer membership to firms. It does not take policy positions nor does it have an institutional view of what is in the public interest. Solicitation for aid from volunteers on opposite sides of issues or causes is possible.

The Council's relationship with the Association of the Bar of the City of New York is good. When the Council was first beginning, the Association gave it moral and financial support —office space and a secretary. The Council of New York Law Associates is not, however, a "bar association"; it is organized around different principles. It concentrates on one specific function: the dissemination of information designed to give a potential volunteer a meaningful choice. The Council focuses on the individual professional—what he would like to do, what he is capable of, and what his responsibilities are under the rubric of professional service:

> The few forms of public service work commonly known to young lawyers all too often either demand skills he does not possess, a flexibilility of scheduling he cannot give or a specific commitment he doesn't feel. Too often, the groups which seek volunteer help are insensitive to the value of an attorney's time or the niceties of his ethical standards; by providing, where appropriate, some measure of central coordination we hope to minimize these problems.[46]

Other brokering organizations, such as the Lawyers' Committee and ACLU, use the exchange facilities provided by the Council. The Council does not represent the client groups as do the ACLU and the Lawyers' Committee, nor does it represent the institution of the law firm. It is a neutral exchange forum.

In many ways, the Council and its *Newsletter* is to public interest law what the coffee house of Lloyds of London was to

46. *Id.* at 313.

the emerging concept of coinsurance. The analogy is to function and form; it does not suggest equal viability.

Boston Lawyers for Housing

This is one of several local operations of a special American
Bar Association project;[47] the Boston operation is one of the
most active ones in the project.[48] It has a highly specialized
brokerage function. Lawyers for Housing operates in one single
area of the poverty problem—the area of trying to bring legal
resources into action to help meet the overwhelming need for
adequate housing. Lawyers for Housing has put together nationally a professional staff which has expertise in housing laws
and in the economic incentives available to developers
(whether they be entrepreneurs or community groups) and
lawyers for the accomplishment of the designated public goal,
the provision of additional housing for lower-income groups.[49]

In Boston the sole staff lawyer has developed an energetic
program, one which includes an educational program for the
general community about existing housing programs. The program provides information about policy goals, economic incentives, and the active role lawyers can play in the accomplishment of announced national policy. This educational
effort is explicitly missionary when addressed to the bar.
Furthermore, Lawyers for Housing actively locates and co-
operates with community groups and lawyers working for
specific housing goals. Frequently this cooperation takes the
form of finding lawyers for interested local groups. Staff support, based on experience and practical know-how, is given to

47. See description by E. Morris, "Lawyers Mobilize for Housing and
Urban Renewal," 57 *A.B.A.J.* 158 (Feb. 1971).

48. The activity level of the Boston operation is partly attributable to
the existence of Massachusetts housing funds, which supplement over-
extended Federal Housing Authority commitments. We felt that the Boston
Lawyers for Housing would be a good working model for us to observe.

49. Data about the national operation were obtained from ABA staff
papers. The data on Boston Lawyers for Housing were gathered for the most
part during an interview in September of 1970 with staff director Richard
Banks.

community groups applying for government subsidies. This support continues during all the stages of planning, completing, and operating housing developments. Boston Lawyers for Housing also uses its expertise, in cooperation with other public interest forms, for the redress of substantive shortcomings and procedural irregularities in the public administration of housing laws and of the public or private mismanagement of housing developments. For example, Boston Lawyers for Housing has worked with two firms brought in by the Lawyers' Committee in a major law suit challenging the way that a developer has operated a housing development for lower-income cooperators and the way that federal authorities have condoned the mismanagement.[50]

The legal talent that Boston Lawyers for Housing seeks to bring to bear is not volunteer talent. There are economic rewards; fees are paid. Unlike the previously described brokerage operations, here the search for legal representation is carried out both among the State Street firms and among the sole practitioners and firms located in the affected neighborhoods. It is not an elitest club. Where local neighborhood lawyers are used, the adjunctive staff work is important; it supplies a support equivalent to large-firm support, and provides tax, administrative agency, and corporate law expertise. Frequently, a large firm is teamed with a local practitioner for the accomplishment of a specific housing development. The large firm sometimes works without fees while the local lawyer has both the client and the fee expectancy.[51]

As we have seen, a State Street firm, Hill & Barlow, considered that working for the accomplishment of designated

50. R1, R2.
51. This pattern was discerned throughout our study. One objective selected by large establishment firms, particularly in economic development work where fees are frequently available through Small Business Administration subsidies or can be anticipated if the venture is successful—if the client becomes economically viable—was the exportation of expertise and technique to local lawyers, particularly lawyers from minority groups. Fees were foresworn by the large firms on the theory that they were contributions toward more adequate long-run local representation.

national housing policy was an ideal method for regularizing a public interest department in its firm and placing it on a paying basis.[52] The potential for specific-goal brokering can be seen in this single example. Lawyers for Housing could interest other firms in a similar approach. In other fields (e.g., consumer fraud, where legislation provides economic rewards for lawyers' efforts), specialized brokers could stimulate law firm activity.

Boston Lawyers for Housing in reality brokers nationally selected public policy goals. It brokers knowledge—general and applied—in addition to making a market for clients and lawyers. The major difference between this brokerage function and the others we have seen is that both the buyers and the sellers of this legal service (the clients and lawyers) are in reality buyers of the federal and state housing programs.[53] Double brokerage is seen to be involved.

Bar Groups Old and New

The educational brokerage functions of Boston Lawyers for Housing have been mirrored to some extent by bar associations. So too have the clearinghouse styles of the Council of New York Law Associates. For a profession sensing a duty to the public, such functions are central to the reason for a bar association's existence in the first place. An association of lawyers, ideally, exists for the exchange of information and the development of skills and as a forum for discussion of those issues which are pertinent to the discharge of professional duty. To the extent that the public good is the focus of a bar association program—whether that focus is implied in an exchange of skill and technique information or is explicit in an exchange regarding alternatives for policy and action—a bar association is an example of an informational, educational, and

52. See Chapter 3 for discussion of Hill & Barlow's department of urban and public law.
53. See E. and J. Cahn, "Power to the People or the Profession? The Public Interest in Public Interest Law," 79 *Yale L.J.* 1005 (1970). We are all consumers of government policies.

policy-brokering clearinghouse, very similar to the Council of
New York Law Associates. Policy and information brokering
are handled through such instruments as committee work,
formal programs, and organizational action dealing with professional responsibility in connection with the selection of
judges, procedural and substantive law reform, professional
skills and ethics, the problem of delivering legal services to
people needing service but lacking the price of commanding
these services, and the problems of reducing costs of lawyers'
services. To the extent that it discharges all of these functions,
a bar association is a prime broker of the real standards for
professional responsibility.

The organized bar has, more or less, dealt with the problems mentioned above. That ideal, however, has been tar-
nished by the energy diverted to such matters as minimum fees
and the unauthorized practice of law. Too often, concern for
gain over service has been the model. There is some evidence
that a counter-bar association is emerging to perform the
central function of brokering professional responsibility. The
Chicago Council of Lawyers typifies such a counter-bar. The
emergence of the counter-bar is dealt with later in this book,[54]
but an examination of this organizational type as it fulfills a
brokerage function is in order here.

Through a program of formal seminars and symposiums,
the Chicago Council of Lawyers has provided a forum for airing
new dimensions of professional responsibility. For example, in
June 1970, the Council sponsored a well-attended Symposium
on Extrajudicial Comment and Conduct, which considered the
roles and responsibilities of lawyers, litigants, the bar, the
bench, and the press. The suggestion was advanced there that
in cases including public issues (e.g., pollution) or in cases
where a public agency is the adversary and has ready access to
opinion-making facilities, a lawyer has a duty to speak publicly
on the issues rather than to conform to the traditionally held

54. See Chapter 7.

view, supported by the formal ethical standards, that he remain mute.[55] In other Council seminars the role of the lawyer in political cases and the role and responsibility of the lawyer in extending specific types of services to the poverty community have been discussed. The focus of these seminars in many ways describes a counter-bar association. Bar associations have always had the duty of defining the professional role in terms of its public responsibilities but have more or less abdicated the duty. The counter-bar starts with the premise that professional standards of conduct must be responsive to public need and public good. The brokerage function is the exchange of insights and policy alternatives as antecedent to policy revision. What is brokered in an ultimate sense is a new conception of professional duty.

The Public Interest Firms

The public interest law firms—discussed in the next chapter—add two important dimensions to information and issue brokering. Most public interest firms use students as investigators, researchers, and brief writers. In this way, public interest firms are participating directly in the education and socialization of prospective lawyers. The students, either during the summer or during the school year, participate in projects like the Citizens Communication Center's study of the Federal Communications Commission,[56] or the Businessmen for the Public Interest's campaign against the pollution of Lake Michigan,[57] or the work of Nader's Raiders at the Center for the Study of Responsive Law.[58] They sometimes receive course

55. "Extrajudicial Comment and Conduct: A Symposium on the Roles and Responsibilities of Lawyers, Litigants, the Bar, the Bench and the Press," a symposium sponsored by the Chicago Council of Lawyers and held at the Sherman House, Chicago, June 30, 1970.
56. Albert Kramer interview.
57. Marshall Patner interview.
58. Ralpth Nader interview. Transcript made available to us by the Yale Law Journal.

credit;[59] sometimes there is a paid internship;[60] sometimes there is academic supervision.[61] In any event, a significant number of students receive an early and systematic view of the lawyer as a policy debater and planner, as a factual investigator, and as a gadfly. These students see law as a responder to contemporary social ills; they also see themselves as participants in the process. What these public interest firms are brokering is a purveyance of a broader image of the lawyer in society— an image that the students take with them when they graduate from law school.

The public interest firm, like the counter-bar, is also a broker of dialogue about new areas of public interest concern and new dimensions of professional responsibility. Much of this is understandable in terms of the ability of the public interest law firms to define their own constituencies and in terms of their disposition to work on situations rather than for clients. They tend to develop lines of factual investigation which help to illuminate an area of concern.

The public interest law firm acts as a broker for career opportunities for a limited number of students. It also provides alternative career options—short term and long term—for seasoned and highly successful lawyers. The directors of several public interest firms are former establishment firm lawyers; Charles Halpern of the Center for Law and Social Policy and Alexander Polikoff of Businessmen for the Public Interest are examples. Monroe Freedman, who heads the Stern Community Law Firm, was formerly a law professor.[62] Recently, Victor Kramer, a senior partner of Arnold & Porter and a litigator, joined the Center for Law and Social Policy for one year.

59. Center for Law and Social Policy and Businessmen for the Public Interest.

60. Center for Law and Social Policy and Citizens Communication Center.

61. Center for Law and Social Policy and Businessmen for the Public Interest.

62. Since this book was written, he has returned to law teaching.

150

The Lawyer, the Public, and Professional Responsibility

Movement similar to that involved in temporary leaves or career switches to enter government is perceptible.

The public interest firms, in common with the organizations discussed above, also make a market for volunteer lawyers. Frequently they develop a matter and then "place" it with a law firm for litigation; like the other brokering agencies, the public interest firm has credibility. It has the clients and can "employ" the lawyers.

chapter 6

The Public Interest Law Firms

The "public interest law firm" is a new phenomenon. Or at least the designation as a description of an extended approach to public representation is new. There is still considerable disagreement over whether either the "public interest" or the "law firm" parts of the designation are accurately descriptive. However, the fact that the phenomenon encompasses a whole new range of organizations, formed and operating as spokesmen for the public, speaks of a public interest character. The use of the term "law firm" comes from an observation of the techniques used and the nature of the staffs of this kind of organization.

Any operational definition of a public interest law firm must take into account our definition of private bar response to public need. Lawyers must be involved in the response, and a law job must be done, whether it is done by lawyers or others and whether or not it is traditional in terms of skills or approach. In this respect both the ACLU and the Legal Aid Societies have long been public interest law firms. Organizations classified as public interest law firms also possess one other crucial definitional element: Public duty is the central principle around which the firm is organized, and it remains central to the existence and functioning of the organization. Public interest law firms characterize themselves by the fact of their creation and by their operation. The public interest response of these organizations is not ancillary to any other function, as it is in traditional firms—even those with bold innovative approaches. It is a reason for their being.

The term "public interest law firm" has been used to characterize organizations with operations as diverse as the delivery of service to the poor, law reform and test case activities, law reform and legislative activities, investigative and muckraking activities, and public relations activities. It covers situations where a client is represented. It covers, more frequently, the clientless or client-light situation where legislative activists or the "lawyers for the situation" take an issue-oriented approach. The Native American Rights Fund, representing the broad interests of Indians, specific Indian tribes, or individuals in their specific grievances is a public interest law firm. So, too, is Ralph Nader's Center for the Study of Responsive Law which has no visible lawyer-client relationship; it has only constituencies.

Whether or not they have clients in a traditional sense, the new public interest law firms attempt to represent broad interests as group "clients," or attempt to serve as spokesmen for inchoate or fragmented interests. The "client" merges with the "constituency." "Public interest" as perceived by the firm is the basis for operation; strategies of approach may differ, but this fact does not.

The funding sources for public interest law firms are varied. Most rely on private foundation support, but some of these "law firms" market their services by seeking broad public support for their programs or by seeking lawyers' fees for specific types of actions (e.g., cases concerning the environment). Some look directly to the clients for fees. The source of funding presents a new set of problems to the firms. Because the organizational form is not for profit, and because support comes from foundations or the public, the tax status of the public interest law firm becomes a question that involves the Internal Revenue Service. Are these firms tax exempt? The immediate consequence of this involvement has been the IRS assertion that "charitable purpose" is an operational definition of this emerging form. A further consequence has been the proscription of lobbying and legislative activities. In the long run, IRS involvement may be beneficial, because public debate and public decisions will be required before the public interest law firm is finally defined and its method of remaining economically viable and stable finally secured.

The problem of defining what constitutes a public interest law firm and the tension between the old and the new styles of public interest representation are dynamically presented in the recent IRS treatment of public interest law firms and the subsequent hearings on the subject held by the United States Senate Subcommittee on Employment, Manpower and Poverty.[1] On October 9, 1970, the IRS announced that it was suspending issuance of rulings on tax-exempt status for "public interest law firms," which, it noted, was "a new phenomenon rapidly proliferating on the American scene."[2] In its suspension ruling the IRS distinguished public interest firms from familiar legal aid groups, which provide "representation for specifically identified persons or groups, such as poor and underprivileged people that are traditionally recognized as objects of charity."[3] Completing the distinction, the IRS found that the public interest law firm was "[o]rganized to initiate, stimulate and handle litigation *broadly* in the public interest."[4] [Emphasis supplied.] It cited, as the specific reason for suspension, the

1. Stenographic transcript of Hearings Before the Subcommittee on Employment, Manpower and Poverty of the Senate Committee on Labor and Public Welfare, "Internal Revenue Service Tax Exemptions," Nov. 16, 1970.
2. Int. Rev. Serv. Bull. No. 1069 (Oct. 9, 1970).
3. *Id.*
4. *Id.*

difficulty of relying on a self-adopted standard of "public interest." It observed that any interests, even private interests, can say they are litigating for the public good: "Not infrequently, opposing sides in a law suit involving substantial private interests claim they are acting in the public interest."[5]

The IRS, however, had difficulties beyond the lack of objective external and judicial definitions of "public interest." The new organizations had left the psychologically safe, statutory haven of "charitable purpose." Public interest law firms appeared as policy-laden groups, groups with a reform purpose. Broad reform rather than specific remedy was their orientation. This opened up a whole host of problems. By the terms of the Internal Revenue Code, public interest law firms were restricted to a litigational or an educational model; for policy promotion, however, where does a test case approach or education leave off and lobbying begin? The new group representation approach seemed contrary to judicial solution. Group representation, class actions, and abstraction of injuries seemed to lie as close to an active legislative approach as to a traditional judicial approach. Traditional models of adjudication were undergoing changes that made even harder the problem of finding the line dividing the two approaches. Subsequently, events showed that the Revenue Service was much more concerned with the Pandora's box of uncharted policy dialogue than it was with the difficulty of definition.

On November 12, 1970, the IRS receded from its October 9 suspension ruling—but only in part. Commissioner of Internal Revenue Randolph Thrower announced that, pending further clarification, public interest firms which pursued a course of litigation or broad representation in the fields of either environmental protection or consumer protection would not lose their tax exemption.[6] The IRS was gingerly stepping

5. *Id.*
6. The suspension may have arisen out of a protest lodged by a public interest law firm engaged in environmental matters. The protest was about a conditional tax-exemption letter the firm had received from IRS. IRS had

out from traditional lines, seeking some of the community's extension of traditional conceptions about who serves the public good. Majority support, or at least consensus, regarding the proper objects of "charity" was being sought. At the Senate hearings the following week, Commissioner Thrower reflected this philosophy. He stated that the public interest law firms claiming to be charitable organizations were

> readily distinguishable from the *traditional* charitable organizations which litigate on behalf of minority interests, such as the poor, the racial minorities, and those who are denied fundamental liberty and rights. . . . The IRS has never questioned the status of these *traditional charitable organizations*. There has never been any doubt that the *typical* legal aid or civil rights organizations qualified as charitable.
>
> They are also distinguishable from the many organizations, such as conservation groups, which were held exempt because they engaged in educational activities, and as an incident to those activities, engaged in litigation in furtherance of their charitable purpose. The IRS never questioned the charitable status of these organizations.[7] [Emphasis supplied.]

The source of trouble, then, was that the focus of the new public interest firms was beyond the traditional conceptions of charity and, further, that their litigation and lawyering skills were the cutting edge, rather than the trailing edge, of education and group representation. It was not the kind of voice or the quality of the voice which seemed to be giving the IRS the most trouble—it was a question of whose voice. Commissioner Thrower expressed concern about the possible cooption of the public interest voice by private interest. This, however, seems to be a disingenuous tactic for evading the real core of concern.

The problem of setting criteria for supporting these firms does not seem as difficult as IRS has stated. It is capable of

---

suggested possible loss of tax-exempt status if major litigation were filed which did not meet the "approval" of IRS.

7. "Internal Revenue Service Tax Exemptions" hearings, *supra* note 1, at 12.

pragmatic solution. In the first place, if fees are charged beyond the amounts recovered in litigation, standards can be set which would preclude tax exemption. (As a matter of fact, no firm which had charged a "fee" had applied for tax exemption by the time of the IRS testimony in 1970.) If "contributions" are accepted from groups whose interests are being represented, criteria can be established which test for the private interest content of those groups. Actually, the public interest law firms we saw rarely received contributions from the groups they represented. We, in fact, perceived an opposite problem: the possibility that contributors might scale down the programs of a public interest firm by withholding grants. This seemed more of a potential threat than the possibility that contributors might purchase affirmative litigation. The funding realities of the public interest firms we observed and the integrity of their staffs made them more susceptible to being silenced than to being coopted.

The question implicit in the continuing governmental attacks on the OEO Legal Services Program may underlie the IRS approach to public interest law firms: How far should government go in supporting or subsidizing (in the case of tax exemptions) an attempt to revise existing rules or practices? Should the IRS support organizations which it correctly perceives to be part of an emerging private-public or quasi-public bar that might set up an attack on a government agency or a government policy?

At the Senate hearings Senator Gaylord Nelson read into the record a letter from Louis Oberdorfer of Wilmer, Cutler & Pickering, which registered opposition to Commissioner Thrower's position. The letter made two telling points: (1) Popularity ought not to be a test of public interest or public good—there should be no disqualification of unpopular public interest positions, and (2) since there is governmental support of private interests which may be in opposition to what some firms perceive as public interest, equity requires subsidization of the public interest form of firm as well. To support the point about unpopularity the letter cited the Restatement of Trusts.[8] Giving further support to the point about equalization, Senator Jacob Javits later argued that since fees to lawyers were deductible as business expenses for private interest, not to do the same for public interest—not to equalize the combat —is to favor private interest.[9]

Charles Halpern, director of the Center for Law and Social Policy, a public interest law firm, asserted at the hearings that the public interest law firm is a new institution which arose in part because government regulatory agencies had failed to enforce existing rules or evolve new rules responsive to the public needs. Even worse, the agencies were sometimes enforcing harmful rules. The public interest law firm, particularly in Washington, came into existence because no other entity was available to meet the public needs:

> The private Bar in Washington unfortunately, by virtue of fees and conflict of interest, is really excluded from providing this kind of representation. It takes a *new* kind of institution.
>
> [W]e undertook . . . to create a new institution which would help to make old institutions work.[10] [Emphasis supplied.]

The function of the new institution, according to Halpern, could be viewed in terms of access. What is available to the public when it is in conflict with government or private interest? By substituting the new entity for the defaulting government, in either litigation or public dialogue, the public interest law firm, if it survived as an entity, would rebalance an adversary presentation of the issues:

> At the present time, for example, there are less than 20 lawyers in Washington who are concerned with representa-

8. *Id.* at 30. The validity of charitable trusts does not turn on the issue of popularly supported goals. Such trusts fail only if they are wholly repugnant to settled public policy.

9. *Id.* at 45.

10. *Id.* at 104, 105.

tion of citizen groups on consumer and environmental problems. In contrast, taking the five largest firms in the city alone, there are 400 lawyers ready, willing, and able to serve corporate clients.

In the communications area . . . there are between 200 and 250 experts in this field prepared to serve corporate clients. In contrast, there are two specialists who are prepared to serve citizen groups as clients.[11]

The Senate hearings, then, show agreement that at the very least the public interest law firm is a new institution. Most of those testifying saw it as representing group interest and the public at large when there is conflict with private interest and with government. Government itself was described by some as too often siding with or apologizing for private interest. The default of the public bar in issue litigation and in rule-formation functions was seen as explaining the growth of the public interest law firm, and helps to explain the growth of that particular form in Washington, D.C. Finally, most agreed that the nature of the public interest bar could not be ascertained by resort to traditional models. The new institution brought with it a search for new methods of conflict resolution or at least the extension of existing methods, such as class action in the judicial process, the public hearing and the less formal ways for participating in the administrative processes, and the accumulation and dissemination of information in the political processes. A quest for new lawyer roles was clearly involved. The quest and the emerging role can best be understood by turning to a consideration of the participants.[12]

Native American Rights Fund is a single-office public interest law firm located in Berkeley, California. It is funded by the Ford Foundation but, as in the case of the Lawyers' Committee, the funding is short term.[13] The Native American Rights Fund

11. *Id.* at 107.

12. For an excellent treatment of the emerging public interest law firms, see Comment, "The New Public Interest Lawyers," 79 *Yale L.J.* 1069, 1096–1105 (1970).

13. The Fund, although supported by the Ford Foundation, is a program of the California Indian Legal Services Program (CILS), an OEO operation.

is now seeking broader community financial support. It has an identifiable client group: American Indian tribes and individual Indians still on reservations. And the approach is traditional—the Fund is counsel to the client. Although the Fund maintains high visibility with its client group, its visibility is perceived as a readiness to do the legal job of representation in specific matters only. It does not engage in broad investigative or educational efforts.[14] David Getches, director of the Fund, does not believe that the broad issue approach is prudent. He explains that the Indians have their own highly developed customs and traditions and a deeper and more immediate sense of injury than any lawyer would have for them. Getches said:

> The client knows a lot more about his problem, and often about how it should be approached legally.

The problems presented to the Fund deal with ongoing efforts to secure or protect fishing rights, water rights, and land rights. In its capacity as counsel, the Fund has tried to secure private lawyers for some tribes on a no-fee or reduced-fee basis. Getches reports that he has not been too successful either in locating counsel for major cases (conflict-of-interest problems are present) or in finding lawyers willing to let the Indian identify a problem for them.

The Center for the Study of Responsive Law, Ralph Nader's organization in Washington, D.C., has an approach opposite to that of the Native American Rights Fund. It does

---

The three-man Fund staff can be, and is, augmented by CILS on a contractual basis. Since this book was completed, the headquarters of the Fund have been moved to Boulder, Colorado, and the operating base of the Fund has been broadened. The Fund is now a backup center for OEO Legal Services for problems about, and affecting, Indians.

14. This can be contrasted with Edgar Cahn's Citizens Advocate Center which deals with Indian matters by means of an educational and investigative approach. Cahn would not consider the Indian his "client" in the same way that the Fund does. Citizens Advocate Center is a public interest law firm operating as an informational and educational broker in other areas, such as urban problems, also.

The Lawyer, the Public, and Professional Responsibility

not have "clients" in any traditional sense, nor does it seek them. It is not a "law firm" within the traditional meaning of that term; it does not handle any litigation—even where the matter requiring litigation has been uncovered and developed by the Center's investigative and research efforts. Yet by concentrating on investigative techniques and by disseminating the results of its investigations, Nader's group is both seeking and representing a constituency—perhaps no less a constituency than the public in its collective capacity as consumer. By switching skill and technique base (relying on investigative techniques) and by shifting voice (participating in the public dialogue), Nader has contributed much to a revival of Brandeis's notion that there must be "lawyers for the situation" as well as lawyers for particular clients. The Center for the Study of Responsive Law is a "law firm," but the role of the lawyer is there viewed differently. The Center studies industries, federal regulatory agencies, and other institutions—even the law firm itself. Its work product (facts and analysis) and its dissemination of the product have produced insights into and dialogue about the automobile industry, the food and drug industry, the Food and Drug Administration, and the Federal Trade Commission. This has led to reform legislation and internal self-imposed reform in some instances and in others to the demand that will lead to such steps.

The Center's research efforts have also provided the factual basis for the work of other public interest advocates. When the Center develops a matter which indicates the need for litigation—for a judicial response—it brokers the matter to other public interest lawyers.[15] Most of the public interest lawyers and firms in Washington have handled referrals from the Center. Ralph Nader does not have faith in the judicial response as a means of resolving broad or endemic social con-

15. This lack of "in-house" litigators may be changing. Nader has established, with his own money, the Public Interest Research Group, which began operating in July 1970. There are twelve lawyers in the Group. They came to the Group directly from law school and handle, for minimal salaries, the public interest litigation developed by the Center and the Group.

flict. The Center's thrust is clearly as a representative in the public forum.

Businessmen for the Public Interest is a Chicago public interest law firm. It operates as a mixed model. It uses the same investigative techniques as does the Center for the Study of Responsive Law and at the same time represents identifiable clients in a lawyer-client relationship. It has, in other words, both constituencies and clients. Gordon Sherman, when he was president of Midas International, established Businessmen for the Public Interest (BPI) to "take on the establishment" under the theory that, once the facts were known, society would be self-correcting.[16] The two initial staff lawyers, Marshall Patner and Joseph Karaganis, had operated, prior to the establishment of BPI, a two-man public interest law firm, Patner & Karaganis. This firm was subsumed by BPI.

One of the first areas of concentration for BPI was the exposure, through journalistic investigation, of political corruption in high places. Marshall Patner explained that the operating philosophy of a self-correcting society flunked its first test:

> Letting the public know that a politician had made a [financial] killing and realizing that no one would do anything about it was both frustrating and nonproductive.[17]

Patner has described an internal competition between what he calls the "lawyer's ethic," which entails withholding the results of investigation while searching for a relevant forum or a relevant remedy, and the "reporter's ethic," which encourages the immediate release of information. The "lawyer's ethic" has proved to be the preferred operating principle, but

16. This statement was attributed to Gordon Sherman in an interview with Marshall Patner, general counsel of BPI. Sherman's extended view of lawyer responsibility and the search for a more active role for lawyers in facing the ills of society is excellently stated by Sherman himself in "A Businessman's Challenge to the Lawyer's Role," 25 *Bus. Law.* 95 (Special Issue, Sept. 1969).

17. Marshall Patner interview.

the investigative style is aimed at a more inclusive audience than merely those attending the judicial forum.

In May 1970, Alexander Polikoff, a senior partner from a large, established Chicago law firm, became director of BPI. The choice of Polikoff, a seasoned lawyer, underscores the prevailing approach to public representation. In addition to Polikoff and Patner, the BPI staff includes an environmental specialist, a sociologist, and a communications specialist. The unique resulting style is described in BPI's annual report:

> ... BPI lawyers, researchers, student interns, and secretaries carry on investigation and research, disseminate information [including public reports and advertising and background information to the media], participate in administrative hearings, and engage in litigation.[18]

BPI's major area of concentration has been environmental protection. In this connection it has: placed in the city's daily newspapers advertisements claiming the city's Air Pollution Board to be coopted by private interests, and advertisements attacking Commonwealth Edison Company for securing a permissive or tolerant city policy toward the Company's burning of soft coal; intervened in the electricity rate case before the Illinois Commerce Commission, urging that the social cost of clean air be accepted as part of the regulatory scheme; and launched a successful bumper sticker campaign against construction of an airport in Lake Michigan—"Don't Do It in the Lake." BPI considers that it represents the environmental concerns of the public at large, but it has also represented groups (themselves surrogates for the public interest) as parties to law suits or as interveners in administrative proceedings.

Outside of environmental concerns, BPI has a more traditional clientele in a variety of areas: police-community relations, discrimination in public and private housing, employment, and education. These clients tend to be nominal, organized for a single matter or typifying the broader public

18. First Report, 1969–70, Businessmen for the Public Interest, inside front cover.

interest. In a recent project, BPI joined other groups in securing the appointment of a special state prosecutor and the calling of a special grand jury to look into the public shooting of Fred Hampton and Mark Clark, Black Panther leaders who were killed on December 4, 1969.[19]

BPI frequently appears in cases as an *amicus curiae,* speaking directly for the public. This, of course, is a traditional device which has long been used before the courts by the older public interest advocates. It is interesting to note that the *amicus curiae* brief, as used historically by groups like the ACLU, represents a pure statement of public representation without the existence of the lawyer-client relationship. The brief speaks to a situation and to the policy considerations raised by a law suit, and it speaks without being limited to the position advanced by either party. In other words, *amicus* has always been above the traditional litigation model and addressed to public interest questions.

While BPI in its basic mixed approach resembles both the Center for the Study of Responsive Law and the Native American Rights Fund, it never quite removes itself from ongoing client groups in the way that the Center does and never quite gets into the chores or the role of day-to-day representation of clients in the way that the Fund does.

The Stern Community Law Firm is a new Washington, D.C., public interest law firm.[20] It is supported by the Stern Family Fund. Monroe Freedman, the director, plans to channel all of the office research into direct litigation and into representation of clients. In this respect, the Stern Community Law Firm is like the Native American Rights Fund. But, unlike the

19. This action followed inactivity by the state and a federal grand jury finding of police mishandling of events. The federal grand jury, however, returned no indictments. Since this book was written, indictments have been returned against the State's Attorney of Cook County and other prosecuting and police officials.

20. The Stern Community Law Firm was opened on July 1, 1970. Accordingly, most of our data about it relates to plans revealed to us in an interview in May of 1970 with its director, Monroe Freedman.

The Lawyer, the Public, and Professional Responsibility

Fund, the clients and the cases sought will be models for law reform issues and efforts. The primary objective, according to Freedman, is to "effect a change in existing institutions, systems, or practices." The secondary objective is to tutor public response:

> Litigation can be very dramatic and therefore we can get things across to the public much more effectively than by other means, like writing a report.[21]

Educational or political objectives are, of course, always present in a conscious law reform approach. Priorities are involved. Even where injured parties or client groups are demanding representation, issues more frequently than not are selected by the lawyers or program directors. One element always considered in the choice is long-run effect as distinct from the immediate result of the law suit.

The policy underlying a preference for law reform litigation is as follows: Symbols, particularly new symbols, are frequently legitimated by litigation, whether they are the prevailing symbols in the law suit or not. Even losing causes frequently advance the content and the symbols of the dialogue. Law suits, even in the older model of single individuals in conflict, are parables by means of which others in the community learn the community's value system, identify the existing issues, and observe the shifting norms.[22] Sophisticated lawyers understand this. And lawyers who direct reform programs must necessarily choose cases and strategies for which publicity will deliver more bang for the buck. The OEO Legal Services Programs were constantly faced with this choice in their attempts to develop their law reform dockets.

21. Monroe Freedman interview.
22. See E. Levi, *An Introduction to Legal Reasoning* (1948). Clinton Bamberger, former director of the OEO Legal Services Program and former partner at Piper & Marbury in Baltimore, who planned that firm's branch office, enunciated the legitimation function of reform litigation at a conference in Chicago on May 16, 1970, sponsored by the American Bar Foundation and the Law and Society Association.

The Stern Community Law Firm is administered and funded through another entity—Lincoln Temple of the United Church of Christ. Its governing board is composed of four church members and the seven people directly connected with the law office. However, in no sense are the church, its social programs, or its parishioners constituencies for the Community Law Firm. The Firm does not attempt to develop ongoing clients or constituencies. Consciously modeled on BPI, it duplicates BPI in its approach to litigation. And, like BPI, it concentrates on local issues or local variants of national issues —hence, the term "Community." The "clients" are the local citizens or consumers.

The Stern Community Law Firm intends to package "model litigation" for other public interest lawyers, communities, and groups faced with problems similar to those in Washington. In this sense it acts as a broker for ideas and information. The Firm intends to copy all relevant pleadings, memoranda, briefs, and evidentiary matter and distribute these materials on a regular basis. The theory is that even if a case loses in the District of Columbia, someone in another locale can "make it go," learning from mistakes and from observing both the style of judicial response and its result. Freedman calls this a "reverberating impact." It is, of course, nothing more than a technical application of the enunciated policy of law reform with educational priorities. Seeking legitimacy for new symbols—new rights and remedies—or more vigorously asserting previously stated rights and remedies is something more than intellectual or emotional shopping. Dialogue takes place among the courts, the litigants, the people, and the legislature. There is always more than one round—discussion is continuous and has formal and informal counterparts.

The six full-time lawyers in the Stern Firm—Freedman, an experienced litigator and a former professor of law, and five young lawyers—have concentrated on cases dealing with employment discrimination, consumer safety, adoption facilities,

The Lawyer, the Public, and Professional Responsibility

and municipal services such as transportation.[23] The Firm avoids duplicating the efforts of other organizations, such as ACLU, the nationally oriented public interest law firms, and the Neighborhood Legal Services offices. Monroe Freedman feels that foundation support gives a stability and a flexibility of operation to public interest work which are simply unavailable to the private practitioner.

The Stern Community Law Firm has actively sought clients and has publicly offered its services by advertising in the Washington daily papers. Two advertisements were drawn into question by the Bar Association of the District of Columbia: One offered legal services to parents who wanted either to adopt a child or to place a child for adoption; the other advised parents of their legal rights against specific makers of hazardous toys (it offered legal assistance as well). After a full hearing, the Bar Association found:

> [T]his new concept [public interest law firms] is consistent with the spirit and letter of the Code of Professional Responsibility. We believe the goals are in keeping with the highest responsibilities of the legal profession. . . .
>
> To the extent that advertising is conducted in the name of the Stern Community Law Firm, we believe that it does not violate the appropriate ethical considerations. . . . [But] we find objectionable the use of the name of an attorney in connection with the Firm's advertising.[24]

The models of public interest law firms we have examined thus far present a range of "client groups." These groups range from the particular client, such as the Indian (who may lack the means of access—financial or otherwise—to traditional

23. See D. Riley, "Objection!" *Washingtonian Magazine*, Nov. 1970, p. 53.

24. In the matter of Advertising Conducted by Monroe H. Freedman and The Stern Community Law Firm, Opinion of the Committee on Legal Ethics and Grievance of the Bar Association of the District of Columbia. There has been prior local bar approval of advertising by Legal Aid and OEO Legal Services Program offices. However, the Stern Community Law Firm matter represents the first time that a local bar has taken cognizance of the new public interest law firm concept and has accepted the implications of aggressive client and issue seeking.

legal services), to public abstractions, such as citizen concern or consumer protection. We have seen, too, a variety of approaches; each form seeks to fill an unmet need.

Notwithstanding the fact that some forms have a service approach, all have a reform look, if not in strategy then at least in style of representation. They are all also similar in another way. Regardless of strategy or style of approach, each is developing specialties. A specialty may deal with the problem of specific clients, such as those of the Indian, or in the skill or technique of opposing the Federal Trade Commission in its indifference to consumer safety. But a specialty is involved— even for the avowed generalist. And the specialization develops in much the same way that it develops in the private interest bar as a method for dealing with the problems of clients. Sometimes the client or clients articulate a pattern of needs which requires a "specialized" approach, and sometimes the lawyers perceive for their clients those institutions, rules and regulations, and interests which pose a regular or persistent problem or threat. In responding to articulated demand for representation, the "corporate lawyer" comes to be viewed as a specialist. But he is more profoundly a specialist in terms of the kinds of interests he represents and not the kind of lawyer skills he applies. The terms "corporate lawyer" and "real estate lawyer" describe an outlook, not a skill. These people see themselves as representing interests as well as clients. In the process of responding to the threats from the real world that bear upon their clients, the tax lawyer, the labor lawyer, and the federal trade regulation lawyer are born. They are specialists in that they narrow the scope of their concern to a single source of problems or threats. More narrowly, they may apply their skills in opposition to or manipulation of a single governmental agency, such as the Internal Revenue Service or the Securities and Exchange Commission. Their task is to seek both favorable rules and favorable rulings.

The public interest specialist, like the private interest lawyer, can be identified either in terms of the clients he sees himself representing—the poverty lawyer, the environmental lawyer—or in terms of the narrow focus of his skill. In the latter case, focusing on the adversary—the FTC or the FCC—and the nature of the issues raised can often give a more accurate description of the particular interests that the public interest lawyer is representing than his own description would give. The same thing is true of the lawyer representing private interests, but that lawyer has long since stopped asking whom he represents. He knows, and the knowledge is thoroughly institutionalized and internalized.

Like the foregoing, the next three public interest law firms we examine are foundation funded. All are located in Washington, D.C. They have chosen a subject matter or skill base approach, and they all deal with the federal government because of their involvement with particular subject areas or because they deal with a single agency. Such an approach used to be reserved for the Washington law firms representing private interests. It is a type of advocacy not heretofore generally available to nonmoneyed or fragmented interests:[25]

> Consumers are a large unrepresented class; it has not had legal advice in the past. And they have been screwed regularly in the past by corporations who have very sophisticated legal advice. And laws enacted for their protection have been subverted.[26]

The Center for Law and Social Policy in Washington, D.C., has a staff of four attorneys. It also employs large numbers of law students and uses volunteer private attorneys from four Washington firms.[27] According to its director, Charles Halpern, the Center is a reaction to "the imbalance in legal representa-

25. Organizations like the Immigrants Service League (formerly the Immigrants Protective League) have represented a nonmoneyed client group before a single agency. So, too, has the Public Defender. But this kind of representation is more akin to private representation before such agencies.

26. Unless there is a strong intellectual reason for attribution, names will be omitted, and assigned code numbers for respondents will be given. The respondent here is R24.

27. Arnold & Porter, Covington & Burling, Shea & Gardner, and Wilmer, Cutler & Pickering.

tion in federal decision making." The Center represents specific individuals and groups before administrative agencies or in federal court and, according to Halpern, undertakes the representation much as do regular Washington law firms. Although the Center represents individuals and groups, it claims in its report, "Summary," to have a broader constituency:

> The Center's attorneys represent the interests of the poor and the ordinary citizens—interests which have rarely been represented before the government agencies, and too often have been overlooked or rejected.[28]

The Center represents clients in three major areas: environmental protection, consumer affairs, and health problems of the poor. Its greatest concentration of effort is in the environmental area.

The representation of "the poor and ordinary citizen" is, in part, facilitated by the representation of organizations which themselves, as public interest groups, represent those constituencies. In the area of environmental protection, the Center has worked on matters for the Wilderness Society, the Friends of the Earth, the Environmental Defense Fund, and the Sierra Club.[29] The activities of the Center are directed at the decision-making and rule-making practices of agencies of the federal government. As specialists, the members of the Center staff have to acquire an intimate knowledge of the day-to-day activities of those agencies. This entails more than a reading of the *Federal Register* or the *Congressional Record* or advance sheets. The staff members "monitor" the agencies just as their private counterparts representing television interests, automotive interests, or food or drug interests monitor agencies relevant to their clients' interests.[30] Halpern, a former corporate

28. "Summary," *Report of Center for Law and Social Policy,* at 1 (1970).
29. *Id.* at 13.
30. As the editing of this book was nearing completion, the Ford Foundation gave a substantial grant to Georgetown University to establish a public interest law center to "intervene with the federal regulation agencies." The new "firm," Institute for Public Interest Representation (INSPIRE), will be headed by Victor Kramer, who, while on leave of absence from

The Lawyer, the Public, and Professional Responsibility

attorney from a large Washington firm, observes this similarity between his present work and his past work:

> Certainly Washington firms frequently monitor decision-making processes in Washington, quite independent of any specific needs of their clients. They inform their clients what their problems are. That's just a reality.

The Citizens Communication Center is much more narrowly focused than is the Center for Law and Social Policy. Citizens Communication Center (CCC) directs its practice toward the Federal Communications Commission and the federal courts, handling "communication issues of social concern and social importance."[31] The stated goal of CCC is to "insure responsiveness of the media."[32] Al Kramer, director of the CCC, was also previously with a large Washington law firm and, like Charles Halpern, is responding to the lack of legal representation in a specific field. According to Kramer, most lawyers who know anything about communications have paying clients in the communications area and are therefore in a conflict position when it comes to developing rules and practices designed to carry out the mandate of the Communications Act that licensees operate their licenses in the "public interests."[33] Kramer stated:

> "Specialists" means that the guy has to be representing the industry, if he is going to make a living out of it. If he is going to [represent] the industry he cannot argue the other side.

The Citizens Communication Center acts as Washington counsel for community groups from all over the country. Many of their group clients also have local counsel. Again there is a

---

Arnold & Porter, Washington, D.C., had spent a year with the Center for Law and Social Policy. It is envisioned that more than 30 Georgetown University law students will receive academic credit for teamwork with the firm. See Washington Post, July 9, 1971, §C, at 6, col. 5.

31. Albert Kramer interview.
32. *Id.*
33. 47 U.S.C.A. §§151 et seq. (1962).

similarity between the Center's style and the style of representation which many of the larger Washington firms give to private industry clients. The Washington lawyer is the crucial eyes
and ears, as well as voice, for the interests he represents when
those interests are affected, or may be affected, by government.
Frequently, Washington counsel reports through local counsel.
Only communication matters are handled by the CCC, but
often communication matters present other legal problems.
When this occurs, the CCC, because of its size and concentration, can bring in other public interest lawyers.

Most of the problems handled by the Center have been
concerned with minority programming, denial of access to the
media, or insufficient community contact by broadcasters. In
most of these cases a community group client is advanced as
the "injured party" with the standing to sue or to intervene.
The Center, to a seemingly greater degree than other public
interest law firms, allows client autonomy:

> The idea is not to take away from the local group its ac-
> tivity. The credit has got to remain with the local group. If
> you're going to be working with community groups, that is
> essential.[34]

Because of the nature of the Center's clientele, many of
its clients' grievances are settled, rather than fought through
the FCC and the federal court. Many times a local broadcaster's
knowledge that a community group has a Washington counsel
can facilitate a desirable result:

> We couldn't get those . . . broadcasters to even sit down and
> talk seriously until they found out there was someone in
> Washington who went to the Commission [FCC] and ap-
> plied for waiver of the rules to extend the time in which to
> file petitions [challenging the broadcaster's license]. They
> realized that there was someone in Washington involved
> who might know how to write a petition, and all of a sud-

34. Albert Kramer interview. There is a similarity here to the client
autonomy seen by David Getches.

den we started resolving problems at the local level that had been outstanding for fifteen years.[35]

This facilitation of settlement is no small point. It goes beyond CCC and its clients. It is the legal process working at its best—providing the framework for informal as well as formal dispute resolution. Informal resolution of specific disputes—and unspecified conflicts, too—is generally possible only when the issues are clear to the parties to a dispute and when the parties have access to formal means of settlement or resolution. To the extent that heretofore unrepresented groups now have access to the law forum, there can be for them informal conflict-avoidance mechanisms, such as settlement and advance adjustment of rules. This process is descriptive of responsive law. Once the industrial polluter is confronted with the potential representation of consumer or citizen groups, it must begin to take steps to settle conflict. Once the adversary is seen to have access to representation, the most the polluter can do is to postpone formal dispute. Similarly, once a government agency perceives group pressure coupled with the availability of an advocate, it must take steps to adjust for conflict. The same thing is true for the clientless lawyer. An advocate with an abstract appeal on behalf of the consumer picks up ability to resolve disputes only as those he may deal with perceive this constituency—and more surely is this so as an identifiable client group emerges.[36]

The Washington Research Project is another public interest firm focusing its efforts on the federal decision-making and rule-making process. Poor southern blacks make up its client group. The Washington Research Project is associated with Clark College, a college in George for blacks, and has a loose affiliation with civil rights groups. Its areas of concentration

35. Id.
36. There is reason to question President Nixon's assumption about the policy-making capacity of a "silent majority." An inert majority may "ratify" policy or tolerate it. But affirmative policy or dispute resolution—rarely functions of an inchoate interest—require participation, or the promise or threat of participation.

have been health, hunger, welfare, and desegregation. Washington Research Project speaks for the poor, but it speaks through or for client groups whenever it can. The staff attorneys stress that the Project's strength really comes from the organization and constituent strength of its clients—southern, black community groups. The Project speaks in specific situations even when it does not have an identifiable client. The staff, however, prefers the more traditional voice:

> I feel more comfortable . . . , when I say I am representing [a specific client] because I know what their interests are.[37]

Washington Research Project is an entity that transcends any one specific client or perhaps even the sum of its clients. It relies on a "community base":

> One of the things I clearly understood after six months was that you could file all the law suits in the world, but unless you had a community base, it wasn't going to make any difference.[38]

This facet, too, can be viewed against the establishment firm counterpart. The law firm, particularly the Washington firm, tends to speak with a prestige that is the voice of the total interests it represents. In turn, its prestige benefits its individual clients. The question to be asked about the public interest law firm is: Does it also speak with an institutional voice that may reflect the total of the interests represented?

Originally, the Washington Research Project was not going to litigate. The Project has found, however, that litigation provides a dramatic way to crystalize public issues and can produce certain results. However, the main thrust—a preventive thrust—continues to be administrative infighting. Marian Wright Edelman believes that what is written into the guidelines of agencies (like the Department of Health, Education and Welfare) which deal with civil rights is often more important

37. R38.
38. Y1. "Y" numbers indicate interviews made available to us by the *Yale Law Journal* (see Appendix, p. 300).

than the law itself. The Washington Research Project appears at hearings on such guidelines and sometimes suggests its own "model" guidelines. Often the Project mobilizes community support[39] and utilizes the press to favorably influence HEW or Justice Department civil rights guidelines.

The foundation-funded public interest law firms we have examined can be seen to have a variety of approaches—publicity, service-style representation of clients, law reform litigation, and investigation. The subject matter of their concentration varies, as does their scope of address. They also have a variety of "clients" from individuals who comprise existing groups to constituencies from which—as areas of concentration are marked out—groups might emerge. Prisoners might emerge as a group when an effort toward prison reform is mounted. So too might local residents who wish to protest a television station's hiring policy after they have observed the resources and the techniques of the CCC. Public interest firms might have constituencies—identifiable interests—from which groups may emerge. Consumers are an example of a pregroup constituency. Given the differences in clients and approaches, the similarities we observed were nonetheless striking. The voice of the public interest law firms is not temporal or isolated even though particular public interest organizations may be. It is an institutional voice. It is a voice seeking to do the public's business. And it is a voice addressed mainly to government.

The most striking similarity among the public interest law firms is the identity of the enemy, the adversary, the defaulting copartner, the biased referee—Government. In some instances Government is the active villain. In other instances Government is a friendly enemy being asked to do something affirmative that it has not done. In still others Government is a referee being asked to make certain decisions which would moderate a conflict between private industry and the public. But one

39. The existing network of group clients is very helpful in this effort.

thing is clear: All roads seem to lead to Government—federal, state, and local; judicial, legislative, and administrative. The pleas to Government are "Do something"; "Don't do something"; "Watch that illegal practice"; "Watch that harmful process which is not illegal and adopt a rule that makes it illegal." In every campaign or project of the public interest law firm, in every case, investigation, or negotiation, Government is involved. This is hardly surprising since it is there that the public's business is done or is supposed to be done.

Private interests have long understood that Government is the arena in which policies harmful, helpful, or indifferent to their particular interests are finally decided. Private interests' contacts with the federal government necessarily increased as government agencies proliferated and Government power increased. Restive watching changed to active opposition and active advocacy. The ensuing debate and dialogue about what rules would be enacted and what decisions would be made found private corporate interests debating public policy and speaking to the public interest, albeit with a self-interest bias.[40] As the focus of the active dialogue between Government and Business moved to "What policy?", self-interest could not be avoided. It was in this context that the growth of the Washington law firm occurred.

When the Washington law firms represented private enterprise, they were arguing what government policies should or should not be. They were arguing, in effect, the balance point between private and "public interest." The private Washington law firm was in a curious way the first public interest law firm, because the issue addressed was: "What is the public interest?" And as long as government was capable

40. C. Reich, "The New Property," 73 *Yale L.J.* 733 (1964). Reich argues that Government is the major source of wealth. This, of course, is an extension of what Bentham said: Property is what the law says it is. Turning his attention to an active government which, among other things, disposes, distributes, contracts, and licenses, Reich takes the next step: Property is what the Government says it is. This is the administrative or large-state restatement of Bentham.

of advancing both the interests of the parties and the interests not privately represented—consumers, citizens, and general public—the end result was in the public interest. This, of course, is the ideal end result of all Government action. There has always been the myth, however, that the public lawyer pitted against the private lawyer could effectively hold a watching or active brief for the public. The public lawyer was expected to play the confusing and conflicting roles of prosecutor, advocate of the Government's position,[41] precursor of public need (here he was in a legislative role), advocate of the public's needs, and judge. The roles were contradictory and would ultimately lead to failure to serve as public advocate. The private lawyer, on the other hand, had one role and one interest. It was no match. Over time the public interest role of the government lawyer and agency became corrupted. Rules and decisions and legislation and policy were more responsive to clearly articulated private need than to amorphous public need.[42] Private desires became "public interest." There was no auditing in the public interest. There was no single-minded watchdog. This phenomenon was not restricted to government at the federal level, but it has been more apparent and more extensive there.[43]

In a literal sense, the new public interest law firms are simply additional public interest advocates. They join the private interest advocates in speaking to the public interest. They add an unmixed regard for the rights of "their clients," and, as we have seen, they speak more clearly and act more effectively because they can locate their clients with specificity. The new public interest lawyer comes as an advocate and watchdog to

41. See C. Reich, *The Greening of America* (1970). The Government develops a line of interest independent of either private or public interests.

42. Reich, *supra* note 40. The process ultimately resulted in considering Government dispensation as "vested right" when it affected interests which were represented and grace or privilege when it affected interests which were not represented.

43. Since the presentation before a government agency was one sided, the public lawyer became sensitized to a single input—an input on behalf of private interest.

redress the balance in what has heretofore been a distorted public interest dialogue.

Commissioner Thrower in his testimony expressed concern that the foundation-supported public interest law firms might, in fact, advance the cause of private interests. But he misses the point.[44] The *private interest* law firms have had their fees treated as deductible items by their clients—even as they have argued public policy and public interest matters. The discussion between the Department of Transportation, the Department of Justice, and counsel for the automobile manufacturers about the timing of the requirement for the installation of antipollution devices on new cars, which led to a consent decree and administrative guidelines, was a public interest dialogue. The problem was that *not all the interested parties were represented* in the dialogue. As Brandeis pointed out, all interests must be represented in order to have enlightened and balanced public-policy decisions.[45] The problem has not been the presence of too many interests, it has been the presence of too few. Private interests might indeed capture a "public interest law firm." In the last analysis, the line between private and public interest is hard, if not impossible, to draw. The issue addressed must be: Are there affected parties that should be heard? The public interest law firm contributes an answer: Yes, there are, and we are talking for them, or some of them. The foundation-supported public interest law firms—particularly the ones in Washington—are doing what their brethren have always done, but they are doing it for new clients and new interests. And what is more important, they have institutionalized a new role.

We did not find any evidence of the captivity of the foundation-supported public interest law firms, but we did see the effects and limitations of foundation control. As far as we

44. Perhaps purposely, because these firms watch government as one of their principal functions.

45. *International News Service v. Associated Press*, 248 U.S. 215, 248 (1918) (Brandeis, J., dissenting).

know, no action was dictated by a funding source. No case or project was a front for unstated foundation interest. But in some instances cases and areas of concern were eliminated as being outside the scope of the foundation grant. This has been in part a reflection of concern over tax status—a realization of the ultimate power of governmental veto—and it has had a chilling effect. The problem, however, goes beyond the issue of taxation. Foundations are neither the clients represented nor the interests thought to be represented; they are the third-party funders. Priorities as envisioned by the foundations are not necessarily reflections of reality. Yet, due to their funding structure, the public interest law firms are presently dependent on meeting the priority choices of the foundations, arrived at by reflection or by default. In the long run, a government by the Ford Foundation may be as undesirable as unaudited policy planning by Government.

The new public interest law firm is an important institution. It has a unique function and role. Although it might escape a conflict of interest problem that would impair its independence and its clarity of voice, its existence is tenuous, being subject to governmental veto and foundation guidelines (which are themselves subject to governmental veto). Charles Halpern sums up the position of the new form:

> The role is clear. The problem is in the future. How are we going to finance institutions of this kind, which I should say are likely to grow less popular as they become more effective?[46]

In addition to the foundation-supported public interest law firms in Washington, a small group of private lawyers there consider themselves, and are considered by others, to be "public interest lawyers." Their style of practice is notably

46. See "Internal Revenue Service Tax Exemptions" hearings, *supra* note 1, at 106.

similar to that of the foundation-funded firm. When one of these attorneys was asked why he did not seek foundation funds, he responded:

> I just didn't want to go through the hassle of trying to get foundation funds. I wanted to see if I could make it as a private practitioner, but doing this [public interest litigation] type of work.[47]

These private attorneys have fewer restraints than their foundation-funded counterparts. No board of directors sets policy for them, and they are free from the tax restrictions on lobbying.

These lawyers often accept referrals from foundation-funded firms if the referred client can pay a fee. Like the foundation-funded firms, they cherish issues; the fee is of secondary concern but necessary for survival. Our study has data about this kind of lawyer from two law firms and one sole practitioner—three operations which closely parallel the kind of representation given by foundation-funded firms. But the economic base of these operations is shaky. While we were making our study, one of the firms was forced to change its operation because of financial difficulties. The remaining two entities admitted having problems making their representation financially viable.

William Dobrovir is a sole practitioner in Washington who specializes in trial and appellate litigation. Most of his docket consists of cases for public interest groups and foundation-funded law firms. Many of his cases come, indirectly, through the Center for the Study of Responsive Law. Although the litigation is rarely brought in Ralph Nader's name, Dobrovir considers Ralph Nader "his client." Other members of the Center staff, as well as Congressmen, are also Dobrovir's clients.

During our study Dobrovir was involved in seven court cases and eight administrative matters generated by the Center. One of the suits was aimed at more stringent enforcement of

47. R66.

the Coal Mine Health and Safety Act. In another case Dobrovir was seeking stricter enforcement of the Freedom of Information Act. The latter was an instrumental action to enable the staff at the Center to continue, and be more effective in, its investigative research into federal agencies.

Dobrovir is an integral part of what some call the "public interest bar" in Washington. And, in a sense, it is a bar. Lawyers from organizations and firms and those who practice as individuals meet regularly to discuss issues, cases, and strategies and to pool a short supply of talent for any big job. The coffee-house brokering of issues, cases, and manpower is at its best among this relatively close-knit group.

The firm of Berlin, Roisman & Kessler considers itself to be a public interest law firm. Like its foundation-funded counterparts, this private firm considers that the public interest revolves around the citizen and the consumer. For two reasons, however, it did not want foundation funding: It did not want to be restricted from legislative lobbying as the foundation-funded firms have been, and, like Dobrovir, it did not want to associate itself with foundations. One of its partners, Gladys Kessler, explained:

> I think you are beholden to whoever funds you; we want to be beholden to our clients.

The firm represents groups and individuals if the partners can see that the issue involved has a public interest aspect. The partners are "forced" to take what they consider "straight legal work" to meet overhead and be paid a draw. Most of their work consists of representing the "public interest" through serving private clients; they decline to serve those whose private interests conflict with what they see as the public interest. When a client is in an economic squeeze they perform additional work free. They have supported disparate interests— tenant unions engaged in rent strikes and negotiations, labor union clients interested in consumer legislation—and have even sought legislation protecting whales.

The members of the firm of Berlin, Roisman & Kessler see the private "self-supporting" public interest Jaw firm as a new type of institution. They see their firm as different from the "straight"[48] private law firm, because they agree ideologically with their clients and are not as susceptible to economic conflict of interest:

> In short, the "traditional" public interest lawyer is forced by the nature of economic realities to cater to big institutional clients who can afford to pay their way. . . .[49]

The self-supporting public interest law firm also differs from the foundation-funded firm in that, free from the control of funding sources, it is autonomous and can lobby for legislation. It also believes that the foundation-funded firm is susceptible to the conflict inherent in the predesignation of policy vis-à-vis the needs of clients:[50]

> [A]nother type of conflict poses a serious problem relating to the role of the lawyer; he is an adviser and a technician, but the client is responsible for setting the ultimate policy.[51]

Although critical of the large corporate bar, the members of the firm of Berlin, Roisman & Kessler use what they perceive as the *modus operandi* of the large Washington firms to achieve their results:

> Here we can and should draw upon the experience of our adversaries at the bar. The successful private Washington firm has made it abundantly clear that full representation of

48. Gladys Kessler's term.

49. E. Berlin, A. Roisman, and G. Kessler, "Public Interest Law," 38 Geo. Wash. L. Rev. 675, 688 (Copyright 1969–70 by The George Washington Law Review).

50. This conflict is often experienced by older public interest forms like the ACLU, where the needs of a client are sometimes in conflict with a desire to advance a constitutional issue. For example, in a police brutality case the ACLU might be interested in marking out lines of duty while the client might have a need to exchange a release for a *nolle pros.* Accordingly, ACLU used to remain above the conflict and enter only *amicus,* thus avoiding direct representation. We suggest that the nonfunded public interest law firm is faced with the same conflict but is less open about it.

51. E. Berlin et al., supra note 49, at 685.

> a client's interests requires vigorous and usually simul-
> taneous representation before four independent forums:
> the courts, administrative agencies, the legislature, and the
> public itself (principally through the press). The effective
> law firm is the one that can supply the appropriate orches-
> tration to achieve a result harmonious with its client's
> interest.[52]

Gladys Kessler suggests that other self-supporting public interest firms could be started all over the country. This brings up a question: What distinguishes a nonfunded, self-styled public interest law firm from other law firms? Is it something beyond self-description?

A public interest law firm seems to entail some introspec-tion about the public good and some selection of policy goals or desirable clients. The stated goals of most public interest firms rarely draw direct opposition. Few would directly oppose health care to the poor, freedom from ecological hazards, or expansion and redefinition of civil rights. But opposition does come in the form of actions or nonactivity. The adversary is usually a governmental bureaucracy looking toward the same goals but listening to other voices and having a different per-spective or bias.

The attorneys making up the public interest law firms that we saw hold their predesignated interest—whether it be health care for the poor, expansion of civil rights, or the responsive-ness of the media—as their highest priority. Clients are taken only if they match goals. Moreover, the individual attorneys seem to empathize personally with the goals and the clients selected. This is the main difference we observed between the new public interest lawyer and the lawyer-partner in a tradi-tional law firm. One public interest lawyer said:

52. *Id.* at 679.

> We react very personally and sometimes overreact to situations. That's our hang-up; we do sympathize very much with our client . . . and feel very much a part of it.[53]

Another attorney put it more directly:

> We have to have a very easily triggered sense of outrage and the ability to translate outrage into a legal theory.[54]

The public interest lawyers view this style of practice as different from the mixture of fee and nonfee work found in the typical small private firm.

One attorney, who had been a member of a *large* private firm, was moved to state the obvious: "We do not represent corporations."[55] As he continued, what he meant became evident—he was not forced to advocate policies which he opposed.[56] The contrast between certain types of regular paying work and public interest work was stated by another attorney:

> You have to be able to immerse yourself in the problems of your clients to see the thing from their standpoint, and not be bothered by the fact that the pile on one side of the desk [represents] money-making amoral work, and that the other side of the desk [represents] nonmoney work you really feel committed to do.[57]

The self-definition of public interest work also invariably included a conception of an interest or a client group either unrepresented heretofore or in need of a new type of representation:

> *To some extent we are defining the public interest [as] the "unrepresented" public interest.*[58] [Emphasis supplied.]

53. Y4.
54. R66.
55. R24.
56. R24.
57. Y3.
58. Y3.

If the definition of a nonfoundation-funded "public interest law firm" turns on enjoyment, approval of clients, a sense of community, adoption of a conscious set of policy priorities, and acceptance of cases according to these priorities, are there other law firms in the United States which fit the definition? We believe there are, but we have no way of gauging this. We do know that many firms bring elements of social conscience, personal styles, and attitudes about clients to the selection of an area of concentration or to the process of case or client acceptance. They do not necessarily consider themselves public interest law firms and would not be called that by others. The shadings are subtle. Does a firm have a conception of serving a new type of client or heretofore unrepresented interests? Does it attempt to make the practice of law more palatable by producing a mix of clients balanced between those determined by conscience and a sense of duty and those primarily determined by economic necessity? One lawyer, who left a large West Coast law firm to go with a much smaller firm, describes a difference he felt:

> I regard this firm as . . . different . . . I joined this firm from a different firm in Los Angeles two years ago, in part because from the top to the bottom everyone was at least somewhat involved in community activities—this is the style of the firm.[59]

The firm he is now with is not a public interest law firm, but by all accounts it pursues a vigorous docket of matters defined in our study as public interest matters. Two points are involved. The closer a firm is to the smaller end of the firm-size scale, the more flexible the style of both its case and its lawyer mix. There is less institutionalization and more room for response to quieter, more intimate appeals for legal assistance. As the lawyer becomes more autonomous so, too, does the line blur between enlightened self interest and public interest commitment.

59. R56.

The Public Interest Law Firms

Two "law communes" which we encountered during the study described themselves as "new public interest" forms. But, again, are they not "traditional" law firms with different life styles, different standards for case acceptance, and a different method for dividing available fees?

CHAPTER 7

THE RESPONSES OF THE ORGANIZED BAR

The organized bar has not played a central role in defining, initiating, leading, or coordinating new responses to public demand or public need. This is not to say that the organized bar has not recognized the need for new responses. In some instances it has even exercised leadership. But it has not played a central part in either the overall response or in the overall address of the profession to questions of professional responsibility to the public.

As we have said, in 1965 the American Bar Association played a central role in the creation of a legal service program in the Office of Economic Opportunity;[1] since then it has been instrumental in defending that program from attacks which in effect were saying that the reform elements of the program were either too controversial or too effective. Most notable of these attacks was the Murphy Amendment, which sought to give state governors a political veto power over the local pro-

1. 1 *CCH Poverty L. Rep.*, ¶6020

grams. At the heart of the ABA defense of the OEO Legal Services Program was an assertion that effective operation in the interest of the poor—or any other segment of society—requires that lawyers be independent. Implicit, too, in the defense is the recognition that groups not now receiving legal representation sorely need it. Moreover, the major revision of the ABA's ethical standards—the Code of Professional Responsibility—reflected an understanding of the need to extend services to new groups through existing forms of professional organization, and contemplated the probable emergence of new forms.[2]

In keeping with the ABA's corporate understanding that new forms of response are undoubtedly necessary we should note three of its pilot efforts.

Legal Insurance Experiments

The ABA was responsible for the initiation of a legal insurance experiment now operating in Shreveport, Louisiana. It is also seeking other field experiments which would test whether pooled-risk and group arrangements would effect a broader use of legal services by people who now lack the price to command legal services.[3] The legal insurance experiment reflects a principal direction of ABA concentration—developing better methods of delivering legal services to meet articulated needs. The program is innovative, but it has a defensive element: Free choice of lawyer is seen to be crucial. The ABA has rejected a group legal service approach in which pooled sums hire a closed panel of lawyers or in which a membership association provides its members with a closed-panel legal service even though the approach has been sanctioned by the United States Supreme Court.[4] The ABA is equally wary of the pooling of

2. Code of Professional Responsibility, EC-25, p. 6.
3. See B. F. Christensen, *Lawyers for People of Moderate Means: Some Problems of Availability of Legal Services* 65 et seq. (Chicago: American Bar Foundation, 1970).
4. The background, issues, and judicial treatment of group legal services is fully developed by Christensen. *Id.* at 225 et seq.

lawyers' services for the purpose of offering them below minimum fee. A paradox appears to be involved. In its support of OEO Legal Services Program, the ABA has endorsed and supported closed-panel group legal services for those who cannot afford to pay at all. The poverty client does not receive his choice of lawyers. Yet the ABA has opposed this approach if the client can pay something, even though without pooling funds with others he cannot pay enough to command equal services in the open market.

This paradox signals some ambivalence about extending legal services; it reveals the opposing pulls of self-interest and professional interest. It also reflects the more traditional charity base of the organized bar's efforts to extend legal services—what cannot be paid for creates no ethical problems. What this ambivalence will mean when applied to the active role of the public interest lawyer in the clientless situation remains to be seen. What will happen when these lawyers actively seek to find or form client groups from fragmented interests in order to structure the disputes of our society into a form which invites the beginning of resolution?

Lawyers for Housing

This ABA pilot project is designed to effectively use the elements of public interest law. We have already examined one of the local operations (Boston) of this form.[5] Here the ABA has fielded staff lawyers who are public interest law brokers. Here, with foundation support, it is experimenting beyond simply meeting articulated need. By bringing lawyers and programs together it is trying to implement a public objective, to locate interest in order to implement an existing social policy. As a pilot program it has possibilities beyond the field of housing. As we suggest later, it may be the responsibility of the legal profession as a whole to seek public programs which, as a measure of public support of those programs, provide for sub-

5. See discussion, Chapter 5; see also E. Morris, "Lawyers Mobilize for Housing and Urban Renewal," 57 A.B.A.J. 158 (1971).

sidization of lawyers' fees directly in the laws. In this way a public interest bar could implement public policy without bearing the full economic burden. The Truth-in-Lending law has such provision, as do parts of our civil rights legislation and some of the new environmental laws. By legislating lawyers' fees into a program, the private bar may be able to support and sustain effort heretofore handled, if at all, for no fee, or relinquished to the public bar for handling.

Public Interest Field Project

On February 1, 1971, the ABA put a project director—Marna Tucker—into the field with a mandate to assist law firms in public interest endeavors. The background of this project is worth noting. The chairman of the ABA Section of Individual Rights and Responsibilities, Jerome Shestack of Philadelphia, put out a "feeler" to the Ford Foundation in March 1970 in an effort to secure funding for a project in the Section's broad range of interest. The letter to Ford pointed out that the Section itself represented a response to "the higher calling of law"— the obligation of lawyers to become involved in the overriding concerns of society.[6] Ford set aside a grant of $75,000 for an action program, subject to approval, which would be aimed at regaining public confidence in the American legal profession and effecting an assumption of a more responsive role for the American lawyer. Proposals were invited. The staff of the Division of Public Service Activities of the ABA suggested the program which was finally adopted by the Section and by Ford. The staff proposal outlined the project director's job as follows:

> [To] select key localities where private law firm programs
> of public interest are negligible . . . . contact the law firms
> in these areas and ascertain their interest in receiving as-
> sistance in establishing public interest branches of their
> firms . . . . direct a general meeting among interested firms

6. ABA staff proposal to Individual Rights and Responsibilities Section for implementation of a Ford Foundation grant.

> .... [spend] time within each individual firm providing as-
> sistance and guidance in creating such a program.[7]

The administration committee of the Board of Governors of ABA approved the program with two important changes. It prohibited a search for firms or any attempt to stimulate interest among private firms. And it insisted that the project title selected reflect that the project was for the purpose of assisting "interested firms." The changes reflect the arguments seen elsewhere—arguments about the old, passive, common law voice versus the new, active, seeking voice.

A close look at the project reveals that, in spite of its limitations, its offer of technical assistance adopts the missionary model of the Lawyers' Committee for Civil Rights Under Law. The limitations eliminate the issue– or case–brokerage aspect of that model. Unlike the Lawyers' Committee model, however, this is the organized bar acting in its official capacity, not simply the "leaders of the bar" acting without affecting official policy or style. And it is the first statement by the bar that a public interest response might have broader professional meaning than simply doing what is fashionable or expedient. The project contemplates reaching into areas not covered by present visible response, areas not reached by the Lawyers' Committee, and areas not affected by national hiring markets. We have no operating performance to look at as this book goes to press. There is important symbolic meaning in this effort, however, because a significant question is being posed by the national professional association: Is response at some level a matter of duty for law firms? By its action, the ABA is sanctioning a style, soliciting a response, and, to an extent, coordinating a dialogue which might lead to an expanded or changed definition of professional responsibilities.

7. Id.

By means of these three pilot experiments and its supporting efforts for an OEO Legal Services Program, the ABA has begun to broker ideas about how legal services should be distributed. In addition, the housing project involves the brokerage of ideas about community policies. By and large, however, the ABA's efforts have only marginally suggested to lawyers that duty rather than grace is involved.

State and local bar associations have not been in the vanguard of innovative responses to new demands and newly perceived needs. The history of their efforts has been dismal. There have been legal aid committees and indigent criminal defense committees, but there has been little discussion of or thought about professional duty to the public at large. There have, however, been moments of exception. In the early 1950s, for example, the organized bar in Philadelphia adopted a plan whereby it would locate eminent counsel to represent defendants accused of being members of the Communist Party.[8] The adoption of such a plan indicated that the Philadelphia bar had a corporate conception of professional duty. But matters of this sort—legal aid at charitable levels, criminal defense, and defense of the unpopular—were in the traditional supplementary mode. They did not touch the central issue.

Two local bar associations have concerned themselves with the operation of local chapters of the LCCRUL: In Cleveland the city bar association is the local Lawyers' Committee; in Los Angeles the county bar association is seeking to occupy the same role. This kind of activity puts these bar organizations squarely into the work of brokering cases and issues, which is something more than coordinating enthusiasm. An active role is involved, one which is new, one which is inconsistent with traditional bar roles. The inconsistency with traditional roles was apparent to the national Lawyers' Committee and caused it to hesitate before it named the Cleveland bar as the local

8. See M. Ernst & A. Schwartz, "The Right to Counsel and the Unpopular Cause," 20 *U. Pitt. L. Rev.* 727 (1958).

chapter. The experience in Cleveland has been a source of some frustration to LCCRUL; Cleveland has been less active than other chapters. This experience, along with some uncertainty on the part of Los Angeles County Bar Association (perhaps reflecting ambivalence about role), is causing a delay in the designation of the Los Angeles association as a chapter of LCCRUL.

But local bar activity is changing in a way that seems to suggest a search for relevance (similar to the search we witnessed within firms) and a quest for action. The Boston Bar Association, for example, has expanded the operation of its Individual Rights Section to incorporate the housing experiment and other new activities, such as paying heed to police-community relations, educational problems, and problems arising from poverty and urban life. The name of the Section was changed to Urban Affairs Section, and subcommittees were established for "Housing," "Environment," and "Human Services." Active stances are now taken on community issues, and information about program, policy dialogue, and specific projects is brokered under the auspices of the bar.

The Los Angeles County Bar Association has formed a new section, the Human Rights Section, to assume the coordination of projects for "*pro bono* work, human rights, and civil rights kinds of things."[9] According to the chairman of the Human Rights Section, projects in these areas had previously been carried out through special *ad hoc* committees, but a recent increase in projects of this sort indicated the need for a co-ordinated approach.[10] The Los Angeles bar, however, appears to be moving cautiously toward assuming a directly active role.

The Beverly Hills Bar Association has formed a foundation for the express purpose of working actively in some sphere of

9. Unless there is a strong intellectual reason for attribution, names will be omitted, and assigned code numbers for respondents will be given. The respondent here is R55.

10. One of these activities was an attempt to open a legal service office in Watts, but the idea met opposition from the Langston Club, the organized black bar.

public interest work. Its plans were not fully developed when we interviewed some of the officers in September 1970, but they were thinking about a service model—a neighborhood office. They did not, however, exclude the possibility of developing a caseload around law reform issues." The Beverly Hills bar has commissioned extensive studies of the options available to it. It has also established a standing committee with a name that suggests a struggle with a definition of professional responsibility: "The Future of the Profession Committee."

Both the Los Angeles bar and the Beverly Hills bar seem to reflect the tendency we have observed elsewhere—a tendency to adopt forms in advance of the articulation of either the role or the content of these forms. As with the public interest partner and the public interest committee of the law firms, changes reflect struggle, but the meaning of the changes awaits the delivery of committed effort. As one of our respondents stated:

> If the price of action is talk, I think it is a price we ought to pay.[12]

The Los Angeles and Beverly Hills experience is by no means atypical. Public service committees or sections have been established by many state and local bar associations. The dialogue starts as with the other forms: "Tell us what to do." Circumspection marks the progress of the dialogue. Most of what has been delivered into action has been in the service mode. Of course, local bar groups engaging in experimental programs—like the Shreveport Bar Association—may be dealing in different and more efficient ways with the problems of delivering legal services. The movement to action is slow, however. What has been done has often drawn criticism from conservative elements. For example, the Association of the Bar of the City of New York received criticism from within because

11. Interview with Messrs. Webster, Robin, Freeman, and Nicholas, officers of the Beverly Hills Bar Association.
12. R9.

the Association's facilities had been used by the organizers of the lawyers' antiwar march on Washington, even though the Association itself did not take part in that activity.[13]

Conversely, specific bars and the organized bar in general have been criticized for not assuming an active leadership role in drawing the attention of lawyers to public interest issues. The counter-bar with its suggested norm of active involvement is in the vanguard of this criticism. The counter-bar movement includes ad hoc groups of lawyers assembled to pursue activities and ongoing projects which are beyond the seeming scope or indicated willingness of the organized bar. The counter-bar movement also includes attempts to restructure the core of lawyer association so that the organized profession addresses itself outwardly, as a profession should, rather than inwardly, as a trade association does. The broader efforts of the movement have produced new bar organizations.[14] The movement reminds one of the revival period which saw the birth of the Association of the Bar of the City of New York and of the American Bar Association.

LCCRUL was a counter-bar effort when it boldly stepped into the central issues of our time, although we are sure that the leaders of the bar who responded to President Kennedy did not view it as such. It was not, however, addressed to a major revision of the definition of the bar's role or of professional responsibility. Paradoxically, its operation has substantially affected that definition.

The Council of New York Law Associates, discussed in Chapter 5, actively sought to perform the function of brokering public interest opportunities, a function which its members felt was not performed by the organized bar. But the scope of the Council's efforts was relatively limited, compared to the activities of a full-service bar association.

13. R10.
14. In the new lawyer groups the term "Council of Lawyers" seems to have replaced "Association" as a generic description. We have no theory about this change in language. Perhaps it is a conscious avoidance of the connotations of "association" or "guild."

The Council of Lawyers of Los Angeles represents a more significant step toward a full counter-bar association. It was formed to have a broad scope, focused on the public interest. The call to join reads:

> The legal profession is experiencing an awakening of social conscience. Lawyers in unprecedented numbers now recognize a responsibility to commit their talents in confronting a broad variety of social and political problems.
>
> The Council is a new organization of lawyers and law students in the Los Angeles area who are vitally concerned about the problems affecting our community and anxious to participate actively in confronting these problems. *Our legal community needs an organization dedicated entirely to fostering and facilitating a more active involvement by lawyers in the public interest.* The Council has been formed to meet this need by transforming good intentions into functional projects.[15] [Emphasis supplied.]

The emphasized portion of the above quote indicates the "counter" element involved in the formation of this council. "Task forces," rather than "committees," have been established for the programs of pollution, prisons, demonstrations, union discriminatory practices, and education. Task forces are being planned for insurance practice in ghettos and barrios, land-use planning practice, consumer protection, and the extension of community legal services.[16] As is true of the Council of New York Law Associates, younger lawyers are the moving spirit and working force of the Los Angeles Council.

The Chicago Council of Lawyers is a counter-bar which comes closest to being a full-range professional organization. A greater percentage of older lawyers belong to it and are involved in its working committees. This Council has been active in "debating" with the Chicago Bar Association the issues of professional standards and standards of judicial selection. It recently found that only four judges on a judicial slate of fifty

15. Open letter from Council of Lawyers of Los Angeles to "All Lawyers in the Los Angeles Community" (undated).
16. *Id.*

candidates were qualified; all had been listed as "qualified" by the Chicago Bar Association. On controversial community issues the Chicago Council has taken positions which either involve questions of professional responsibility or invite the participation of lawyers. It coordinated the call to Chicago lawyers to participate in the antiwar demonstration in Washington and entered the case calling for a special grand jury in the Hampton-Clark deaths.[17] It believes that a professional organization should, with the approval of a majority of its members, take affirmative stands and should not avoid controversy in deference to the qualms of some of its members.[18] We see this belief resting on an assumption that a response to higher calling necessarily implies controversy. To be sure, controversy is avoided by speaking for the lowest common denominator—speaking only when consensus can be had—but so also is professional responsibility avoided. This truth seems to apply equally to questions of passing on judicial competence, seeking methods of acting for the poor, or speaking to controversial community issues. The counter-bar movement, viewed against the existence of the traditional bar, is, in a way, a macrocosmic reflection of the choice presented each individual lawyer and law firm: whether to adopt a neutral or a value-laden approach.

Another counter-bar association, born in the 1930s, is still active in some of the places we visited, particularly on the West Coast. The National Lawyers Guild has supported the formation of private public interest law firms and law communes. Its members have actively assisted young lawyers who seek, from the standpoint of their greater social consciousness, a client mix. The Lawyers Guild has also brokered issues and cases. It

17. See discussion under Businessmen for the Public Interest in Chapter 6.

18. Organizational structure allows committee reports to be acted on with celerity by the Board. Style allows for committee reports to be accepted with the presumption that the working committee knows the issues and the need for action.

publishes a loose-leaf service which covers contemporary cases and issues.

There seems to be a stirring among the organized bars. Symbols are changing; some counter-cultural forms are emerging. The principal new focus of the traditional bar has been to ask how legal services can be more effectively extended to groups not heretofore represented. The primary departure of the counter-bar has been to assert that a lawyer *must* take a more active role in the affairs of the community, that a lawyer *must* address community conflict and not wait for the representatives of conflicting parties or interests to find their way to his office.

PART THREE

THREE

The Meaning of Public Interest Response

cHApTER 8

Why Is tHE PublIc INTEREST REspoNSE OccURRiNq Now?

In exploring the nature and scope of the public interest response, we must attempt to understand why this activity is
occurring now. This can be best understood by viewing the
conflict between demands for a change in the lawyer's role
and the resistance to change which is based on adherence to
the traditional ways that law has been practiced in this country.
Both the demands and the resistance are occurring inside as
well as outside the profession. There has been a more rapid
change in rhetoric than in action; this, too, can be understood
in terms of the conflict between demand for change and resistance to that change.

The New Professional
The sought-for change in the professional role of the lawyer
entails abandonment of the traditional concept of professional
neutrality, a concept in which the lawyer does not identify
himself with the goals of the client or with the outcome of a
matter or its social consequences. The new, policy-oriented

202

lawyers, and those who consciously extend existing service facilities, seem to envision a new profession. They see the roles of both client and lawyer changing. And they see new ways of presenting issues for resolution. The committed lawyer is seen as taking a role which allows him to express personal values as well as to assume an ultimate personal responsibility for his professional actions.[1]

> It is important to recognize explicitly that whether he is engaged publicly or privately, the lawyer will no longer be serving merely as the spokesman for others. As the law becomes more and more a determinative force in public and private affairs, the lawyer must carry the responsibility of his specialized knowledge, and formulate ideas as well as advocate them.[2]

The new demands call for a shift in primary loyalty—from the corporate interests of the establishment toward the unrepresented interests of society. A new language is emerging. It includes talk of representing the indigent or the consumer as a class, of monitoring federal agencies, of seeking desirable social goals. The lawyer using this language can be likened to the doctor speaking to issues of public health:

> Where doctors act as spokesmen for the physical health of the community, lawyers feel that this aspect of their role calls for informing, educating, and protecting Americans in regard to the exercise of their political rights.[3]

The legal profession is conservative by nature; the nature of law and the legal process is the basis of this conservatism. The doctrine of precedent says: What is past is present and, by

1. Comment, "The New Public Interest Lawyers," 79 *Yale L.J.* 1069 (1970).
2. R. Nader quotes professor Charles Reich of Yale Law School in "Law Schools and Law Firms," 3 *Beverly Hills B.J.* 13 (No. 10, 1969).
3. D. Lortie, "The Striving Young Lawyer" (Ph.D. diss., University of Chicago, 1958), p. 140. Both the legal and the medical professions have dealt with this aspect of professional role in the past in their respective public sectors, i.e., the public lawyer and the public health physician.

implication, even future. Moreover, the resulting rules and laws—legislative or judicial—in themselves seek to respond to sought-for stability. The burden has always been on the one who seeks change. The people who have entered the profession of law have sought stability, and their socialization in law school—concentration on precedent—has for the most part reinforced its quest. Not that adjustment to change is not stressed as a major function of law: It is. But the basic orientation of the system is toward securing what is. Beyond the nurture of law school, particularly for those who have opted for the mainstream of the profession, the socialization process continues to reinforce and reward the conservatism reflected in career choice.[4] The dominant client group is in business enterprise. The dominant organization of practice consists of departmentalization and specialization aimed at efficiently serving the interests of corporations. Harold Laski in 1948 noted that specialization itself engenders conservatism.[5]

There have always been voices seeking to drive, shame, or lead the profession away from its role as conserver and toward a more active role in seeking responsible social changes. In the mid-1960s, the voices became louder and listeners more attentive. Mr. Justice Brennan,[6] in an often-cited address at Harvard Law School, reiterated the point that the profession, dedicated to the service of business, had neglected its social responsibility. He doubted then that the legal profession was fully capable of or even willing to carry out its professional charge. He noted a cleavage in the profession whereby public interest work was done mostly by government lawyers and professors, who had (in 1967) just recently been joined by the young lawyers associated with neighborhood legal offices or

4. It goes without saying, even for the new breed, that lawyers make lousy revolutionaries.

5. H. Laski, *The American Democracy*, 575–79, 590–91 (1948).

6. Brennan, J., "The Responsibilities of the Legal Profession," *The Path of the Law from 1967* (A. Sutherland ed., 1968).

with organizations serving public "causes." The practicing bar, at the time of his address, had for the most part remained nonsupportive.[7]

Mr. Justice Brennan concluded that additional outside pressure was needed, that new problem areas, such as consumer protection, welfare, and landlord-tenant conflicts, required a departure from or a supplement of traditional methods of legal solution. His address was a call to the profession to be responsive to need and to act in advance of the explicit declaration of that need. The profession was asked to enter the realm of policy and public responsibility, seeing to it that the rules were fair and that all had access to the system.

Actions in the direction suggested by Mr. Justice Brennan were being taken even before his speech. Mississippi Summer 1964 and the new law reformers—typified by the OEO attorneys—were visible examples. These actions can be viewed not only as responses to pressures emanating from the events and changes of the outside world but also as responses to pressures from within the profession. The actions themselves contributed to a state of conflict within the conservative profession, and they created a more explicit conflict with traditional values and traditional forms of organization.

Pressures from Within the Profession

Pressure for change in the ethical standards and ideals of the profession came from the law students who were emerging from law schools in the late 1960s. Much of the observable change since then has been in response to that pressure. All the law firm respondents in our study cited the law student demand as a major factor in their adoption of a public interest form, or at least a public interest image, and most respondents cited the students as the single or final factor which led their firms to formally address the problem of public interest re-

7. *Id.* We do not here imply that all this has, in the intervening years, changed in any massive way.

sponse.[8] The reason for this effect is simple; it was dictated by economic necessity. Moral force may have been involved. We think it was. But it was moral force impelled by a strong economic lever. The establishment law firm is the major employer of law school graduates, the young lawyers. Large establishment law firms compete vigorously for talent. They have been pushing forward the recruitment timing; summer internships are a way of lining up future prospects after their first year of law school, and employment interviews are scheduled almost a year ahead of graduation.

The demand for talent is fed by a discernible growth pattern of the establishment firms, which in turn reflects the increase in dollar demand by clients for the services of these firms. (The demand for new lawyers has always been inflated by the high dropout rate among large firms.[9]) The growing excess of demand over supply is dramatically revealed in the 40 percent increase in the salaries of beginning lawyers over the last two decades. Since the mid-1960s, the already disproportionate rise of demand over supply has been heightened by factors which operate to diminish the supply of lawyers available to the large firms. New career options, such as the OEO Legal Services Programs, the Peace Corps (legal and non-legal), and VISTA, offer satisfaction to the student's heightened appetite for community service. An involuntary career option, the draft, also adversely affects the supply of young lawyers.[10] These market pressures, along with the obvious message communicated to the firms when students not infrequently chose alternate career options, led directly to the offering of non-dollar inducements; the opportunity to gratify the desire to

8. We do not suggest, nor did our respondents suggest, that student demand was the sole input. It was not. Pressures for change already existed within many firms. The student pressure was, however, the catalyst for change.

9. E. Smigel, *The Wall Street Lawyer: Professional Organization Man?* 74 (1964).

10. The increased draft, fed by the undeclared war in Southeast Asia, of course, affects more than supply. It has been a pervasive factor in forcing the emergence of and shaping a heightened social conscience.

respond to social need became part of the law firm's offer to young law students. The offer was tutored by articulated student demand and, in some instances, by threatened boycott. One firm considering the adoption of public interest forms demonstrated its concern by writing in the fall of 1969 about the "market" competition in a memorandum considering the adoption of public interest forms:

> It has become increasingly evident that there is a tendency among younger lawyers, particularly those with *highest academic qualification,* to seek out public service-oriented careers as an alternative to practice in the larger metropolitan law firm.[11] [Emphasis supplied.]

Law Students and the Law Firms

The political consciousness of the 1960s, added to the rebelliousness and life-style experimentation which characterize present-day American youth, has produced a generation of law

---

11. Unless there is a strong intellectual reason for attribution, names will be omitted, and assigned code numbers for respondents will be given. The respondent here is R34. The memorandum reflected the statistics available at that time about law school graduates entering private practice. These statistics showed drops in rates of entry: Harvard dropped from 54 percent in 1964 to 41 percent in 1968; Yale, from 41 percent in 1968 to 31 percent in 1969; and the University of Virginia, from 63 percent in 1968 to 54 percent in 1969.

For the class of June 1970 these rates were reversed. At Harvard the percentage of students entering private practice rose dramatically. The factors which may have contributed to this reversal are the economic recession, a closing off of significant career options in OEO Legal Services Programs and the Peace Corps, and a diminution of the effect of the draft on graduating law students. The student looking at OEO in June 1970 was indeed looking at a dwindling short-term career option, which, after the Murphy Amendment fight, had looked less attractive anyway. All things taken into account, many factors were affecting the job market. Because of the proliferation of public interest forms and the even more extensive proliferation of public interest rhetoric—which in some instances has sounded like an invitation to join Robin Hood and the group in Sherwood Forest to practice high-paying law for the sole purpose of giving to the poor—there is reason to believe that many students were able to make peace between their desire to serve and their need for income. They joined the private law firms, where starting salaries were $18,000 a year in some instances.

students who are not satisfied with the legal profession's traditional career lines. Youth is a time of searching for commitment and identity, and the adoption of a particular life style serves to confirm a chosen or sought-for identity:

> It is the young who, by their responses and actions, tell the old whether life as represented to them has some vital promise, and it is the young who carry in them the power . . . to renew and regenerate, to disavow what is rotten, to reform and rebel.[12]

In the 1960s, activism, born of outrage at injustice, was prevalent on the campuses of major colleges and law schools throughout the country. Kenneth Keniston reminds us that those students who are in the vanguard of social change tend to be among the brightest and the most idealistic. Such students—intellectually oriented, politically liberal, and from professional families—gravitate to the major universities in the country.[13] Erwin Smigel's statistical analysis in *The Wall Street Lawyer*[14] shows that lawyers with these same characteristics are the ones most coveted by the large firm. The social consciousness of the more able students, with their attendant career options, became, therefore, a direct factor affecting the supply and price of talent available to large law firms.

The new ideals are an integral part of the law students' definition of professional responsibility. The recruiting process is a good perspective from which to view the kinds of pressure the students have put on the law firms. Traditionally, the law student applying for a position in a law firm has been passive, accommodating, and willing to answer questions in a way he thinks the firm would like. Over the last few years there has been a departure from the traditional recruitment interview. There has been a role reversal, with the law students becoming more aggressive—inquiring about the amount of public inter-

12. E. Erikson, *Identity: Youth and Crisis* 258 (1968).
13. K. Keniston, "Harvard On My Mind," 15 *New York Review of Books* 6 (No. 5, Sept. 24, 1970).
14. Smigel, *supra* note 9, at 113–41.

est legal work performed by the firm—and the interviewer listening and responding.[15] Some of the major law schools (or student associations within those schools) even ask firms recruiting on campus to respond in advance to questionnaires concerning firms' policies and attitudes toward public interest work.[16]

The increase in career options available to the younger lawyer undoubtedly, while it lasted, served to increase his sense of autonomy during the recruitment process. If he were not offered a type of practice which would give him an opportunity to fulfill his public interest aspirations, he could join a legal service program.[17] Indeed, the nature of the options open to him accentuated the central issues in the bargaining process—focus was on public interest work. Monroe Freedman described the student attitude toward the law firm as

> a concerted movement—almost to the same effect as if they had said, "We are a union now, and we are not going to work unless we have these conditions." It has been that widespread. . . . The firms have become quite aware that they are not going to get the better people if they do not make time available.

It is important to point out that rhetoric about public interest work is the basic currency of exchange between the students and the firms, but the actual level of public interest activity in the law firms, for both those who do the hiring and those who are hired, in many instances does not support the weight of the rhetoric. Many firms, confronted by students' questions concerning their public interest work, responded with "public interest memoranda." These memos frequently used offhand references to a firm's associations or affiliations

15. R12, R44.
16. The students at the University of Buffalo and Georgetown University used a questionnaire developed by E. and J. Cahn (reproduced in "Justice, the Rule of Law and You: A Challenge," mimeographed, pp. 5–6). Harvard law students used a model developed by Ralph Nader; Stanford, Yale, and George Washington students have developed their own.
17. See note 11, *supra*.

with organized efforts such as the Lawyers' Committee for Civil Rights Under Law or Community Law Offices. Or they alluded to a firm's "public interest partner" or committee. These symbols were useful in the rhetoric of recruiting, and in many instances seemingly became more important in the process than the actual substance of the public interest efforts. Rarely was there an attempt to describe specific public interest efforts; instead, the listed formal affiliations with public interest organizations seemed to be substitutes for candid discussion about role changes. In other words, appearances and forms were the tools used in the recruitment of law students. "We work with the Lawyers' Committee" was the law firm's counterpart of "Let's have a meaningful dialogue."

Large law firms have traditionally had specific policies about the approval of "nonfirm" work by associates. The policies have not always been formal; there are informal—sometimes subtle—ways of discouraging nonpaying work. The new institutional promises that law firms make to job-seeking law students do not necessarily mean that the way in which arrangements are made for carrying out these promises has drastically altered. Abstract commitment has not changed working relationships. There are still the individual views of partners to consider—partners whose views about their firms' announced *pro bono* policies may vary. Individually and collectively, they, not "the firm," supervise associates and reward them for their work:[18]

> Although the public service commitment of many private law firms has been increasing, the attitudes of individual firm members toward such work often conflict. Young lawyers desiring to do *pro bono* work are often wary that the firm, even if purporting to support or allow such work on firm time, will in fact penalize those engaging in it.[19]

18. See in Smigel, *supra* note 9, at 97, a chart of what an associate can do to help himself become a partner.

19. Comment, "Structuring the Public Services Efforts of Private Law Firms," 84 *Harv. L. Rev. 410* (1970).

Thus, even within the firm, conflict remains. The pull of tradition is countered by the push for change. In those firms where older associates and partners have been committed for some time to public interest actions because of dissatisfaction with the way in which they have had to carry out their professional roles, we found real and substantial change.

A few lawyers have taken major steps away from traditional law firm roles: For example, after many years in establishment law firms Alexander Polikoff (who had been a partner) and Charles Halpern (who had been a senior associate) each left his firm to assume the direction of a public interest law firm. Many private firms have made no discernible moves toward a public interest response, but their struggle with the problem has already affected their ultimate commitment to a public interest response.[20] Still others have remained completely unconcerned. Ultimately, the issue of change will turn on how the lawyer sees himself and is seen by others as a professional relating to injustice in the world and, further, on how the lawyer himself relates his personal—human—responses to his profession.

Practicing Lawyers

There exists in American society a tension between "work" and "living."[21] A man's work constitutes one of the more important parts of his social identity;[22] at the same time, however, work is frequently viewed as something necessary so that something else—living—is possible.[23] Professions generally, and the legal profession as it is followed today in particular, require that much of the living take place outside the confines of professional life. The norms of the legal profession dictate

20. R35, R65.
21. K. Keniston, The Uncommitted: Alienated Youth in American Society (1965).
22. E. Hughes, Men and Their Work 43 (1958).
23 K. Keniston, supra note 21.

that one be unemotional and objective at work. Response to beauty or ugliness lies outside professional life—or tends to.[24] Although there have been feelings that certain *pro bono* work is a legitimate outlet for charitable propensities, such efforts have frequently been conducted outside the professional life of the firm and the lawyer. The work identity of the lawyer— the specialization, unemotionality, and neutrality demanded from him, especially in large law firms—is alienating. In reaction, lawyers may reach out for more meaningful endeavors, such as public interest work, with commitment, enthusiasm, and dedication; it is in their role as humans, not as lawyers, that they respond to social problems. Even in the public interest field the attorney *must* have commitment, enthusiasm, and dedication, because public interest work, particularly when it is embraced vocationally, also seems to fall prey to the norms that rule out emotionality and subjectivism. Just as the neutral lawyer who narrowly served his client had to remember that he was "doing justice," so the public interest lawyer has to hold in mind the beauty of the call:[25]

> Guys coming out of law schools see it as a very romantic thing—to go out and change the world through litigation; and soon they find out, however, that it isn't so romantic. *It's just a lot of hard work.*[26]

Firm associates who are several years out of law school and have done public interest work seem to be crucial to the effective formulation of their firm's address to public service. Perhaps their stage of career development has made them

24. The novels of Louis Auchincloss, lawyer turned author, reflect this insulation from human value. To underscore this flatness, Felix Frankfurter once whimsically suggested that law schools give a course consisting of field trips to art museums. The field trips to the ghettos and to Mississippi may have served the same purpose.

25. A. Fortas, "Thurman Arnold and the Theatre of the Law," 79 *Yale L.J.,* 998 (1970), speaks of the ideal lawyer in the ideal system. The public interest lawyer may be simply a lawyer who, working in an un-ideal system, has to contend with the problems arising from that situation.

26. R63.

secure enough to ask the questions: "What am I doing? Why?"
Perhaps, too, the questions are shaped by their associations
with colleagues in other firms who are asking the same questions. Although associates, even older ones, very rarely have
any say in the management, intake, or administration of a firm's
regular work, they do have a say in these matters as they relate
to the firm's explicit public interest work.[27] These lawyers are
sensitive to controls over "nonfirm" work, and conscious, from
their own experiences, of the sense of liberation that accom-
panies reaching out for public interest work. They are also
sensitive to the difference between "firm" public interest work
as a part of professional duty and a simple encouragement or
permission to do independent public interest work. They are
more sensitive to the implications of these differences than are
the younger attorneys or law students, who might look grate-
fully at the allocation of firm time to "do their thing." The
younger lawyers may fail to realize that, as long as they have
to finish paying work after hours or on weekends, permission
to do public interest work does not alter the fact that the work
remains avocational.

Paralleling the push for redirection of efforts within the
firm is a new vision, among the young and even the not-so-
young lawyers, of acceptable professional goals:

> Involvement in legal problems of the poor and in environ-
> mental issues is replacing participation in bar associations'
> corporate law sections, and aspiration to lead local aid
> programs ranks with the ambition to head the local bar as-
> sociation.[28]

A new kind of legal work is replacing the old, approved activities. And, in the process, the kind of work which was once
thought of as charity begins to look like an integral part of
professional life.

In summary, those very lawyers who had been to Mis-

---

27. R28, R61, R62.
28. J. Robson, "Private Lawyers and Public Interest," 56 *A.B.A.J.* 332,
334 (1970).

sissippi, who have taken ACLU cases, who have defended indigents accused of crimes, and who have volunteered hours for legal aid work, together with their younger colleagues who have, more recently, been in the Peace Corps or OEO Legal Services, have been those most responsible for the present proliferation of public interest activity. They have brought the pressure that has caused the senior partners to change at least the symbols of commitment; perhaps ultimately the pressure will cause the partners to bring commitment into full reality. It is these lawyers who are urging upon their colleagues a new conception of their profession, or, perhaps more accurately, an old conception which had been abandoned:

> A profession is a line of work in which, so long as he who professes it can eat, his job is service.[29]

The new view of the profession is that one can have pride in his craft and at the same time actively serve society. One can do a job which has both social and personal rewards. Unfortunately the prevalent view remains that service means service of those interests which bid for the lawyer's time— professional work and personal gratification do not mix.

Pressures from the Outside World—New Demands, Chaos, and an Indictment

The "new" conflicts raging in the 1960s, some of which were simply dramatic proofs that major social injustices had been festering unattended for years, had a major impact on many law students and also on the more sensitive of those people already in the profession. The outrages of racism, poverty, hunger, and the fouling of our own nest (the environment) burst upon us as a new lexicon. These were not new problems (they were, after all, very old problems), but there were new imperatives. Events evidencing the severity of these problems

29. K. Llewellyn, "The Bar Specializes—With What Results?" 167 *Annals* 177, 190 (May 1933). Llewellyn posed an additional definition: "Service ahead of gain."

were dramatic and urgently compelling. Our institutions were in crisis. National policies were adopted to meet some of the new crises—the Civil Rights Act of 1964, the Economic Opportunity Act of 1964 (the "War on Poverty"). Violence and upheaval revealed the festering wounds. Moderate men, such as the members of the President's Commission on Civil Disorder (the Kerner Commission), were able to reach an unprecedented and unanimous finding: We live in a racist society. The fact of the conflict was inescapable. The law student, contemplating his chosen profession, could not help wondering why the law had not worked to eradicate these problems and what would make it work. He would not accept the idea that the profession continue as it had in the past; this was simply untenable. It was untenable to the thinking lawyer, too. Or at least it was becoming so. Unmet need was getting very noisy.

In our society, any attack on institutions, and indeed any crisis, must ultimately be viewed in terms of how it relates to the law and the legal profession. Presumably the function of law, and of those operating the legal system, is to structure the conflicts of society so that they are capable of peaceful resolution. Any realistic view of the present catalogue of unresolved conflicts, including an understanding of how long some of the problems have been swept under the carpet, leads to a fairly grim assessment of the legal profession. There is no escape from the conclusion that the job of dealing with society's conflicts has not been done.

The people who in the 1960s were articulating the conflicts in the loudest fashion presented the legal profession with a haunting bill. They were the people who had been inadequately represented, or not represented at all, in judicial or political dialogue. They had not been represented by the people in government or by the private practitioners of law. Nor were the private practitioners of law watching to see that government functioned to meet the needs of these unrepresented and underrepresented groups. The demands, which had been repressed, were for both what was in fact already due under existing rules of law and for new rules. The inadequacy of past legal response from public and private sectors was apparent.

When asked why the public interest response is now occurring, a Washington lawyer told us:

> There is a new awareness on the part of the bar that the country is in serious trouble and that we better begin working within our institutions to straighten things out. Right now![30]

This belief was echoed by many of our respondents when we asked them to reflect on the reasons for a public interest movement. It was echoed by respondents who were trying to meet newly articulated demand and by those who were seeking to formulate issues in order to generate new demands. The relationship between present crisis and past performance was also understood by the respondents. The difference between the ideal of equal representation before the law and what has really existed is vast. That difference has delayed an articulation of conflicts to a point beyond politeness. In addition to meeting the emergency, it will be necessary to bring delivery of legal services permanently into line with the promise of equality.[31]

The LCCRUL[32] was the result of an early effort of a segment of the bar to bring the bar's prestige and problem-solving skills to bear on a major problem which had been long ignored by the bar—civil rights. Ironically, LCCRUL's first project was to supply lawyers for legal problems in Mississippi, where the local bar simply refused to give the needed representation. There is additional irony: It was not very effective delivery of services:

> A lot of volunteer lawyers helped, but it was impossible to

30. R34.

31. Charles Morgan of the ACLU, speaking of constitutional precept, made a statement which has application to the efforts of the public interest lawyers. He said, in effect, that the Bill of Rights is not a bad document; we ought to try it someday. Similarly a system of equal justice under law is not a bad idea—we ought to try it someday.

32. See description in Chapter 5.

> supervise 10–15 volunteer lawyers who stayed only two weeks and when they left were just beginning to learn how to file the right paper. It was rather a bad scene when all of them left in September and we were left with maybe a thousand cases pending. . . . I would never use volunteer lawyers anymore. . . . Too much hassle.[33]

Although there was little difference between the past indifference of the bar as a whole and the Mississippi bar's refusal to serve (both unpardonable), ineffectiveness in delivering or attempting to deliver services to the unrepresented can be pardoned—and cured, as long as desire to serve remains. Therefore it is significant that the leaders of the bar—the top leaders—said, as did President Kennedy, that a responsible bar should go to Mississippi.

There is further and more recent evidence of a shift in the view of professional duty by some of the bar's leaders—the senior lawyers. A new style is emerging, typified by the delegation of 1,000 Wall Street lawyers from New York, led by a prominent senior partner, who were in Washington on May 20, 1970, to protest this country's involvement in Cambodia.[34] They, too, are attempting to meet the new demands for professional leadership in the crucial affairs facing the nation. In the process they are having an effect on the entire profession.

Response to the demands of the outside world by both young and senior lawyers and the pressures from within for a new professional identity have already profoundly affected the symbols and, to a lesser extent, the forms of professional address to public service. The bulk of the profession, however, still slumbers on, aware of the new symbols, but unaffected by them. Yet the very pressures that have led so far to the forms of response we have considered are still working on the conservative element in the profession, because the causes of the initial changes still exist.

33. Y1.
34. Wall Street Journal, May 20, 1970 at 1, col. 1.

Why Is the Public Interest Response
Happening Where It Is Happening?

The visible and formal public interest responses of the private bar are not occurring evenly throughout the country. They are concentrated in Boston, New York City, Washington, and Philadelphia, and—to a lesser extent—in Chicago, Los Angeles, and San Francisco. In addition, isolated pockets of formal response are scattered throughout the country. In part, the concentration of public interest activity is explained by the nature of the national marketplace—that is, where the clients are and with whom they do business, where the law firms are and with whom they compete for business and talent. The way in which law is practiced in the cities where public interest activities are taking place is relevant, as is the ambience of those cities. By and large the most innovative public interest responses have occurred in major cities where there is a constant demand for legal work on a grand scale. Competition for business, talent, and prestige is the matrix of the public interest response.

Competition for law students in a national market is, of course, a key factor in explaining why the public interest response occurs where it does. We have talked about the persistent demands of the law students. A factor of differentiation between cities and between firms within those cities is the degree to which the pressure of business forces law firms to seek talent in a national market. Cities and firms compete with one another in that market: cities as desirable places in which to live and as "stimulating places" in which to practice law, firms as the best alternative in the country or in a particular city. The competition is both national and local. We have already seen how the public interest symbols are used as currency in the marketplace. The forms themselves may be explained in terms of meeting the competition in the marketplace. For instance, if one firm belongs to the Lawyers' Committee, other firms feel obliged to either associate with the Committee or come up with a comparable attraction. Firms which do not compete in the national market because they traditionally accept law school graduates from local schools are not under this kind of pressure—unless those graduates are being sought elsewhere in the country. The quality and prestige of the local school is critical here: The large Boston firms hire much of their talent from a local school—Harvard. If students do not have an outlet to a national market, they do not usually have the leverage to demand that prospective employers be making public interest responses.

The more intense the competition for law students in a given city, the greater will be the likelihood of a visible public interest response in the city. The briskness of competition not only puts pressure on the levels of public interest response but also works as incentive for the boldness and inventiveness of the forms. The most innovative responses are occurring in New York City and Washington, where the competition for students is keenest. In San Francisco, by contrast, both the level of response and the style are muted by the sunshine factor— more students want to locate there and will place less demand on the market. (The trading of good works for easy living may come more easily in such a market.)

Once a law firm within a given city announces a particular public interest response, other firms in the city counter with their own forms—matching or otherwise. The first firm in a city (particularly in a city where there is intense competition) to adopt a form is a trailblazer and a stylesetter. Other firms *must* make their own responses for fear of being outdone by "the competition." One of our respondents stated:

> Once several firms got into it, they escalated to keep up with each other. . . . If other firms did CLO work one night a week, it would be easier for us to do it also.[35]

The ever-present frame of reference within which law

35. R12.

firms compete to attract law students consists of a variety of public interest forms. Forms of public interest response become as regularized in the hiring process as salaries, although not as capable of being quantified. The firms are offering a kind of fringe benefit. And, like most fringe benefit packages, the offerings reflect the realities of the marketplace.

In the process of competing for talent a firm builds a public image. This may not be the only reason for building the public image; the image is not always directed to the world of the law school only. A view of the law firm in relation to other law firms is involved—both for the lawyers in the firm and for those in the community. In any event, a competition for good public image takes place.[36]

Local custom and tradition—legal and general—as well as responsiveness play a role in moderating or compelling the nature of public interest responses. In Atlanta, for example, law firms have not established any new forms, even though some lawyers within firms are, as individuals, engaged in new-form responses. The firms have traditionally considered all outside activities—professional and other—as being no part of their concern. This style of professional autonomy continues, in spite of the change in the nature of the lawyer's activities. The tradition has promoted harmony within firms. One lawyer can support the Klan while another lawyer in the same firm supports fair housing; neither jeopardizes or compromises the firm. In Atlanta, as we have seen, the LCCRUL had to break away from its usual procedure of approaching a firm *qua* firm. There it contacts lawyers as individuals and is one of the externally added community ingredients which supply outlets for the new lawyer. The firms have no competitive advantage

---

36. We do not mean to suggest that even in places like New York City or Washington all firms adopt forms or get caught up in the competition of providing forms. From the level of public interest response, it is evident that this is not the case. Firms may simply compete with dollars for young lawyers, or, because of their size or situation, with attractive professional opportunities: more rapid advancement into court, into a specialized practice, or into the partnership itself.

or disadvantage thereby. Through the Lawyers' Committee, cases have been brought charging discrimination in the police and fire departments, a rare move for an established lawyer in a northern city, rarer still for a private attorney in the South. The lawyers, the firms, and the Lawyers' Committee itself have all had some of their response to situations shaped by the fact that they function in Atlanta.

Little of the formal structure of the public interest response *qua* firm in New York City approaches the level of response we observed in Washington. Yet because New York City is New York City, firms there are able to compete for personnel especially well by using a public interest currency. It is a currency that assumes the urbane, cosmopolitan nature of the professionals. New York firms can plug into dozens of active programs which use volunteers, and can count on young lawyers to extend the frontiers opened by those programs. The Council of New York Law Associates and the CLO are examples of such active programs. As in Atlanta the inputs for involvement in public interest work come from outside the firms. But, unlike the firms in Atlanta, the firms in New York City need to identify, for competitive and traditional reasons, with public interest activity. The effort for that activity, however, is born of the city's élan.

In Los Angeles a geographically dispersed and loosely organized private bar predisposes toward efforts for a group approach.[37] There is a tendency to organize multifirm efforts, such as the ill-fated consortium office in Watts or the *ad hoc* projects carried out through the bar association, examples of which are the attempts to support scholarships for black students in law schools or to monitor parades where violence might occur. Effort is mutual; this fact may in part reflect less interfirm competition about public interest work than in other cities, and most surely results in diminished competition. Competition is muted, not because a firm is doing something in a

37. The dispersion of the bar and of bar organizations in Los Angeles is like the oft-stated description of the dispersion of the city of Los Angeles: "Seven suburbs in search of a city."

way similar to that of other firms, but because it is doing the *same* thing at the same place *with* other firms.

The development of public interest work in the city of Washington, where the private law firms have produced the greatest innovations in public interest forms and where the new form, the public interest law firm, sprang into being and blossomed, is a story unto itself. The forms have proliferated, but the reasons for this proliferation are complex. The fact that Washington is the center of policy making and decision making is the basic reason for the city's uniqueness. The size and the centralization of the city's enterprise, the pervasiveness of Government (it is a company town), and the effect that these things have had, over the years, on the character of the Washington bar describe the city's essence for our purposes. Washington attracts young lawyers of a special type—those who seek to do public service, who aspire to high purpose, or who are drawn to the corridors of power by their desire to be at the heart of vital decision making. The market for lawyers is brisk in Washington. If the supply of lawyers there is greater than in other cities, it must be remembered that government is the largest single user of legal talent. Notwithstanding younger lawyers' disenchantment with government, the abovementioned facts keep the competitive edge high.

Dollars alone have probably never been enough to hold a lawyer in private practice in Washington. Even before the emergence of new forms, Washington firms had to allow their lawyers to participate in the city's exciting rule-making and policy dialogues. This participation frequently took the form of leaves of absence for government service, but participation short of that has always been tolerated, even encouraged. The tradition is clear. It was noted by Mr. Justice Brennan in the speech we cited earlier that the Washington lawyer has always passed freely from private practice to government and back again.[38] The Washington lawyer has always been active, through established organizations such as ACLU or through *ad*

38. Brennan, J., *supra* note 6.

hoc committees, when an issue arose or when a task needed doing.

The fact that the Washington law firm is set up along specialized lines in order to deal with a government set up in the same way may have allowed this tradition to develop. It means that clients hire Washington counsel for specialized tasks, more often than not on a matter-by-matter basis, and not as general counsel on a regular retainer. A client of a Washington firm does not seek from that firm a general allegiance beyond his particular needs:

> Washington lawyers are disposed like the spokes of a wheel. They practice down the spokes against the hub which is the common opponent—the government—but seldom do their activities extend to what is doing on another spoke, even though it be only next door or across the street.[39]

Too, the clients of Washington lawyers are usually remote from that city. They know little of what their lawyers are doing beyond what the lawyers are doing for them.[40] These factors of specialization and remoteness have provided an atmosphere less hostile to the emergence of the new forms within the law firms in Washington.

The Washington lawyer, public and private, to some extent has always been situation oriented. For the private lawyer the situational view may be limited by, and to, his specialization. But he does participate in dialogue about rules and policy. It is a participation, however, that is usually limited to holding an adversary or watching brief for private clients. Paradoxically, the specialization which has given the Washington lawyer a greater latitude for public interest response has frequently inhibited him from taking public interest clients before certain

39. C. Horsky, *The Washington Lawyer* 160–61 (1952).
40. Throughout our study the subject of whether clients were concerned about the behavior of their lawyers remained nebulous. Some of our respondent lawyers point to the subject, or at least to their own concern about it, as central. We agree with one of them (R34), who said, "The clients do not care. It is a great illusion that they do." At any rate, it is an illusion which many seem to hold.

agencies—those agencies where he practices for his regular clients. This inhibition has become critical for the new lawyers, particularly as they have begun to see that government service no longer provides an alternative way for addressing issues.

As Government emerged as the active or defaulting adversary, and as the private firm was seen to limit effective representation of the public—particularly in the watchdog or monitoring areas—the public interest law firms were created. The founders of these firms are the Washington lawyers who seek to find a new voice in the void between the private law firms and Government.

chapter 9

Who Are the "Public Interest Clients"?

Clients have not yet been discussed in this book, which has focused thus far on how the private sector of the legal profession organizes its efforts to deliver needed service. Service is needed not only by clients who are articulating demands but lack the means for gaining access to the legal system; it is also needed by those groups and interests in the community which are not yet vocal but bear injuries. Although those groups do not articulate demand for legal services, they need those services to gain access to a broader policy-making dialogue. This need in turn suggests a need for new methods of delivering lawyers' services and more active roles for lawyers. In the previous chapters, the public interest client has been used as a symbol of unmet need. Now we have to look at what a public interest client is.

Several elements are important to an understanding of the "public interest client": how the client defines his problem (whether or not he defines it as one of public interest), how the client defines himself (whether or not he sees himself as a "public interest client"), and the way in which clients are defined by lawyers. Understanding who directs the relationship between lawyer and client and who chooses priorities is also crucial, as is the question of whether the client speaks for himself or for others. The problem of understanding the nature of the public interest client is compounded by the fact that some of the clients are not associations, or corporations, or people —they are abstractions of interests, albeit sometimes fragmented. When the clients are actual people or organizations they may be private clients with problems that affect the public interest or clients with problems completely concerned with a public interest issue, at least in their conception of themselves. The Urban Coalition is an example of the latter. Such a client usually speaks for interests not heretofore represented.

The ultimate question is whether or not we can define either the "public interest client" or the "public interest" content of a matter. In the last analysis, we will have to discover whether there can exist for clients, lawyers, and the community a test for determining what is worthy of being called "public interest." We doubt, from the outset, whether such a test can be formulated. Further, we doubt the wisdom of trying to formulate one. But in the interests of objectivity we are led to examine the possible validity of tests which have been suggested.

One always available test is an economic test—saying to the individual client "Put your money where your mouth is." But it has serious defects when we are trying to locate the best way to allocate legal services for the common good. Whatever utility an economic test may have in weeding out the important issue from the unimportant, it is restricted to those who can pay for legal services but choose not to for a particular problem. It cannot, however, in any way be seen as a workable test when applied to those who lack the means to pay. Even for those who can pay or—and this in part is why public interest groups come into existence—who can find someone to pay for them, the dollar test does not provide a sure way of certifying the social utility of a matter. The client may be willing to pay and the matter may have economic utility, but few today subscribe to the notion that economic utility to individual interest has automatic utility for society. Individuals lack equal access to the public forum; this fact alone frustrates an economic utility–social utility model. Over and above this fact, social policy should not be made in the interests of the highest bidder. If an individual feels strongly about something, he may be able to find the price for seeking redress, but his inability to do so does not remove the possibility of the seriousness of his injury.

There is a collective version of the economic test. It has been argued that any idea worth advancing will receive financial support from groups or social support from legislative policies. The statement which describes this position is: Public interest is those policies or priorities that the public is willing to pay for. The statement fails to distinguish accepted goals from the process of arriving at that acceptance. Some economic test may possibly suffice in the long run as a test for social policy. In the long run we may be willing to pose the issues in this way: Are we really willing to support by self-taxation a better educational plant or a more expensive system for maintaining a healthy environment? In the short run, however, a dollar test would inhibit some who ought to be heard in the process of arriving at a balanced social policy. The public interest dialogue is essential for arriving at enlightened policy. It is in this dialogue that the public interest lawyers are needed and where we must hear from a multitude of interests. In advance of a hearing or debate we cannot tell what interests should prevail and what points or issues have the greatest importance or social utility. After a policy is adopted, we can perhaps test our seriousness of purpose by ascertaining whether society, through its representatives, is willing to pay for enforcement of that policy. But we cannot impose a test in advance that is based on a dollar model. We cannot rule out interests because they lack dollars.

Some public interests or clients do gain access to the public forum by using dollars. Sometimes payment is made by third parties for the benefit of clients or for the benefit of others who are not clients. For example, a campaign by Businessmen for the Public Interest to save Lake Michigan will, if successful, benefit more than "clients." Or the named members of a class in a class suit may be benefiting "others similarly situated." When money is available, the means of access takes care of itself. But it is not possible to tell in advance how much potential a matter has for enlightened policy. In such situations it is not important to try to differentiate between those asserting self-interest and those seeking public interest. It is only important that they all be heard. The more the merrier. The point is that an economic form of access should not be the *sole* test for public importance; on the other hand, for those who have gained access by dollars, it should not be a disqualification for public importance.

Most of the public interest clients now being served do not gain access to lawyers by using dollars. Without a dollar test, lawyer choice of priorities and third-party choice of priorities frequently determine who gets served and who does not. It is important to see what tests the lawyers and the third-party groups purport to apply.

The volunteer lawyer, doing public service work as an individual (with his firm's permission) or as a member of a group formed by his firm, more often than not works through service models like the Community Law Offices or the neighborhood legal assistance programs. This lawyer serves poverty clients. The client selects himself (although the brokerage agencies define eligibility standards) and has usually already defined his need for a lawyer's services. He directs the lawyer's work; that is, his problem determines the nature of the legal task to be performed. Interaction between lawyer and client is generally subdued, particularly for the routine cases—divorce, creditor problems, and eviction. The client usually selects the program or agency which renders him service but does not select the individual lawyer who handles his case. This has an effect on the working relationship. The criteria that the lawyer applies are the criteria of the legal service program or agency through which he works; he has already given some general indication of his priorities by choosing to work through that outlet. His more particular concerns are for the most part not reflected in the needs of the clients assigned to him and in the type of service he renders. We have seen that this situation is frequently dissatisfying to the lawyers. They feel that service directed to the areas selected by the poverty clients may not be the most significant public interest contribution possible for them.

Piper & Marbury serves poverty clients through its branch office, but the firm, not a third party, makes the decision about who will be served. The clients present the issues, and this fact plus the firm's insistence on autonomy of operation for the branch office give the staff lawyers a close relationship to the individual case. The client, however, is the principal director of the lawyer's energies.

The Native American Rights Fund serves a specialized segment of those who cannot afford services—the Indian. The client, however, appears to have a substantial amount of autonomy and directs the lawyers' efforts to a greater extent than in the other service models.

In the service model, with the described variations, the clients appear to be certified as public interest clients through the application of a reverse financial test—the absence of means to command services. A paradox seems to be involved: A dollar test is not qualifying, but an absence of dollars may be. The matching of eligibility criteria, set by the offerors of legal service, with a client's application for service is said to serve as some kind of "test" for the merit of the poverty client's case. When a client with a real problem requests service that the agency is willing to give, the public interest is said to be met by extending that service. However, aside from the existence of eligibility criteria which are set by others, not the client, there is little assurance that the matters presented by the clients have importance for society as a whole. Matching eligibility criteria and demand may give only the illusion of public importance.

We do not criticize the absence of a valid "importance test" in poverty law. We do emphasize it here, because the poverty client and the clientless approach to issues pose *exactly* the same problem to a lawyer. There is no standard in either situation for certifying a problem as worthy of consideration: no standard, that is, beyond what would come from tutored instincts, a sense of equity, an ability to feel community injury, and an enlightened judgment by those seeking to allocate legal skills and techniques on other than a price model.

The lawyer who does volunteer work other than through his law firm often has public interest clients other than the poor. These tend to be the "sexy" clients, the ones who bring the big issues or the big cases. They might be draft resisters, street gang members, arrested protesters, or individuals who have been discriminated against in employment, housing, or education. Sometimes a client consists of a group involved in big case litigation; some of the school desegregation cases have been handled in this manner. The volunteer lawyer not working through his firm is likely to handle individual and group clients under circumstances in which the client selection has been made without his participation and the priorities have been set by someone other than the client or the lawyer. His clients have usually come to or been found by the brokering agencies, such as the Lawyers Committee for Civil Rights Under Law or ACLU. Rarely does the lawyer-client relationship go beyond the single case. The clients are clients precisely because their cases or situations are models for public interest issues—test cases or affirmative litigation. These models measure up to the eligibility criteria or the rationing or priority principles set by the brokering agencies. Clients in these situations have usually given up some of their autonomy of direction over the lawyer's efforts. Direction comes from the principle or the nature of the inquiry.

As we have already pointed out, there may be some doubt about the case which has elements of private or nonpublic or self-interest. The lawyer and the agency and the client together have to decide whether the principle, the public issue inherent in the case, is paramount. If it is, the client gives up power of direction (or at least directs as agreed). The client agrees to be *the client for the situation*. The lawyer, in his turn, agrees to be *the lawyer for the situation*. If private interest is seen to be paramount or equal to public interest, some power of direction is retained by the client. In some ways the public issue versus the private issue problem may be present in most situations with private clients, whether they be individuals or groups. Depending on how issues are framed, points of broad or narrow interest may be emphasized. It can be said then that a public interest client is a regular client who has gone to a public interest lawyer because of the primacy of public interest issues in his matter. Analyzed in this way, degrees of difference can be seen. At the level of private client–private lawyer relations, a public issue can emerge as of primary or secondary significance, depending on the characters and personalities of the client and the lawyer, the nature of the circumstances, and the attention that may be paid to the matter by outsiders. In common law theory all cases are public issues for someone, and all derive meaning both from how the issues are framed and what is done by others with the eventual result.

In contrast to the situations just noted, when a public interest client comes to and is accepted by a large private firm, or when he comes directly to a lawyer working through such a firm and is accepted as a client of the firm, he generally retains a greater power of direction. He makes more of the decisions and selects the public interest goal. The intake process, of course, allows the lawyers to match their priorities with those of clients. Once the case is accepted, however, the client directs. The lawyer's priorities are important only if the client asks for or allows the lawyer's participation·in goal selection. This fact derives in part from the nature of the public interest clients who come to large law firms. Even the case brokers seek to send special clients to large firms—those clients who will utilize the complex of talents available in those firms. The public interest clients of those firms tend to be groups rather than individuals. They tend, in fact, to be groups which seek continuing relations with the firms. Even for single matters the groups seem to have a conception of themselves which preserves for them a higher degree of autonomy. Invariably the groups see themselves playing a role in the furtherance of interests which *they* define as matters of public concern or as matters which *should* be of public concern.

In LCCRUL's early stages, efforts were made to place economic development groups with large law firms. This, however, is tapering off. As the law firms have developed their own community contacts or as lawyers within the firms have come to be identified by the community as ready to respond to public matters, the firms have relied less on the brokers. But the kind of clients they get still tend more often than not to be the larger groups, who possess a public interest identity of their own.

A client might be a "pure public interest" client. By "pure" public interest client we mean a group which defines itself as working for the public good rather than primarily for economic gain. Its constituency and goals may be parochial, directed to the interests of a single group or interest, but the definition holds. Pure public interest clients are groups like the Urban Coalition, the Sierra Club, and the National Minority Contractors Association. They state policy goals at the time of their formation and periodically reevaluate and revise these goals. Some pure public interest clients have additional characteristics. A group like the Young Great Society in Philadelphia has programs and offers service outlets. The Center for Democratic Institutions and the Cambridge Institute are groups in which lawyers are in directing positions. The Western Center on Law and Poverty or a local legal service program office are comprised of lawyers who deal with a complex of problems. When they use the services of a law firm, the lawyers in the firm being used are really lawyers' lawyers. In most of the instances which we have listed, the clients' preferences and priorities direct the energies of the lawyers. The lawyers may participate in a dialogue with the client, but the client sets policies and priorities.

The public interest groups have another dimension. Not only are they centered around policies or outlooks attracting issue-oriented cases and matters, they also have internal affairs relating to their viability as organizations. These internal matters contain the classic material of legal representation—tax status, corporate organization, property, and trusts.

The public interest group may divide its legal work into that which is traditional and that which is done on behalf of the public interest. The Sierra Club, for example, has Arnold & Porter do its work on its tax status. At the time of this writing Arnold & Porter was pursuing a situation in which the IRS had found that some of the club's activities consisted of "lobbying." Many of the club's matters dealing with specific environmental problems, however, are handled by the Center for Law and Social Policy, the public interest law firm directed by Charles Halpern (formerly with Arnold & Porter). Can it be said that the subject matter or case content of the Center's work for the Sierra Club is more public interest oriented than the work of Arnold & Porter? We doubt it. The survivability of the client and the viability of the client's program both touch directly on the public interest nature of the client.

Does the self-styled public interest nature of the client bring with it an assurance that the client's problems are a proper object of public concern? Particularly where an ongoing group does not have money to command legal services, is there some way of authenticating the public interest content? Again we doubt it. As in the case of the poverty client, some may draw small comfort from the fact that the priorities of the nonpaying clients have to be matched by the similar priorities of lawyers willing to serve for no fee. This can reassure us about cases taken but not about the worthiness of rejected matter. What happens to interests that cannot locate a lawyer with similar goal priorities? We cannot say that the goals or priorities of the rejected groups have less pertinence simply because they lack lawyer "approval." The situation may be analogous to the unpopular client who can pay.

Frequently the public interest client is representing or directing its attention to interests which are not its own—other people's private interests or quasi-public interests which are seen to have public interest character. In many instances the client is really not the interest ultimately served. This is true of clients like the Sierra Club, the Urban Coalition, and the Young Great Society. Community people are served at the Mantua branch office of Saul, Ewing, Remick & Saul at the request of the Young Great Society.[1] Similarly, the Western Center on Law and Poverty as a client of O'Melveny & Myers in Los Angeles directs to that firm legal work on behalf of others.

The lawyer working for the large public interest client may be addressing a broad community injury—an abstract situation—but he has someone who selects goals and tells him what to do. Some lawyers like this, because, as with their traditional counterparts, it leaves them free to devote their time to applying their skills as tacticians. The big cases and big issues seek the services of lawyers who address themselves to the injury, lawyers who, in Brandeis's words, are "lawyers for the situation." In the new public interest endeavors the lawyers find that in many instances they have actual clients to direct them and that the clients are called public interest clients because they too have addressed themselves to the

1. In some ways this example is like the situation of corporate employees whose personal problems are handled by their companies' lawyers. Who is the client?

situation—as we have said, they are *clients for the situation*. When such clients are setting priorities and are paying for or otherwise directing legal services to meet demands already articulated in the community, they are addressing one part of the public interest challenge. When they are the ones who articulate the demand in the first place they are addressing another part of the challenge. In the latter instance they are defining for themselves what is or is not in the public interest or in the interest of the group or constituency that they, the clients, represent or seek to represent. Here again the client is like the lawyer without a client. If matching issues with lawyers is an illusory procedure for authentication of priorities, how are priorities to be authenticated? How do those speaking for constituencies test their premises?

There may be little difference between the Urban Coalition directing in the name of the public the work of its lawyers and United States Steel Corporation directing in the name of the corporation the work of its lawyers. Both select the priorities. But United States Steel can test priorities against their economic utility. The decision to use a lawyer, and to what extent, can be tested against the goal of maximizing profits— short run or long run. No equivalent test is available for public interest clients.

It is when we look at the public interest law firm that we encounter the most difficulty in locating the client. To begin with, when the public interest law firm has a sense of constituency but no real clients, the law firm may be its own client. Or the firm and the funding source may be "the client," although neither are the intended beneficiaries of the work. They select the priorities. As one public interest law firm director said:

> Every year we pick out one or two things that are doable in addition to the long-range things. To show people that change can occur, you pick out a small issue that you can get a handle on and can translate into direct benefit to the community—which the community cares about. . . . You

need to figure out who your enemy is and what kind of an issue you can make out of it.[2]

Frequently, even when there are real clients who are ultimately served by the public interest law firm, client demand is a response to priorities set and work done by the firm —demand follows rather than precedes policy selection. Citizens Communications Center might stimulate local group action and channel demand about discriminatory broadcasting. So, too, might an antipollution campaign of Businessmen for the Public Interest stimulate public protest and local group action. Real clients emerge after a program is initiated. This resulting demand may be a form of testing for the validity or importance of an issue. Policy selection is authenticated through its ability to stimulate demand or its capacity to be adopted by resulting clients as statements of real injuries. The test case program of NAACP preceded the proliferation of actual clients demanding integrated school facilities. Long before *Brown v. Board of Education*,[3] NAACP's directors selected a goal reflecting their belief that segregated schooling was wrong. The plaintiffs were at first simply symbols for selected policy goals; they were nominal clients. Later the injuries were articulated by real plaintiffs who, having experienced the injuries all along, finally felt them and demanded a remedy. For public interest firms as well as for NAACP, priority decisions are untested when first made.

Sometimes the clients or a demand are present before the public interest firm is formed. But in instances of this kind, just as in the case of the private law firm, the demand is matched by the firm's selection of priorities. The firm chooses, on the basis of circumstances, compassion, or interest, in what area or with what groups it will work. Whether the demand is from environmental groups or from minority groups, priorities selected by public interest law firms frequently accomplish

2. Y1. "Y" numbers indicate interviews made available to us by the *Yale Law Journal* (see Appendix, page 300).
3. 347 U.S. 483 (1954).

the same objectives as do the neighborhood offices for poverty law. Service is extended to groups that have evidenced need but have never been represented.

It does not appear that any effective test for public interest content is available to either clients or lawyers. Self-selection in the public interest field appears to be an extension of the common law model: self-identification of injuries and self-selection of remedies. Frequently what is identified is injury to others or to the community. Compassion, in other words, may be a validation of sorts. We have here the same simple test for the public interest responders that we had for the poverty client: Is someone willing to speak to the issue? That may be enough.

If we cannot test for importance, can we test for the bare reality of issues? For the reasons already advanced, we do not think so. We can comfort ourselves, however, against the feeling that the energies of the public interest responders may be squandered. Most of the priorities of public interest responders—clients and lawyers alike—are chosen as reactions to something: racial discrimination; pollution; war; the conditions of poverty, such as bad housing, hunger, disease; the malfunctioning of government, including police abuse, failure to regulate business in the interests of the public, and non-extension of services to the poor. The list is endless. Few of the items are in the control of the responders. They are reacting to and objecting to injuries they perceive. The adversaries —the perpetrators of present practices—are the best test for concern that public interest responders have. The responders very frequently refer to their own efforts in terms of the identity of the opponent. The public interest clients and the public interest lawyers object to existing conditions and practices in this country. In this sense, who is to say that the focus of their work is not real?

For the public interest lawyers, the funders, and self-styled public interest clients, the problem is the same: Who has the right to speak in the name of public interest if there is no ultimate test for content? How can a client say that he speaks for the public interest? If a client represents a single group or a particular view, how do we know that the group or view should be heard? The answer is simple. We do not know. We know only that in a pluralistic society it is far better to hear from all than from some or none. The logical definition of public interest—a totality of all interests in the community balanced for the common good—supports a hospitable view of the self-arrogated or self-elected public interest client. No single interest and no single client can ever speak for the common good. They can only speak to a part of it—usually their part of it. A public interest response is not disproved if we sometimes find public interest clients on opposite sides of the same case; the efficacy of the notion that *all* ought to be heard is probably thereby proved. Two cases illustrate this point.

In the Alaska pipeline case, one public interest client, the Wilderness Society, was arguing completely against the pipeline. Other clients, Indian tribes in Alaska, were arguing for environmental protection, but wanted to secure jobs and other economic return from the pipeline. Even among the Indian tribes in this matter there were competing views and positions.[4] Should a decision be made without hearing from all sides?

In *Doe v. Scott*,[5] the Illinois division of the ACLU asserted the unconstitutionality of the Illinois abortion law. The plaintiffs were doctors, hospitals, and a class of women, who contended that a woman's right to decide these questions for herself was beyond the powers of the state. The court allowed the Committee for the Right to Life to intervene on behalf of all unborn children in Illinois and appointed that public interest group as guardian *ad litem*. On January 29, 1971, a three-judge court held the Illinois law unconstitutional when ap-

4. Unless there is a strong intellectual reason for attribution, names will be omitted, and assigned code numbers for respondents will be given. The respondents here are R24, R31, R48.
5. 70 C395 (D.N.D. Ill.).

plied in the first trimester of pregnancy.[6] Few doubt the right of both sides to speak to this important issue.

A close look at the *Doe* case really illustrates two variants of the public interest question. The appointment of a guardian *ad litem* is in traditional terms a recognition that interests not in being can and sometimes ought to be heard from. The courts have done this in trust cases for a long time. Even in the public dialogue about other concerns a voice often speaks for those yet to be born. Environment and defense issues are both sounded in this voice. The clientless situation—in which the client lives but is not present—may be just as important for a balanced public policy.

We observe in Chapter 10 that arrogance is involved for the public interest lawyers, but it is a special type of arrogance. So, too, for the public interest clients who dare to speak out and suggest policy. Dare we not hear them?

6. Doe v. Scott, 70 C395 (D.N.D. Ill., Jan. 29, 1971). Several nontherapeutic abortions were subsequently performed in Illinois before Mr. Justice Marshall stayed the injunction against the enforcement of the Illinois abortion law pending the outcome of a full hearing by the United States Supreme Court. The three-judge federal court's treatment of the issue of fetal viability raises some interesting public interest questions. By holding the Illinois abortion law invalid only for the first trimester, the court in effect ruled that the embryo up to that time did not have rights which could be protected by the state, but that thereafter it had interests as a living being and could be represented by the state.

chapter 10

The Individual Lawyer and the Quest for a New Professional Role

We have examined the new forms and some of the reasons why they have emerged. In the process we have seen that new-style lawyers are placing explicit and implicit pressures on traditional legal institutions to shift the base of overall professional response toward the representation of a broader client group and toward the assumption of a more active role in the affairs of the community and of society. We have seen, too, that the responses to new demands and the representation of new interests is thus far limited to a small percentage of the bar's total effort; the institutions of the legal profession—the firms and the organized bar—have not changed as rapidly as the rhetoric. Ultimately the question of whether the profession as a whole will adopt a new definition of role and responsibility —whether there will be a "new profession"—will depend on two factors: (1) the depth of the new-breed lawyer's commitment to the new professional role, and (2) the extent to which the experience gained by these lawyers can be incorporated into the daily life of the institutions in which they work.

239

The Lawyer, the Public, and Professional Responsibility

We will examine in Chapter 11 whether the new responses have altered the institutional definitions of professional responsibility. Now, however, we must understand that the individual lawyer's commitment will be heightened, dulled, or frustrated by the ways in which law continues to be practiced and the ways in which it incorporates change. Ultimately, the committed lawyers will either change the profession's definitions of responsibility or will themselves be coopted by or lost to the profession.[1] The direction of change will depend, to some extent, on how the individual lawyer perceives or defines his role.

The individual lawyer defines his role or has it defined for him from four perspectives: (1) his view of himself as a human being living in a social context; (2) his view of his skills and techniques as they relate to the accomplishment of goals that he or the community sets; (3) his view of the demands placed on him by those in the community who seek to use his skills or by those he aspires to serve; and (4) his view of the demands placed on him by the professional institutions which employ him, establish standards for his performance, define his skills and tasks, and judge his performance. Certainly there is much overlap in the four areas; standards, pressures, and inputs from each are related in complex ways to the others. The individual lawyer's eventual role definition will depend on how he identifies and blends the separate and sometimes competing inputs.

The Lawyer as Citizen in the Community
We identified in Chapter 8 the quest for a work-living identity as a factor in the emergence of a public interest response from the private bar. Here we will deal with a particular aspect of that work-living relationship. We are concerned with the lawyer's view of himself as a citizen, but more particularly with his behavior as a citizen.

1. It may be that the individual will remain a "professional" and the profession will become or remain lost.

The most striking thing about the new public interest lawyers is their belief that their skills and training do not disqualify them as active participants in the community dialogue. The majority of the lawyers we saw told us in effect that, independent of their roles as lawyers, they felt compelled to participate in the controversies of their time. They seemed to echo the admonition of Oliver Wendell Holmes, Jr.:

> I think that, as life is action and passion, it is required of a man that he should share the passion and action of his time at the peril of being judged not to have lived.[2]

Our respondents realized that they would have to enlist their professional skills and involve their professional lives in their social concerns. In responding to us they spoke as citizens. They indicated their lack of neutrality about contemporary events. Their lack of neutrality was evidenced by their specific actions, such as participating in antiwar demonstrations,[3] environmental groups, or civil rights groups,[4] or acting as monitors at demonstrations or parades at which community passion and interaction with officialdom threatened to blur the distinctions between dissent and disorder.[5] In these activities they have *not* moved to disassociate professional identity from civic identity, as others in the past have been moved to do if they were at all active about contemporary issues. The new lawyers have also had new professional roles suggested to them in these contemporary activities. The lines are not clear between citizen and lawyer when a lawyer does more than observe.

As an antiwar demonstrator or a member of an antipollution group, a lawyer may be involved in mapping policy strategies, monitoring official behavior, or certifying facts.

2. Memorial Day address of O. W. Holmes in 1884, cited in J. Bartlett, *Familiar Quotations,* at 786b (1968).

3. Unless there is a strong intellectual reason for attribution, names will be omitted, and assigned code numbers for respondents will be given. The respondents here are R10 and R44.

4. R63, R65.

5. R36.

242

The Lawyer, the Public, and Professional Responsibility

These are less traditional lawyer skills than those employed by the lawyer who incorporated the symphony orchestra, but our new lawyer-participant relates them to his essence as a lawyer more readily than did the incorporator of orchestras. He sees his capacity to deliver effort to the public goals he espouses as a function of a skill he has always used—the orderly isolation of facts which are relevant to the consideration of issues. The skill is not a new one. The new lawyer believes that he has a civic duty to associate himself with policy-oriented groups and to bring to that association whatever skills may be relevant to the requirements of advocating particular programs. In the process he extends his function as a lawyer.

Traditional party politics have long been an acceptable form of activity for some of the lawyers in firms. Law firm custom has traditionally dictated that lawyers either take leaves of absence for political work or disguise their role as lawyers or the identity of their firms in order to do it. Professional identity has not been emphasized during a period of political work. The new lawyer seeks a greater degree of social and political activity—activity not restricted to traditional party politics—and, although his identity as a lawyer may be secondary in this seeking, he does not try to hide the identity nor does he attempt to call his broader advocacy of issues something other than lawyering. In his own eyes and in the eyes of the public he is a lawyer-citizen. Difficulties still exist if a vocational label is placed on a lawyer's social and political activities, but the difficulties relate to the law firm that pays the lawyer far more than they relate to the lawyer's problems of self-identity.

The Lawyer as Responder to the Needs and Demands of His Clients

The lawyer cannot avoid seeing his role and even his skills in terms of the clients he serves. This is true for the public interest lawyer, the public lawyer, and the traditional private lawyer. It is a function of his loyalty and his training. To the extent that the public interest lawyer serves clients he has not previously served, the needs of these clients, the nature of their problems, and the demands that they make are bound to affect—extend—his view of his role. The lawyer in the public interest law firm and in the public interest section of the traditional law firm is necessarily reshaping his view of his role just as surely as if a commercial client that the lawyer has not previously dealt with—one with specialized needs —had retained him. The public interest clients "educate" the lawyer. He is exposed to new problems. He learns a new language. And he may develop a sensitivity to the needs of those clients. This does not always happen with celerity; sometimes it does not happen at all. There have been peculiar insensitivities to the client's needs. It may be that the lawyer has been "turned off" by mundane problems important to the client but not the lawyer.[6] Or it may be that the lawyer has attempted to control the client's judgment about the client's needs in a way that does not really serve those needs.[7] But, by and large, exposure to new clients affects perspective and sensitivity.

If the lawyer is extending his services through a service agency, such as Community Law Offices or a neighborhood legal assistance program, he has a limited range of response. He meets a real client, one who usually has a well-defined problem. He may begin to think about his client's general situation, but does not reach the heart of the client's problem, which lies much deeper.[8] As the public interest lawyer builds up and provides service for a regular clientele, thoughtfulness leads him to see that particular problems are common to many clients; inevitably he begins to serve as a lawyer for the situation. At present he is not asked to engage in a reform approach and, indeed, is stopped short of it, but he is responding and he

6. R9.
7. R48.
8. Stephen Kass, director of CLO, points out the difficulty: The lawyer wants to respond fully to the general situation of the poor but is directed to a specific complaint.

is getting ready to respond to more total need. What this means is that a Peter Smith from the Piper & Marbury branch office or a lawyer working through CLO have through their daily work learned about broader issues in an intimate way and are now capable of speaking to the policy issues under consideration by legislative or administrative bodies or by the community. The senior partners of firms also pick up, through their contact with work taken in and with the people doing that work, an understanding of new issues. The broader implications are important for two reasons: (1) Private firms are not inhibited by tax laws from seeking legislative change; and (2) participation in policy dialogue is an aspect of representation which has always been excluded because of traditional *pro bono* views. (For example, individuals in the poverty group may have always been represented, but the problems of poverty could not be discussed or placed at issue.)

The group client provides a broader education for the public interest department or firm than does the individual client. Lawyers with such clients come more easily to a realization that they are representing a situation or an interest. The group client is in itself a statement of common interest and cohesion. It exposes lawyers to problems in greater depth than do individual clients. In turn, the lawyers see more clearly the need to take active reform steps in the interest of these clients.

The lawyer without a specific client—the lawyer for the situation, who may search for socially relevant facts or audit the operations of governmental agencies—is also learning from and about the new styles of representation. As he uses his ability to research and analyze a situation, his understanding about social need and possible solutions for current problems is increased. If he thinks honestly, his instincts for compassion will be heightened by reality. This lawyer is subject to the charge that his concern for the "public interest" involves a type of arrogance, because he speaks with a brief that he has handed himself. And, in a sense, the charge is irrefutable. Arrogance is involved, but it is a special type of arrogance.

We feel that as long as the lawyer's policy-laden role is limited to a diligent search for facts and a careful identification and analysis of issues the danger of excess is small. The risk to society is much greater if the lawyer does not speak—for others and for himself—to the issues as he sees them. The fact that the public interest lawyer speaking in this mode has selected such a role for himself may make him peculiarly suited to the task. Given his exposure to and thought about public issues, it may be far more arrogant of him to withhold his representation of the public. There would seem to be a special kind of courage involved in the transition of the lawyer to an active spokesman for the situation. The lawyer who runs for office so that he may legislate for the public good also has these special brands of arrogance and courage.

The Lawyer as Affected by His Institutions

The public interest lawyer working in a public interest law firm may be relatively unaffected by tradition. There are no traditional definitions of his role. The public interest lawyers in the firms we saw felt, like Mr. Justice Brennan[9] and Harlan Fisk Stone,[10] that traditional ethical standards had to be rewritten and redefined to allow for their roles.[11] Their relationship with the organized bar is made easier because of the absence of standards for judging performance.[12]

The public interest lawyer in the private law firm, on the other hand, does not feel the same ease about his role. He has to contend with the interpretation of others as to the ethical and economic considerations involved. He may see his public interest work in a way that is different from both the view of

9. Brennan, J., "The Responsibilities of the Legal Profession," *The Path of the Law from 1967* (A. Sutherland ed., 1968).
10. H. F. Stone, "The Public Influence of the Bar," 48 *Harv. L. Rev.* 1 (1934).
11. R23.
12. Bar associations become far more concerned with professional standards in cases where fees are cut than in cases where fees are waived entirely!

the law firm employing him and the view of the organized bar as expressed in the Code of Professional Responsibility. He may have one image of professional responsibility and his firm may have another.

The competing views of professional responsibility do not rest on philosophical differences alone. The life styles of public interest lawyers and the managers of firms are apt to be different, and these differences turn on sought-for levels of economic and social comfort. They indirectly affect the definition of professional role—principally through the mechanism of client selection or rejection. Clients selected by the firm are those who represent the interests that make the partners comfortable or enable them to attain the standard of living that they want to have or have to have. Whatever they may say about professional duty to all comers, the older lawyers' choices of public interest clients are moderated by the life styles of those lawyers, just as the public interest responders' choices are moderated by theirs. The younger lawyer has, of course, to contend with the choices of his firm's managers more than they have to contend with his. It is in this area that the young lawyer in the private law firm may feel the greatest tension. He may see full-range public interest work as a duty to be fully integrated into the daily life of the law firm. But the fact remains that the professional ethic that dominates the private law firm relegates all but a few of the new-breed lawyers to an avocational pursuit of professional responsibility as they see it. Even with changed symbols we find little integration of firm and public interest work. The latter is still viewed by the law firms in terms of the acceptable levels of dispensed grace.

The young lawyer must, therefore, put it together for himself. He must find an institution that allows him to integrate his conceptions of professional role with his daily work; or he must attempt to modify the law firm in which he works; or he must modify his own views of professional duty and accept, temporarily or permanently, an avocational pursuit of that duty.

The full-time public interest lawyer has made his choice. Although there may not yet be ways of assuring the stability of the public interest law firm, the lawyer in that firm has a clear idea of his role. A statement by Alexander Polikoff of Businessmen for the Public Interest perhaps best describes the role as it represents the disappearance of the split between vocation and avocation:

> Now I can spend my spare moments, like when I am shaving, thinking about the implications of my work day and the matters we are handling.[13]

The lawyers with nonfoundation-supported public interest law firms and the members of the law communes have also attempted to integrate their work-living identity. Their failure to

---

13. The vocational approach of the full-time public interest responder seems to liberate a great deal of the lawyer's inventiveness as well as his facility of response. Marshall Patner, also with Businessmen for the Public Interest, while representing a coordinating council of community groups seeking more jobs for blacks in the construction industry, was faced with the harassing tactics of construction workers picketing the United States Department of Labor hearings being held at the Customs House in Chicago in September 1968. Witnesses for the black coalition were being intimidated. From an office of one of the affiliated community groups, Patner sent a long telegram to the governor of Illinois, Richard Ogilvie, and to United States Attorney General John Mitchell, asking that protection be given witnesses entering and leaving the building. He discovered later in the day that the telegram had not been sent by Western Union because that company would not extend credit to the telephone account of the community group. Investigation revealed that Western Union extended credit to some telephone exchanges and not to others and that the exchanges where credit was not extended were all in minority areas. Immediately Patner sent another telegram—this one to Attorney General Mitchell and to the FCC—asking that Western Union be placed in federal receivership because of its discriminatory extension of a utility service. The night manager at Western Union asked Patner to withdraw the telegram. At Patner's insistence it was sent, and shortly thereafter an "agreed" order was entered by the FCC, prohibiting the discriminatory extension of credit. In the midst of a difficult case—the controversy which led to the adoption of the Chicago Plan—Patner was able to perceive a separate and significant injury and respond to it appropriately and effectively. (Patner interview, May 1970.)

date to locate a stable base for this integration underscores a basic problem. There is no broad social and economic base that will reward these law jobs—if they are indeed law jobs that ought to be done or that the community wants done. We deal further with this question in Chapter 12.

Unless society finds ways of subsidizing the price of entry into the law forum, or unless the profession as a whole changes its cultural (life-style) base and professional outlook enough to drop or reduce that price—so that the poor, the unpopular, the isolated, and the abstract or fragmented interests in our society are represented on an equal basis with all others—the public interest responder has identified for himself a professional role which is isolated.

The Public Interest Lawyer Affecting His Firm and His Profession

The policies and organization of law firms are ultimately affected by the participants. So, too, are the operating standards of professional organizations as a whole. The new-breed lawyer has already effected a change in the external symbols of the law firms. We have seen, too, that the content of even the least-committed of the law firm forms of response—the public interest partner—is a direct result of the commitment of the lawyers participating in that response. The new-breed lawyer, then, can and does have an effect on his institutions to the extent of his commitment to an integrated view of professional role.

It is here that we must again remind ourselves that the new-breed lawyer's attempt to arrive at a definition of the lawyer's role may be struggling closer to the classic definition than to the definitions implied by the way in which the modern profession operates. The classic definition may be a more appropriate answer to the question of how the entire society can have its law jobs done. The public interest responder is raising for himself and for his profession the question whether the law is a profession after all if it will not relate its daily occupation to the very core of the legal imperative: resolution of social conflict and the evolution of fair and just rules for the society. In this sense the new-breed lawyer's search for a definition is painful and confusing—particularly so when viewed in the light of historic development and of the legal profession's current attempts to become more relevant. Again, the charge most frequently leveled at the public interest lawyer is that he is arrogant. The charge of arrogance can be coupled with an assertion that all law is public interest law. To the extent that the public interest lawyer has an integrated view of himself, he would concur with the statement and emphasize the goals: "Of course! That is all I have been trying to say. I want to be a lawyer. Not a public interest lawyer, just a lawyer. I would be perfectly willing to see 'public interest law' pass from compensatory effort to ordinary effort incorporated into the day-to-day workings of the legal profession." In this way the public interest lawyer is reminding the profession of the true meaning of service ahead of gain. It is here that present experience may tutor the profession as a whole.

Thomas Jefferson stated the broader principle implicit in the new breed's plea to the profession:

> When a man assumes public trust, he should consider himself public property.[14]

14. T. Jefferson in 1807, cited in J. Bartlett, *Familiar Quotations,* at 472b (1968).

chapter 11

What Do the New Lawyer Roles Mean for the Profession as a Whole?

We have examined the forms of the private bar's response to growing demands and needs for broader representation. We have suggested why this response is occurring, and we have examined who the clients are and what public interest efforts mean to individual lawyers. The true test of the new responses is not in what they mean to individual lawyers, however, but in what they mean to the profession as a whole.

The level of public interest work by those parts of the private bar that we observed is low; the delivered efforts of private firms represent only a small part of the available energies of those firms. For the bar as a whole the response appears to be even smaller; indeed it appears to be infinitesimal. Certainly one cannot say that the bar as a whole has fashioned a public interest response unless some of the institutional definitions of professional responsibility are being affected by its efforts. One way of determining what effects have occurred is to see whether those institutions which have consciously thought about and publicly discussed and engaged in

250

public interest responses have changed their central definitions of professional responsibility. Here we will focus on the large law firms we studied.

The overall response of the private bar of course includes more than the responses of the large establishment firms. The responses of sole practitioners and lawyers in small firms are important too, both numerically and in terms of style. But for the same reasons (low visibility and absence of statements of declared policy and formal allocation of energies to public interest work) that the sole practitioner and the small-firm lawyer were beyond the focus of our study they are beyond the scope of this inquiry into shifting definitions. Shifts in the individual views of lawyers who work alone or in small firms will more directly affect intake decisions. The sole practitioner and the small firm make intake decisions which reflect an ongoing effort to balance self-interest and professional responsibility. These decisions are moderated by directly felt economic realities. The potential of these lawyers as public interest responders is intimately tied to the way in which society does or does not choose to reward a public interest response. This we will discuss in Chapter 12.

The totally new form—the public interest law firm—is part of the overall response. Public interest law firms are small in number as are the total lawyer hours that such firms can now deliver, despite their extensive use of volunteers. To date they have had a primarily symbolic effect on the bar's overall definition of professional responsibility. It has been an important effect. In the long run, the new approach that they offer may have a more profound effect on the definition of professional responsibility than all the other efforts now being delivered.

The large firm, however, is of primary interest to us because in that context we can see the new forms within the framework of a going institution—an institution with tradition and continuity. The large firms we observed had made explicit changes in their symbols and had advertised their efforts to reallocate a portion of their enterprise. They most greatly evidenced the dissonance between those responsible for the outlook of firms as to a proper definition of the lawyer's role and the individual lawyers within the firm. Our general impression is that the way in which large firms practice remains substantially the same after they have adopted public interest forms. For the most part public interest responses are mere diversions for those firms—they remain ancillary to the practice of law. Public interest work there, though explicitly directed, continues to look like a dispensation of grace rather than the discharge of professional duty. The ways in which these law firms make their money, relate to their regular clients, and practice law limit—or threaten to limit—a fully integrated public interest response. The response is limited by the heavy competition for the available resources of the firms, by the firms' conceptions of which clients or interests can be "properly," safely, or even feasibly handled, and by the firms' style of handling law work.

The large law firm is more than an economic organization; it is an institution. Its institutional character centers for the most part on the way in which its lawyers do their work. To the extent that the practice of law is considered by attorneys in large firms to be a way of life, it is a way which involves the pursuit and attainment of excellence in employing the skills of the craft. Perhaps every lawyer starts with this ideal, but only the lawyer in the large firm finds himself continuously faced with this ideal as a standard. It is the standard of the firm. It is defined by the firm, although not necessarily stated explicitly. It is simply there, nurtured by the history of the large firms, by the prestige of the lawyers who have been and are in those firms, and by the prestige and magnitude of the clients and the matters handled as part of the daily routine. The sheer size and versatility of the large firm further supports the standard. It would be hard for the lawyer in the large firm to be unaware of the set of expectancies. This lawyer is recruited in the first place because he shows the promise of excellence in skill—he came from the top ten percent of the class in the "best law schools." Careful attention is paid to his training after he joins a firm. He is "brought along" by guided exposure to a variety of skills and specialities—even his public interest work may be tolerated or explained in terms of training. He in turn observes that his firm has a policy of hiring for the most part only those who have just finished law school, not trusting any alternative process with the training or socialization of its lawyers. The message is clear: Excellence in skill is expected at all times. The lawyer comes to expect it of himself. And whatever his view of social responsibility, he expects to bring that kind of excellence to *all* his work. When the large-firm lawyer is working on a matter, he knows that he is being observed and judged by fellow practitioners. And not just any fellow practitioners, but lawyers whom he respects. Until recently there was no conscious attempt by this kind of firm to relate excellence in skill to broad social concerns. This was seen as simply happening. The assumption was, and, we feel, to a large extent still is, that the craft of law is employed in a neutral fashion and that it is available to the clients of a firm for whatever legitimate use they might want to make of it. Thus the prevailing image of the law firm depends on who its clients are; it does not have a voice of its own.

The extent to which a large firm can change its external image by announcing a public interest response and by taking new matters and new clients may be limited by the institutional ways in which such firms pursue the craft of law and by an economic dependence on large clients that seems to follow therefrom. The assemblage of talent and specialized skill in large firms not only reflects who, in the past, has demanded and paid for the services of those firms, but also dictates who, if the firms are to survive in the future, must receive the lion's share of the firms' available services. It must be those who can pay for the specialized skills, for the flexibility of operation, and for the built-in inefficiencies of practicing law with a standard of excellence. Two paradoxes are involved.

The Lawyer, the Public, and Professional Responsibility

PARADOX 1
The standard of excellence, which provides the potential for a quality public interest response (a job should be well done no matter who the client is—"when it's firm work it has to be good"), is the very feature that creates an economic dependence on regular paying clients.

The institutional identity of a large firm depends on the delivery (or potential delivery) of high-quality work. The large firm invariably lives up to its standard of excellence; in fact, for certain matters there is often more skill available than is necessary in terms of the economic utility of the matters handled. While this surplus seemingly makes the law firms potentially able to divert their excess to public interest work—which they only occasionally do—that very surplus and the attendant inefficiencies lead to a greater dependence on regular retaining clients.

The surplus of skill over economic utility is due, in part, to the compelling necessity to satisfy the professional standards of the lawyers and the firm far beyond what is necessary to solve a client's short-term problem, indeed, far beyond what the client may demand for a problem's solution. Frequently, law firms expend time and energy in developing a professional judgment, in giving advice, or in fighting the "principle of the thing" for clients, although they do not or cannot bill directly for these things. They recognize that their pursuit of resolution is motivated by a desire to gratify their own professional needs and is not as meaningful to their clients as it is to them. The "extra" work is not seen by the large firms as optional; it is necessary. Whether the law firm admits the fact or not, the extra effort is marketed. The paying clients rely on this "overkill"—which law firms see as professional pride. It is insurance for the large clients, and they ultimately pay a premium for it, either in the form of a large retainer or in higher bills across the board, which they know are padded by this general quest for certainty. It also describes, for both the lawyer and the client, an element of the large law firm's prestige. Most law firms recognize the merchantability of this overkill and direct it toward ultimate payment for effort rather than treat the ability to expend the effort as a surplus available for use by nonpaying clients. Frequently, the rationale for including this effort in a bill is explained as gaining greater familiarity either with a client's recurring problem or "affairs" or with attainment of a skill so that a "better job can be done next time." Indeed, much of the public interest work of large firms is justified in these terms. A young lawyer's work on a public interest matter of his own—under the watchful eye of the firm—is, from the firm's point of view, one of his opportunities to acquire skills and self-assurance "so that he can do a better job for the regular clients." And, there is less risk of loss of regular business while he is acquiring the skill. Better to risk a conviction of an indigent prisoner than the loss of the Acme Steel account.

The prestige arising from overkill frustrates the public interest client who is not able to retain these large firms. It is a prestige that could work for the public interest clients, too, and does work for them when they are successful in retaining these firms. Opponents and potential opponents—whether they be government agencies or private parties—of clients of the large law offices give up untenable or marginal positions more rapidly than when they face less prestigious firms or lawyers. They know that the large firm will fight an issue all the way. The leverage of this factor facilitates settlement and resolution. When government—with a unique overkill of its own, born perhaps of bureaucratic inefficiency rather than pursuit of skill—is the opponent, the large law firm is a desirable match for it. Without the prestige of the large firm, tons of dedication are needed from the public interest lawyers if those lawyers are to build up comparable prestige.[1] The prestige of a large firm is for the most part made available to a nonpaying public

1. As has been done by the lawyers of the Citizens Communication Center in their dealings with the Federal Communications Commission. There the skill and dedication of a single-purpose public interest law firm have begun to match those of a governmental agency. See discussion in Chapter 6 at pp. 170–72.

interest client for one time only. The public interest clients cannot and do not rely on the large-firm prestige in their daily comings and goings, as the paying client can. Overkill is reserved for regular clients.

PARADOX 2
The external factors that led to the creation of public interest forms in the first place impose an immediate limitation on public interest efforts and may ultimately lead to either their curtailment or their liquidation.

Paying clients demand the assemblage of large pools of talent both for the reasons we have indicated and as a reflection of their own level of economic activity. Their steadily growing demand for services has led to a steady increase in the size of large firms. The needs of the firms for a continuous supply of young lawyers capable of pursuing excellence in skill has given top law students an economic lever which makes them free to demand time for public interest work. The demand for talent, by both the firms and the clients, remains real once a student has entered a firm and has been socialized to "do a good job." In short, he was hired to do a job and use his talent for the paying client.

In this context it can be seen that survival of the public interest response in the large firm is not automatically assured by a simple change of symbols. Unless public interest effort is formally separated from the economic aspects of the practice of law, that effort will probably dwindle. To the extent that the large firm has succeeded in this separation it has changed its definition of professional responsibility. It has not necessarily made a central change, but it is paying a tax or tithe.[2] It is saying that a portion of its resources are *not* available to the paying client.

The large clients, however, do more than merely command the reservation or deployment of large-firm energies. As

2. G. Sherman, "A Businessman's Challenge to the Lawyer's Role," 25 *Bus. Law.* 95 (Special Issue, Sept. 1969).

we have suggested, a part of the law firm's resources can be removed from the marketplace by conscious interdiction and insulation. Can the regular paying clients of Piper & Marbury command the services of a branch lawyer? Can the regular clients of Covington & Burling use the lawyer who is released to the neighborhood legal service program? They cannot. These lawyers have been hired elsewhere. Paying clients, may, however, determine *how* the services of these lawyers will be offered to public interest clients. Even where paying clients lack such influence, managing partners, in their thoughts and plans, often attribute to these clients the power to direct the manner in which allocated public interest energies are spent. It may be an illusion that regular clients can, would want to, or even have the power to determine the character of the large firm. Regular clients may be more dependent upon their lawyers than the lawyers realize. Washington firms are especially needed by certain clients. And these latter firms have sought a community voice more fervently than have firms in other cities, perhaps for the reason that they may feel more isolated from those of their clients (many in number) not based in Washington, clients who hire them for particular matters only. The business firms that Washington counsel represent usually have general counsel elsewhere.

When large firms first consciously sought a community voice, they may have discovered that they already had a community voice. At least they found that they had an identity, because an overview of the clients whom these firms represented indicated that these firms represented more than clients; *they represented interests.* The identity of those interests has been and continues to be influenced by the needs of these firms to meet an expected income level and pay large overhead. The new voice—the public interest voice—is one which has to be in harmony with the old voice. A little counterpoint may be tolerated, but nobody wants to write a fugue. The name that the large-firm responders give to the exercise of avoiding dissonance is: Conflict of Interest.

An analysis of conflict of interest, or the things that are

called "conflict of interest" by the large law firms, will provide us with an understanding of why the public interest response of these firms is not only minimal—an allocation of some surplus—but also, for the most part, benign. The number and type of clients turned away because of "conflict of interest" may be a gauge of how much the central definition of professional responsibility has or has not changed.

In an ethical sense a conflict of interest exists when a firm is on both sides of a given controversy or has a dual interest in a given transaction. It is based squarely on the concept of loyal service to a client or to the public. It is a fiduciary principle often explained, when lawyers use their priestly language to "laymen," as "a man cannot serve two masters." The large firm does not confine its view of conflict of interest to a *strict* conflict of interest, but extends it to the firm's felt necessity to avoid *broad* conflict. We must observe how strong the master's voice is and how faithful the lawyer remains beyond the strict bounds of conflict of interest. As the concept of conflict is extended, we have to ask why it is being extended. Moreover, we have to ask how the public interest client is handled in the process.

In one sense the problem of the large firm's response to the public interest client is present even when strict conflict of interest is present. The public interest client is usually not treated in the same way as is the regular client. If two regular clients of a firm are in controversy with each other, the firm, with the assent of both parties, may try to mediate the controversy as a neutral third party. Given full disclosure, this is consistent with ethical standards. If the importance of the clients—or at least the sizes of their annual legal fees—are unequal, the firm may not trust its neutrality and may avoid *any* kind of involvement. More important, the firm may not trust the clients' views of the firm's impartiality. In any event, the firm usually steps completely out of the situation—particularly if both clients are retainer clients—and assists each client in retaining other competent counsel. Sometimes when one client is large or on a regular retainer basis and the other client is either applying for service for the first time or has used the firm only casually, the firm will continue with the large or retainer client and reject the other client. Even here, however, the firm will consider the rejected client a "client" and seek counsel for him. The public interest client, who is not a regular client of the firm from whom he seeks service, usually receives less. If he is rejected, no referral is made. He is left to determine for himself whether he has a legitimate suit against the rejecting firm's regular client. Sometimes he is not even told that conflict of interest is the basis for rejection. Rejection that is accompanied by a referral may cure a potential client's doubt about the possible legitimacy of his case. There is a vast difference between "You have a case, but we can't handle it" and "Go away!" Rarely does a firm treat the public interest client as it does its regular client and attempt to locate other counsel for him.[3]

Part of the problem of rejecting or accepting on a conflict of interest basis is seen in sharp focus when the conflict is strict. Despite rhetoric, public interest clients are not treated like regular clients. Even the language is different. Labels such as "real" and "casual" segregate regular clients from public interest clients. Economic and long-range professional sustenance is not expected from the latter. When a public interest client is a group or an organization with an ongoing relationship with a firm, these labels begin to disappear, and the public interest client begins to look more like a regular client. Perhaps this explains in some small part why the ongoing public interest clients of the large firms—the Urban Coalition and the Sierra Club, for example—all look so "establishment" themselves. The danger of blowup from clash with regular clients is minimized because "responsible" people serve on the governing boards of such organizations.

It is at the intake stage that we see the public interest

3. We saw only one firm which insisted on locating a lawyer for the public interest clients who were rejected because of conflict of interest; however, those public interest clients who have come to firms through brokering agencies can go back to the agencies, which will locate other counsel (R12).

client scrutinized more thoroughly than the regular client. It is there we see the broad definition of conflict of interest applied to the public interest client.

When a firm decides whether or not to accept employment from a paying client, only narrow and immediate conflict of interest is considered. Even in the process of forming a continuing relationship with a paying client a firm rarely goes beyond scanning for existing or presently emerging or obvious future strict conflicts. True, in this process it does review the clients it currently represents in order to avoid possible future conflict. Speculation about conflict, however, rarely ranges far afield. That way lies madness, for the large law firm represents many large clients, each of which has diverse operations and interests. Potential conflict between clients lies everywhere. The prevalent view is that classic conflict can be dealt with as it arises. Meanwhile there is the salient point: The interests of regular clients are all substantially the same except when they are in strict or classic conflict. Law firms may think they represent clients, but they really represent *interests* after all. That is, they represent clients who have similar interests. Few clients of large law firms have system grievances. Few seek major changes in the distributive system. The similarity of basic interests is understood, as is the possibility that these interests will occasionally come into conflict with each other.

The law firms scrutinize the public interest client in a more searching manner. Threats are seen; conflicts are imagined or manufactured. At the intake session the unseen regular client is a silent partner, a role he does not have in the usual course of business. The reasons for this are simple; the excuses are complex. The mere imputation of a regular client's veto of a public interest client may be a projection of economic self-interest. Since the firm has only a small amount of time available for public interest work and since economic return for that work is not expected, choices are involved. The public interest client who poses the least risk to the firm's economic stability and the least threat to the interest of the regular clients can be accepted. This is the crux of the broad conflict of interest notion. It is because of overwhelming risk that many firms have ducked the question of public interest intake altogether ("That's not firm work") or have sent their lawyers to CLO. The firms that do take public interest cases as firms proceed with caution. Even when the public interest client comes to a firm for a single matter every implication is studied. The regular client's foot is more germane than the chancellor's foot in fashioning a yardstick for measuring who among public interest clients is worthy. If the public interest client has a variety of ongoing problems, the risks of accepting him as a client are greater. Few firms take these risks. And, as we have said, when they *are* willing to take them it may be because the client is the very model of a "nice" public interest client. (Remember the hospital and the symphony orchestra we mentioned earlier.) To *fully* understand a firm's confusion about conflict of interest as applied to public interest clients one should consider that groups like the Black Panthers may present less conflict of interest to a firm than groups like Indian tribes in disputes over land. It may be easier to represent a generalized grievance with society than it is to pick through a maze of particular competing interests. (It is easiest, of course, to represent the aforementioned "nice" public interest client.)

Four cases which typify reasons for rejection of public interest clients fill out a portrait of law firm interest and of the broad view of conflict of interest:

> 1. A law firm which represented a city in some of its law work, but which had never represented that city's police department, would not accept a public interest client with a police-abuse suit because of "conflict of interest."[4]

> Query: Would a paying client who was suing the water department get the same treatment? Is there irony

---

4. Unless there is a strong intellectual reason for attribution, names will be omitted, and assigned code numbers for respondents will be given. The respondent here is R13.

in the fact that representing a public body is seen as disqualifying another piece of public business?

2. A firm which represented a bank would not accept a poverty client wanting to sue another bank about a form note.[5]

3. A firm appeared regularly before a federal agency on behalf of a large client but would not accept a public interest client who wanted to be represented before that same agency.

Query: Would the firm reject the representation of another paying client before the same agency?

4. An attorney, funded by a large foundation, organized the criminal defense of street gangs through a metropolitan law firm. The arrangement was amicable to both parties. However, when it was suggested that affirmative action suits against the city also be undertaken, the firm declined to participate. The firm represented a large utility which did a great deal of business with the city. It was proud of that representation, and felt that action against the city was a type of conflict.[6]

Sometimes the perceived threat to a firm's general interests is worked through, and the firm finds that in reality a community of interest exists. The following example is rare:

[I] went to a law firm that happened to represent a number of banks, some of which have provided loans to the developers guaranteed by the FHA, and that looked like a clear conflict. . . . After a while we decided that there was in fact a community of interest. A bank was getting screwed. The bank, which looks to the FHA to see that the work is carried out, had at least been partially injured, and there was a community of interest between the bank and tenants, each providing a kind of clout, political and economic, against the developer and the FHA, which had acted to-

5. R18.
6. R43.

gether in at least passive collusion. The lawyers went to the bank which said to go ahead, and, if needed, it would become involved, but not initially . . . so I think it is a matter of looking past the initial horror of the two interests involved.[7]

Sometimes a firm's willingness to accept risk from broad conflict rests on a sense that professional duty outweighs perceived self-interest. For example, a senior partner in a law firm wrote to a close friend who was an official of a company explaining that the younger lawyers in his office had determined that a public interest client had a suit against the company in question. The partner felt that, because of his close friendship with the defendant, he should apprise the defendant of the suit in a nice way but that he would not interfere with the professional judgment of lawyers in his office.[8] By and large, however, the quest for community of interest or for professional duty gives way to a *quest for conflicts*. A broad view of conflict of interest assists in the process of converting what should be duty into a dispensation of grace. Self-interest and "economic reality," not a code of professional ethics, lie at the heart of this conversion.

The profession as a whole, in its attempts at self-regulation —the Canons of Ethics and, later, the Code of Professional Responsibility—does not help the law firm extend its own definition of professional responsibility. Rather, its ethical statements simply mirror existing ambivalence. The law firm and the profession as a whole sense a duty, and the law firm may even grope to do it; but the absence of clear standards for what constitutes duty allows "economic reality" and self-interest to prevail. Canon 2 of the new Code of Professional Responsibility reads: "A Lawyer Should Assist the Legal Profession in Fulfilling *Its* Duty to Make Legal Counsel Available."[9] [Emphasis supplied.]

7. Y2. "Y" numbers indicate interviews made available to us by the *Yale Law Journal* (see Appendix, page 300).
8. R47.
9. Code of Professional Responsibility, Canon 2, p. 6.

The Lawyer, the Public, and Professional Responsibility

The profession has a duty. Fine! But nowhere has the Code spelled out a duty on the part of the individual practitioner. The Ethical Considerations in Canon 2 prayerfully suggest that the individual will take the responsibility of serving those who cannot normally pay for services.[10] What is prayed for in the Ethical Considerations is negated by the Disciplinary Rules. There one finds not the slightest hint of disciplinary action against a lawyer who refuses to take a client who cannot pay, or an unpopular client, or a client who is unable to get service elsewhere. In fact, the old ethical standards are retained. Discipline is promised only to those who would seek to aid a client through other than approved channels.

We will suggest, in Chapters 13 and 14, economic, social, and professional alternatives which would enable the bar to respond more fully. For now, what are the implications of the existing public interest responses of the private bar?

10. Code, EC–25 & 26, pp. 6–7.

cHApTER 12

Conclusions

The private law firm—particularly the large establishment law firm—has interests that transcend the interests of the individual lawyers in the firm. As an institution, the private law firm did not, in the past, include in its definition of professional responsibility a sense of duty to the public which went beyond economic self-interest and loyalty to regular clients. The activity of private law firms in the area of public interest has directed a modicum of energy toward the representation of new clients and has had some effect upon a redefinition of professional responsibility, but too many clients have been excluded because of real or felt conflicts of interest. Without a more substantial alteration of the definition of the law firm's institutional role, it is unlikely that many of the needs of the unrepresented will be met by the establishment law firms. There is, in fact, some reason to believe that present effort from this source will, over time, diminish. As going institutions with established clientele, these firms must insulate whatever public interest response they do make. There has been far less change in the character of the law firm as an institution than there has been in the character of the lawyers as individuals within the firm.

Some of the lawyers in firms, including some of the older senior lawyers, have changed their definition of professional responsibility. And to the extent that firms require allegiance from their lawyers, the policies of firms have shifted toward a more permissive attitude about public interest work. A shift in attitude, however, does not produce a change in the core content of the legal profession. It is possible that prolonged exposure to public policy debate and contact with new public interest clients and other elements of low-level public interest response will sufficiently motivate enough lawyers to force an alteration of the law firm's ethic. This could be accompanied by a change in the personal expectations of partners about income and social reward. It is unlikely, however, that this change will occur. Even with external supports for public interest goals—subsidization of public interest work—it is unlikely that the large law firm will become a significant public interest responder. Housing programs can perhaps support money-making professional work, but what about class actions against discrimination in employment or against polluters? Even if the latter kind of work were supported routinely, as it now is occasionally, it is unlikely to become a significant portion of the docket of an establishment firm. In all probability a specialized segment of the bar outside the establishment firms would be a more likely responder, as in the case of antitrust plaintiffs' lawyers who bring antitrust actions in furtherance of public policy against economic concentration. This sort of public interest work, subsidized with treble damages, has led to a distinct and even profitable specialized bar.

Given the individual lawyer's shift in personal attitude and in perception about professional role and responsibility, it would seem that the sole practitioner and the small firm are more likely to become significant public interest responders. These lawyers, of course, will have the problem of economic survival. The seriousness of the problem, however, will depend upon how well the profession as a whole and society in general make arrangements to reward the doing of public business within the framework of the private sector of the legal profession. The point is this: The individual lawyer is likely to have a greater impact on the definition of professional duty through his actions than through his words. In action he may eventually affect the large law firm's institutional definition of professional responsibility.

The public interest law firm is the most significant development in the private sector of the profession. It *is* new. It is a counter-institution. It does have the potential of influencing, through action, the overall definition of professional responsibility to the public. The view that the legal profession did discharge its responsibilities to the public was shattered when the myth was put to rest that the public lawyer—i.e., the government lawyer—represented the public. It is the public interest law firm—as an institution—which seems to represent the clients and interests previously thought to be represented by government and not then or now represented by the traditional law firms. Moreover, as with its predecessor the single-purpose volunteer agency, the public interest law firm frequently or usually views the government as the adversary.

The public interest law firm, being new, does not have long-established relations with the interests it represents. Further, we could find no evidence that the basis of its income is at this time related to the advancement of the funders' interests. Its general purpose makes it relatively free from conflict of interest problems. Like the large law firm, however, it ultimately acquires constituencies whose interests it advances. Ultimately, it, too, defines a standard for client eligibility, that of loyalty to causes and proponents of causes. Conflicts of interests, constituencies, and a standard for eligibility are all identified for the single-purpose public interest law firm by the subject matter and the philosophy of the firm.

Because it is situation-oriented, the public interest law

firm by and large has greater flexibility than does the private firm in meeting situations as they arise and in responding to the dictates of those situations. This facility is enhanced by the relative independence of the public interest firm and by its necessarily casual view of some of the formal statements of legal ethics. The public interest law firm comes into existence with a mission—to represent a given segment of the public. It feels a duty to search for "clients" when real clients are needed as nominal parties to a lawsuit and to inform clients and constituencies about specific wrongs. It also feels a duty to comment on pending cases when both the content and the outcome of those cases will profoundly affect public issues or identifiable public interest. All these factors, plus that of a full-time vocational approach—the ability to allocate all available hours —make the public interest law firm suited to bold issue structuring and case handling. In contrast, the traditional law firm generally makes only a supplemental effort.

The public interest firm, by its actions and by virtue of the attention paid it by both the counter-bar and the established bar, is affecting the way in which the private legal profession as a whole will have to define its relationship to the public— particularly to those groups who either cannot pay for legal services or whose "injuries" are not injuries in a traditional sense. The standing of those groups to sue about an issue related to continued life on the planet, for example, is no better than the standing of the rest of us, but the importance of allowing them to be heard on the issue is beyond question.

It may be that the public interest firm, like the traditional firm, will be found to fall short in the matter of taking "all comers." Public interest firms may ultimately identify with interests that are seen to be inimical to other interests of the public. The alignment of interests in the Illinois abortion case is in point:[1] There, one group of public interest lawyers took a position for a woman's right to elect abortion, a position which

1. See discussion of *Doe v. Scott* in Chapter 9 at 237.

was opposed, in the name of all unborn children, by another public interest group. In the last analysis, all effort by public interest and private law firms—whether for regular or public interest clients—must be viewed against a single ideal: the maximization of representation so that *all* relevant parties are heard from on any issue touching on decisions of public policy. Dependence on the proliferation of public interest law firms alone for the realization of this ideal would be misplaced. It is unlikely that this new form will give voice to all who need to be heard, at least in the short run. As the definition of professional responsibility is enlarged, the traditional private firm may and, indeed, should have more of a role, not less, in reaching a part of the unrepresented public.[2] This could be accomplished through private outreach programs; in that context it would be less important that the range of those represented be narrowly circumscribed by possible conflicts of interest.

When we look at the law firms and make judgments about the viability of forms, we find that the more structured forms (the department, the branch, the released-time program, and the conscious allocation of minimum levels of money and manpower) are likely to survive in some manner. All are, in one sense, ways of tithing.[3] The department insulates the lawyer from the firm's regular paying business or relieves him of a portion of his responsibility to the firm's regular clients. So, too, in varying degrees, do the branch, the released-time, and the more formal allocation programs. Upon a closer look we see, in embryo, public interest firms within private firms (departments) or owned and/or operated by private firms (branches and released-time programs). The operations and functions of these firms are separated. The question really becomes: *How long can a private law firm with one set of*

2. Until the rules on lobbying are relaxed, either the private firm or the sole practitioner will have to perform this function if it is to be performed at all. Because of their relative freedom the sole practitioner and the lawyer in the small firm are more suited to this function than is the large firm.
3. G. Sherman, 25 *Bus. Law.* 95 (Special Issue, Sept. 1969).

premises operate a public interest law firm with different premises before the nature of one or the other is changed?

The public interest law firm, like the sole practitioner and the small law firm, may be free from the control of invidious interests, but, like them, it has the problem of economic survival. The problem consists of locating a stable economic base for discharging professional responsibility to the public. The public interest firm is not likely to survive as a creature of the foundation. The tax problem is only one aspect of the limitations. As long as this type of firm is foundation supported, the matter of setting priorities for selecting matters—in particular, clientless matters—runs the *risk* of being concentrated in a few hands. Ultimately, government by the Ford Foundation could be as dangerous or as indifferent to the public good as either the United States government or entrenched private interests. Statutory supports in the form of allowable attorneys' fees—from the wrongdoer or from public funds—for doing the public bidding seem to be a necessary ingredient in funding firms of all types. This idea will be discussed in the next chapter.

PART
FOUR

THE FUTURE?

cHApTER 13

Who Pays for Public Interest Work?
Who OughT to Pay?
The Burdens—Economic and Other

We have seen that the phenomenon of a public interest response by the private bar, such as it is, reflects a recognition
that the two principal mechanisms for allocating legal services
have major defects when viewed against the premise that the
central function of the legal system is the structuring of individual and community conflicts so that they are capable of
peaceful resolution. The two mechanisms for allocation are a
price demand system, in which legal services are allocated to
those who can pay for them, and a rationing system, in which
services not allocated in the price system are allocated to individuals or issues according to selected principles. The first
mechanism, of course, describes the delivery of legal services
in the private sector of the legal profession. The second describes the public sector, supplemented in a minor way by the
private sector. Broad representation, beyond the confines of a
litigation model, has long been practiced in the public sector.
The lawyer in a governmental agency has not always had a real
client—the "client" has been the "public" in general or in its

role as an air traveler, a user of public parks, or a consumer, to name a few. The wholesale delivery of legal services to represent interests had been the principal mode of allocating legal services in government long before OEO Legal Services Programs came to grips with the "law reform" issue and long before the class action emerged as a significant tool in private litigation against public agencies.

The two mechanisms for distributing legal services are inadequate, primarily for two reasons. First, there are individuals in the society who bear substantial recognized injuries, but who lack both the price to obtain redress by hiring the services of a private lawyer and the political power to command representation from a public lawyer. Second, there are inchoate injuries and conflicts in the community which, in both their nonpeaceful and urgent forms, suggest that their complete resolution requires a broader participation in the rule-making process—broader than has heretofore been afforded by either the private or public bar. The private bar has shown some disposition to look for supplements to or substitutes for the present mechanisms. It seems to have faltered not only because it is so strongly wedded to past practices, but also because there has been no inducement to depart from them —no professional or social system for distributing the burdens of service, no overall mechanism for supplementing the price necessary for entry into the legal system or for augmenting delivery of services to the public.

Services are most needed now in situations where persons or groups cannot pay and in abstract, clientless situations. It is evident that the question of who should bear the burden of representation becomes crucial if sustained levels of broadened activity are desired. The economic burden is not the sole burden involved; social and psychological burdens are involved, too.

There are four basic alternatives for bearing or distributing these burdens: (1) The potential client or a specific group can bear the burdens by retaining either the injury or a sense of injury, or by bearing the cost of seeking redress; (2) the lawyers handling these matters can bear them; (3) the regular clients who do pay can be taxed for those who do not; or (4) society as a whole can bear the burdens. A variant of the last alternative might involve a shift of the burden to specific wrongdoers, such as industrial polluters, through an assessment for the costs.

The Present

Potential clients and unrepresented interests still bear the major part of the burdens for their injuries and frustrations. The public interest responses of the private bar may have provided some innovative forms and supplemental services, but, overall, these provisions are minimal. There is no system for delivery of service; there is only a search for alternatives to the price mechanism. Price still remains the major mechanism for allocating legal services. The public interest law firm has picked up a very small part of the challenge of making government responsive to public need. The private firm has picked up even fewer matters involving policy. Neither segment of the bar has picked up a substantial part of the burden of representing those without money. All efforts fall short and leave the major share of the burden largely where it has been—on the injury-sustainers and -bearers. This can be called *the burden of a nonpublic interest response by the American legal system.*

It is neither likely nor evident that injury-bearers have paid the entire cost of maintaining such a situation. The deep social conflict which we witness represents attempts to shift a substantial part of the cost of bearing injuries or dissatisfactions to society as a whole. Society pays in terms of riots, alienation, guilt, and the erosion of the social fabric. Direct economic costs are experienced because of the increased use of external and artificial means (e.g., police) for holding society together.

When the needs of the public are responded to by public interest work, the major part of the economic burden falls on society. This is because most of the work in this area is still being done by the public lawyer—including the agency lawyer, the public defender, and the OEO Legal Services Program lawyer.

When the private bar does public interest work, the economic burden falls for the most part on the individual lawyers who do the work. There are, of course, exceptions. This is not true, for example, for staff lawyers in the foundation-supported public interest law firms, for the staffs of older-form public interest or volunteer agencies (such as Legal Aid) or for the newer-style agencies like the Community Law Offices or the Lawyers' Committee for Civil Rights Under Law. In these cases, the staff lawyers are salaried, and the expectation is that they do this work to the exclusion of other professional work.

In many cases the pain of facing one's legal problems may increase rather than decrease a short-term frustration with a situation or a condition. When public interest law work is accepted by lawyers, a burden still remains on the clients served. Poverty clients, for example, bear a special burden even when accepted by lawyers. Public interest clients who are fighting injuries which they perceive on behalf of others carry two kinds of burdens. In many instances these clients—frequently group clients—pay for service and hence are accepting all or part of the economic burden. They are also taking on for society as a whole *more than their share* of the social burden of being responsible for one's fellow man.

In the large law firm the burden on the lawyer handling public interest work may be hidden, but it is there. For the most part the responders in large firms are associates, who are paid a salary. The associate receives a good income for his professional work. His high-level income is the factor which assures that he will personally bear the major burden of the public interest work accepted by the firm. He is not paid high wages to accomplish public interest work; he is paid to produce fee-generating work. Public interest work notwithstanding, he still has to "pay his way." He still works on fee-producing matters as many hours as do his nonresponding colleagues. This fact is not altered if he produces public interest work during office hours; it means merely that he does fee-generating work after hours.

The only way in which the large firm can lift from its associates the burden of doing "the firm's" public interest work is to reward public interest work monetarily and not discriminate in *any* way between responders and nonresponders. The public interest responder in the large firm who is paid a salary or shares in the firm's earnings and is *not* expected to produce a share of fee-generating work equivalent to that of his nonresponding colleagues is being rewarded monetarily for public interest work. This is true for John Ferren, the full-time public interest partner at Hogan & Hartson, for Peter Smith and Edwin Villmoare, the associates at Piper & Marbury's branch office, and for the associates of Covington & Burling who are paid by the firm during their six-month rotating stints with the neighborhood legal service program. These lawyers resemble the staff lawyers of volunteer agencies or public interest law firms. Their firms bear the costs of their services.

The firm of Arnold & Porter, too, would in part shift the burden of public interest work from the lawyers of the firm to the firm itself if the 15 percent draw on lawyers' time were an across-the-board tithe rather than an allowable limit. (As it is, with reliance placed on volunteers, only the full-time department partner, Bruce Montgomery, is rewarded by the firm for a public interest response.) The fact that the firm has made promises about a percentage of time available for public interest response may be illusory.

For the most part, the absence of relief from an equal share of paying work, the absence of an across-the-board tax, and the absence of a perception that public interest work is a duty are clues that the firm leaves the burden for public interest work squarely on the lawyer who desires to do it. A firm's volunteer lawyer has to determine for himself what the risks are if he makes an allocation of his time which involves a substitution of some public interest work for paying work. And he has to take those risks. Even if he does not substitute public interest work for paying work, he may take a risk if he shows greater enthusiasm for doing public interest work than for doing regular work. These risks may be in terms of slower advancement in salary or status within the firm or a halt to advancement entirely. The full-time public interest responder in a firm is not free from risk either. He receives money for not doing his firm's paying work, but how far will he advance? Has he accepted a subsidiary role as a lawyer akin to the secondary role allotted to the public interest response itself? Will he be the equivalent of the lawyer who used to be retained in the large firms to handle traffic cases and other mundane matters —a lawyer not really thought of as such?

The lawyer in the small firm and the sole practitioner also bear most of the economic burden of the public interest cases they accept. It is, however, a more clearly understood and direct burden than is the burden of the lawyer in the large firm. Each matter taken is within the ambit of autonomous choice. Lawyers in the self-designated, nonfoundation-funded public interest law firms such as Berlin, Roisman & Kessler provide clues, however, to another relevant question: Do any of the public interest responders, working in any of the forms of public interest response and willingly accepting the risks of doing so, personally bear a burden in responding? For many, real income is psychic return, which is bargained for and received; these lawyers may be balancing service and self-interest in a way satisfactory to them. It may be only when a public interest response interferes with economic survival that a burden is seen to clearly rest on the individual lawyer. And many times economic survival *is* at stake.

For the individual lawyer and the firm alike, some of the economic burden for handling public interest work is shifted whenever public subsidies or allowances are available. Not many are now available. But they serve to illustrate how the burden is or may be shifted from the individual lawyer or firm.

The Federal Criminal Justice Act of 1964 provides fees for lawyers on assigned cases. The Truth-in-Lending Act allows lawyers' fees for class actions, payable by the breaching party as an element of damages. Title VII of the Civil Rights Act of 1964 also allocates fees as an element of damages in cases of discriminatory employment practices. Another example has already been examined—the National Housing Act; we saw there how rewards could provide the basis of plans to do the public's bidding. Hill & Barlow never accepted the main burden of public interest work when they established their department of urban and public law. They put their energies into an area in which the burden had been systematically divided among the lawyer, the client, and society generally.

There is no way of estimating the true economic cost of the public interest work done by the large firm, the small firm, or the sole practitioner. The associates and younger lawyers in the large firm are likely to do the bulk of that firm's public interest work, and to the extent that they do the amount of paying work expected of them the cost to the firm is zero. True economic cost is involved only when the public interest work of a law firm or an individual lawyer reduces the amount of paying business or increases the amount of overhead necessary to produce an equal level of fees. The elusive concept of "billable hours" is not helpful for our purposes, because nobody has adequately defined the term and because the concept may not have the same meaning for a large firm that it has for a small firm or sole practitioner. Everybody knows that a fee-earning day is less than a working day. *The Lawyer's Handbook* estimates that there are approximately 1,300 fee-earning hours for each lawyer each year:

> There are only approximately 1,300 fee-earning hours per year unless the lawyer works overtime. Many of the eight hours per day available for office work are consumed in personal, civic, bar, religious and political activities, general office administration and other non-remunerative

matters. Either five or six remunerative hours per day would be realistic, depending upon the habits of the individual lawyer or the practices of the particular office.[1]

The new lawyer, whether in the large firm or on his own, may have replaced the nonremunerative "personal, civic, bar, religious, and political activities" with public interest lawyer work. If the concept of billable time were the accurate one, this replacement would produce no economic costs, even if "firm time" was seen to be involved.

In the large firm the problem of using billable time as a standard is compounded by the probability that young lawyers in large firms always have more billable hours than most lawyers—their marginal time is always in demand.[2] Nevertheless, even in the large firm there is always an excess of working hours over fee-producing hours.

Given the amount of time that we have seen allocated to public interest work, we doubt that true economic costs are involved. If the firms claim costs for public interest work (as many do), they should also see that costs are involved for the time a lawyer spends eating with or playing tennis with his wife.[3]

Cultural and professional values are also involved. The lawyer's life style and the style set by the firm may determine whether an alternative economic return is expected for the hours allocated to public interest work or whether billable hours should be restricted to those which are necessary for economic survival. "As long as a lawyer can eat, he owes service," said Karl Llewellyn. If this kind of standard is accept-

1. In The Lawyer's Handbook 287 (ABA Comm. on Economics of Law Practice ed., 1962). This figure, however, is arrived at by including Saturday as a half-day. Others have placed the annual figure closer to 1,000 or 1,200 billable hours.
2. The large firms do not have a concept of "eight hours a day."
3. The claim of costs may suggest the possibility that it is the law firm and not the law which is "the ancient and jealous mistress."

able to a lawyer, he cannot put an alternative hourly price on his service to the public.[4]

Many of the lawyers we talked with felt that their law firms shifted the cost of public interest work to regular retainer clients. We do not believe that this happens; the levels of response indicate no real cost and therefore no need to shift cost.

The lawyers who take public interest work and the law firms that accept or support this work regardless of what it may or may not cost in economic terms share a social burden with the public interest lawyers and the public interest clients who are addressing injuries borne by others or society generally. They are accepting for the nonresponders in society a part of the responsibility of ministering to the needs of their fellow men. In a significant way they are civilizers. This fact does not make heroes of the responding lawyers, but it does entitle them to honor. And it underscores the default of the profession as a whole.

The burden of responding to social need is one of the responsibilities of the legal profession. This is made clear in the classic definition of profession: service ahead of gain. The public interest lawyer, therefore, is not doing something that he does not have a duty to do; it is only in contrast to the lawyer who does not respond that we say "burden" is involved. To paraphrase Reginald Heber Smith, every time the public interest lawyer takes a case, he is discharging for the profession as a whole a moral and legal obligation.[5] The term "public interest lawyer" is truly redundant. There are lawyers and there are tradesmen. The lawyers are carrying a burden for the tradesmen; they are retaining for the non-

4. When a lawyer talks about an activity "taking bread out of his mouth," is he talking about bread?—or cake?

5. R. Smith, *Justice and the Poor* 243 (1924). Smith was referring to the Legal Aid lawyer, but the observation has the same force when applied to the lawyers engaged in the whole range of public interest responses.

responders a semblance of dignity that those nonresponders cannot truly claim until they have paid for it.

If a law firm charges a fee to a public interest client, the fee may be marginal income for the firm rather than a shared "cost." In this situation the client has a real economic cost, which a group client may shift to its members or supporters. If the client is tax exempt, part of the cost is shifted to the public. An allocation of social burdens is involved in this process, too.

We have to ask who bears the economic cost of the work done by the public interest law firms. To the extent that there is foundation support the cost is borne by the foundation and, through tax exemptions, by the public. If the public interest law firms are not tax exempt, the cost is borne by the clients.

The position of public interest law firms and clients who do not have tax-exempt status, and who are contesting a governmental practice or policy, or a corporate practice, as being harmful to the public interest, is indeed anomalous. Society, taxed to pay for government, bears the cost of the defense of a government practice, but not the cost of questioning the practice. The scrutiny of, or attack on, the practice can be seen as leading to society's benefit, but the economic burden remains on the examiner or objector. The outcome of the defense of the practice may be harmful—as it frequently is when a bureaucratic policy is defended—yet society bears the cost. When the attack is on a corporate practice—one that does violence to the environment, for instance—society, because of the corporation's use of business expense deductions, bears the cost of defending the practice, but not the cost of doing what is really society's business. The argument about tax exemption for the public interest law firms reaches only one part of the problem. Is there a way in which society can arrange to bear the burden of specific cases, if the resolution of the issues in question is going to be of possible benefit to society as a whole?

The Future

Three basic strategies can be employed toward the ideal end of assuring that the legal system is responsive to the needs of all interests and parties: (1) Government, by providing a separate delivery system, can augment the price method of gaining access to the legal system; (2) a system of subsidies can be worked out which utilizes the price model for distribution of legal services, but which operates to equalize it; (3) a *duty* can be imposed not only on the legal profession as a whole but also uniformly upon the *individual practitioner*—a duty perhaps externally imposed—so that each lawyer has at least a minimum duty to supplement the price model on his own, allocating a percentage of time to render service as needed, independent of the question of payment.

The first strategy has been the one used for the most part, and it has been deficient. The public lawyer has not adequately represented the interests of the unrepresented groups; instead he has become a principal apologist for interests which already have representation or the price to acquire representation. This does not mean that we will not have to rely on help from the government's legal or public services in the future. We will have to. In a democratic society, government must be the spokesman for all of the interests in the community. If it is not to the public lawyer, it is at least to the public servant that we must look for a balancing of interests. When a major part of a public interest problem, however, is caused by the breakdown of a governmental function, we cannot be too optimistic about looking to government for a solution. The history of the OEO Legal Services Program reveals some of the government's potential for extending services to and providing an outlet for heretofore unrepresented groups and individuals. It also indicates the limiting power of the political veto over government-funded efforts to correct the deficiencies of government operation. Moreover, some of the strengths of the OEO Legal Services

The Lawyer, the Public, and Professional Responsibility

Program rest on lawyer independence, due, in part, to moral and professional cosponsorship by the private bar, to the decentralized character of that legal service program, and to the good character of the lawyers who staff the program. These are strengths more frequently found outside government than in. By possessing an independence from government, the private bar is a potential auditor, correcter, limiter, and director of both private and governmental policies, practices, and excesses.

The other two strategies—economic inducement and enlistment or draft—are ways of getting the private bar to respond: Economic inducement, of course, would be the most palatable way for the bar. It is also a way which would cause the least dislocation to the prevailing system. By drastically extending a scheme of legislative grants (such as is found in the National Housing Act) and by adopting legislative schemes which would provide that reasonable attorneys' fees be assessed against those who intrude on public interest (such as is provided for in Title VII of the Civil Rights Act, in present environmental legislation, or in the Truth-in-Lending laws) it might be possible to induce substantially more effort from the private bar than now exists. The Sherman Act provided a way of placing the doing of public business in the hands of private business and of the private bar and of offering a socially sanctioned bounty for the doing. And certainly in the antitrust field there have been plentiful rewards for the private bar. An extended legislative scheme of subsidies or bounties for those who respond to public need would have the added feature of putting a monetary emphasis upon the importance of declarations of policy: By showing that society is willing to pay money for the execution of a policy or—through enforcement procedures—to see to it, at least, that someone will pay, the legislature would be expressing more than hope, more than a naive belief in self-executing policies. Further, it would be adding economic worth to the lawyer tasks involved.

The legislative scheme of subsidies, grants, and bounties

has thus far been reserved for auditing abuses by private parties (or applying to private enterprise the affirmative or negative sanctions of adopted public polices) or for carrying out affirmative governmental programs in fields like housing, shipping, and veterans' benefits. An element is missing from the scheme: Government can be the wrongdoer. The governmental agency that does not carry out an affirmative or corrective policy can be an injury-producer. This is frequently so. There seems to be no reason why bounties and subsidies cannot be extended to the function of watching—and seeking to correct or direct—Government. When a suit is brought against a federal agency, the legislative system should recognize that someone should be rewarded for doing the public's business in having brought the suit. Legislative policies should weave the auditing function directly into the scheme of governmental regulation.

A built-in auditing system could ideally provide for financing both the part-time public interest responder and the public interest law firm. Congress, for example, could provide a budget allocation for each agency, which in effect would say to an agency: "Where private parties come forward and want to be heard on matters affecting your agency, yet lack the means to pay counsel of their choice, you, as part of the continuing need to have your process audited and to provide for broader participation in your decisions, shall pay the fees." Affidavits would be involved. Judicial review would be involved. The method and the contents of the plan would be complex. But in the end, the process could look very much like the Federal Criminal Justice Act of 1964, whereby in many instances funds are disbursed to "appointed" counsel. The scheme would really be a plan to fund federal ombudsmen, with one very important element added: Reliance would be placed on individuals and lawyers to come forth on their own. There would be no single, potentially cooptable agency or group. The public interest firm could thereby have a funding source which could provide greater independence for the firm and the wherewithal for additional cases. Other public interest responders could also be eligible to use the plan. In the process, the administrative agencies might thereby be rendered more efficient.

Tax deductions provide another possible way of subsidizing the public interest responder. These could be available to both individual and group clients and lawyers who do a piece of sanctioned public business. Tax deductions or tax credits could be given to the lawyer who represents those who pay no fee or in situations where there is no "client" in a real sense. A scheme like this goes much further than that which simply gives tax-exempt status to foundations and to certain public interest clients and public interest law firms. Deductions would be available on a single-case basis for anyone doing the qualifying work. Congress can define the qualifying areas by looking into those pieces of legislation that require or invite lawyer participation for the better execution of adopted policies. The deduction would be analogous to the deduction given to businessmen for lawyers' fees: Clients or lawyers would receive deductions for doing the public business. This would be something completely new for lawyers. The business lawyer receives a fee, often a large fee. A tax deduction or credit for the public interest work done by a lawyer might serve to equalize availability and access.

The deficiencies of both affirmative subsidization and tax subsidization are obvious. Subsidization works only after policy has been decided—after a law is passed. Subsidies work for audit and correction. There still remains, however, the large amount of necessary public interest work which precedes the evolution of a policy and the passage of a law. We still need a bar responsive to need as need arises, to demand as demand is made, and to issues far in advance of demand. How can we assure that a bar, on its own, without compensation, will be willing to enter the fray?

The standard, applied internally or externally, of compelling service from all lawyers at a certain minimum level (apart from the price structure) has two advantages. First, lawyers are particularly capable of locating policy responses which would shift the burden of representing the public to society at large, particularly if that burden, in the absence of such policies, is imposed on lawyers to begin with. Second, it may assist in the process of converting the practice of law into a profession. The duty to respond was always the lawyer's. We deal more fully with this issue when we discuss the third method of allocating services in Chapter 14.

The Practice of Law Is a Public Utility

The grant of a monopoly license to practice law is based on three assumptions: (1) There is a socially useful function for the lawyer to perform; (2) the lawyer is a professional person who will perform that function; and (3) his performance as a professional person will be regulated by himself and more formally by the profession as a whole. In view of the practices of the American legal profession, only the first assumption seems warranted. We have seen too little evidence of professional as opposed to trade performance by the individual lawyer and no evidence of serious professional self-regulation toward diverting the profession to the pursuit of the common good—the public interest.

A monopoly is tolerated by society under only two conditions. Either a function is performable by only one group—a natural monopoly—and regulation assures the performance of that function (this is a classic description of a public utility) or society has been sufficiently corrupted to permit the continuation of a dysfunctional monopoly.

288

The central function that the legal profession must perform is nothing less than the administration of justice; this necessarily requires maximum participation in the rule-making and decision-making processes. The monopoly grant to lawyers provides for access to the process of adjudication and rule making in the courts, and for the giving of advice about the legal consequences of action or forbearance. But the monopoly has further consequences because of the way in which the American legal, political, and social systems operate. Because of the interaction between the judicial, legislative, and administrative branches of government, the legal profession controls meaningful access to the formal decision-making and rule-making processes in our legislative and administrative bodies. Moreover, because of the heavy reliance in our social system on the rule of law—whereby shifting community norms and ideals are sustained, sanctioned, tested, and legitimated or rejected by the law in an endless cycle of dialogue between society on the one hand and society's formal adjudicative and rule-making bodies on the other hand—many of the informal processes of decision making and rule making are moderated by the legal profession. In short, access to the entire policy dialogue is controlled by the lawyers.

Given the function that the lawyer has to perform—structuring the conflicts of society so that they are capable of peaceful resolution—we feel that even without a monopoly grant of power the legal profession is a public utility. The law is a calling which by definition deals with public interest, not self-interest. The monopoly grant simply makes the need for regulation by self or state more urgent.

In many ways the legal profession is like that sensitive area of the field of radio and television in which licensees control access to public discussion. In the communications field, the announced public policy—the Communications Act—requires that a commitment be made when a license is granted, that the licensee affirmatively undertake to "operate its license in the public interest." The licensee has a duty to so operate, and the licensee's discharge of that duty is reviewed when a license is renewed. The question is faced directly:

At what level of public responsibility must the licensee operate to retain the license?

The review is in terms of public interest. There have not been satisfactory answers to the question, but at least the question is directly put. And the duty of each licensee—each outlet—is perceived.

The license for the practice of law is perpetual; regulation is illusory, and the question is *never* put:

At what level of public interest *must* the lawyer operate as a condition of retaining his license?

The issue of the right to practice has never been put in terms of what a lawyer's *duty* is.

There are no disciplinary procedures for the lawyer who refuses to take a case; there is only the suggestion that it would be nice if he would. The absence of controls over the lawyer with respect to what he turns away is socially dangerous. It is more dangerous than the risk involved in drafting or socializing a percentage of a lawyer's time. The latter would be a drastic step but less drastic than socializing all of a lawyer's time. To some this will be a shocking notion. But why?

One of the issues now being debated in the field of communications is whether network time should be coopted for the public interest during presidential and other important political campaigns. The effect of the high cost of purchasing time on the networks or on the major station outlets is that officials are elected on the basis of who buys the most time. The cooption idea, or a competing one that would limit the amount of time which candidates can purchase, is aimed at equalization to avoid or limit the auction effect. So, too, is the idea that the time should be sold at lower rates. We have

precisely the same problem with respect to the sale and allocation of available lawyer time—it goes to the highest bidder.
The result is the same, too, although more subtle and perhaps
more pervasive: Policy on a day-in, day-out basis is made by
the use of lawyers' skills allocated mainly through a price
system. Policy is therefore auctioned to the highest bidder.
Can this be tolerated? Most would say "No," but few would
argue that services to supplement the price system should be
allocated on other than a voluntary basis.

We feel that reliance on a voluntary system will be enough
only if the kinds of subsidies and grants which we discussed in
Chapter 13 support enough lawyers who, as a matter of self-
imposed duty, are willing to respond to those who need representation but do not come within the ambit of any support
program. On the basis of past experience and present projection, there is little hope that a voluntary system will be
sufficient.

A draft of lawyers is not outrageous when one considers
that we draft children from the ages of six to sixteen so that
they can acquire the skills of good citizens. This is compulsory
education. We draft into the military—and at the risk of their
lives—men from the ages of eighteen to twenty-six who may
have no particular qualifications for the draft other than
citizenship. The military draft is supported on the premise that
the country's security is involved. Yet when one examines the
policies of our country, arrived at without hearing from all,
and then sees the lawyers, who possess unique skills for arriving at balanced social policy, exempting themselves from their
professional duty or being exempted by others, why *would* a
draft for lawyers be outrageous?

If a draft is not acceptable, what about a tax on the lawyer's time? Perhaps a set of penalties could be assessed through
the tax structure on those lawyers who are unable to certify
that they have operated their licenses with balanced programming for the public good.

We do not think it likely that these drastic measures will

be taken. But we think that they should be taken if the profession is unwilling to regulate itself.[1] We are talking about professional regulation that is real, not the myth of self-regulation. Perhaps one of the reasons for the exemption of the legal profession from the external—state—regulation imposed on other public utilities is that it appears to be self-regulated. Lawyers are skilled in rhetoric. They have given the appearance of self-regulation. Even when making public interest responses they have often managed to make what is vocation look like voluntarism and what is duty look like grace—at least to the casual observer.

As a start toward internal regulation, the legal profession will have to drop the minimum fee and the self-aggrandizement evident in its definitions of and approach to the unauthorized practice of law. As long as there are clients and interests in need of service and representation, the profession is ill-advised to talk of protecting the public against inadequate representation. The profession's excuses for minimum fee and vigilance against unauthorized practice are weak in any case. The profession should attend to those receiving little or no service. In the process it might find its own integrity and forget about devices which sustain a dysfunctional view of law as a profession. Karl Llewellyn expressed these thoughts in 1938,[2] but no one listened. Perhaps some are listening now. The public interest response evidences a degree of maturation in the bar.

In reality there is little public interest response from the legal profession as a whole—and even less self-regulation. All that has happened is that some have made many look good on the surface—and very, very bad in the final analysis. Arrogance *is* involved when a lawyer calls himself a public interest responder, but it has been, for the most part, the arrogance of

1. We are not sugesting that the other professions have not similarly defaulted in self-regulation. They have. But we are concerned with the legal profession.

2. K. Llewellyn, "The Bar's Troubles, and Poultices—and Cures?" 5 *Law and Contemp. Prob.* 104 (1938).

the nonresponsive bar which necessitated the special vocabulary—"public interest lawyer." Although the responses have been minimal overall, the efforts of some lawyers have been exceptional. The real value of these lawyers has been to point out the default of the many. The few will be happy without praise.

Appendix

Methodology

When we designed our approach to this study, we assumed that the participants in the public interest efforts of the private bar could tell us what they thought they were doing and why they thought they were doing it. After all, they were the ones who seemed to be asking and responding to the question: How can we, as lawyers, serve the public? On the other hand, we anticipated that the participants would not be able to fully express what they were doing and why they were doing it, or what were the implications of their efforts. We therefore expected that the respondents' actions and the context of their actions would be at least as meaningful as their words. Additionally, we rejected an approach which would produce an exhaustive catalogue of all public interest work. Such an approach would not be likely to further an understanding of the character or implications of the public interest response of private lawyers. Alternatively, we decided to study the public interest phenomenon by identifying and examining the various types of professional response. This decision was aided by our belief that the totality of public interest efforts was as yet a small percentage of the total enterprise of the private bar.

The data for the present study were derived principally, but not exclusively, from interviews. We selected our interviewees not randomly but rather purposively, because they occupied certain positions or performed certain functions which were directly related to our public interest concerns. We eventually located representatives of the various new public interest efforts and interviewed until we had gained sufficient understanding of how each variant operates. To understand what was new and different, it was also necessary to interview participants from some of the older and more conventional public interest forms.

We constructed a list of potential interviewees, starting with members of those organizations which had already received some attention for their work in the public interest. In February 1970, the senior author, prior to designing our study, had attended a symposium conducted by the National Legal Aid and Defender Association (NLADA) in Atlanta, Georgia, entitled: What Private Law Firms Are Doing to Provide Legal Services for the Poor. We started with this meeting and interviewed at least one person from each of the firms or organizations represented. We also talked with Richard L. Woodward, field consultant with NLADA. Woodward gave us a list of organizations, firms, and individuals who had announced or revealed a formal commitment to public interest work up to that time. Stanley Keller, of the Beverly Hills, California, bar, also spent some time with us. Keller had traveled extensively, assembling information on private efforts in the public interest both for NLADA and for a report he was making to the Beverly Hills Bar Association, which was then in the process of setting up a foundation for the purpose of entering into active public interest work.

We interviewed sixty-eight lawyers in all: forty-two from large private firms (twenty-seven partners and fifteen associates); five from small or medium firms; and twenty from public interest firms or agencies. Some of the lawyers with firms also had contact with public interest agencies but were counted only as firm lawyers. We interviewed the following individuals:

Atlanta, Georgia
R. LAWRENCE ASHE   Kilpatrick, Cody, Rogers, McClatchey & Regenstein
DAVID CROSLAND   Executive Director, Atlanta Lawyers' Committee for Civil Rights Under Law
A. JAMES ELLIOTT   Alston, Miller & Gaines

Baltimore, Maryland
PAUL CORDISH   Cordish & Cordish
PETER SMITH   Piper & Marbury

Boston, Massachusetts
RICHARD BANKS   Director, Boston Lawyers for Housing
STEPHEN BING   Associate Director, Lawyers' Committee for Civil Rights Under Law
FRANK HEFFRON   Foley, Hoag & Eliot
CARL SAPERS   Hill & Barlow

Chicago, Illinois
ROBERT HOWARD   Associate Director, Lawyers' Committee for Civil Rights Under Law
MARSHALL PATNER   General Counsel, Businessmen for the Public Interest
ALEXANDER POLIKOFF   Executive Director, Businessmen for the Public Interest
DAVID TATEL   Director, Chicago Lawyers' Committee for Civil Rights Under Law

Los Angeles (County), California
CHARLES BENDER   O'Melveny & Myers
WILLIAM BOGAARD   O'Melveny & Myers
LOUIS M. BROWN   Irell & Manella
JULIAN BURKE   Chairman Executive Committee, Human

Rights Section of the Los Angeles County Bar Association;
Tuttle & Taylor
ALAN FRIEDMAN   Munger, Tolles, Hills & Rickershauser
TERRY HATTER   Executive Director, Western Center on Law
and Poverty
MELDON LEVINE   Wyman, Bautzer, Finell, Rothman & Kuchel
PAUL POSNER   Wirin, Rissman, Okrand & Posner
STANTON L. STEIN   Wyman, Bautzer, Finell, Rothman &
Kuchel
MAYNARD TOLL   O'Melveny & Myers
SHARP WHITMORE   President, Los Angeles County Bar As-
sociation; Gibson, Dunn & Crutcher

New York City, New York
HÉNRY ARONSON   Director, Manhattan Court Employment
Project
J. TRUMAN BIDWELL, JR.   Donovan, Leisure, Newton &
Irvine
ANN GARFINKLE   Lefcourt Garfinkle Crain Cohn Sandler &
Lefcourt
NEAL JOHNSTON   Chairman, Counsel of New York Law As-
sociates
STEPHEN KASS   Director, Community Law Offices
MARK LEVINE   White & Case
BEVIS LONGSTRETH   Debevoise, Plimpton, Lyons & Gates
FRANCIS T. P. PLIMPTON   Debevoise, Plimpton, Lyons &
Gates
J. ASA ROUNTREE   Debevoise, Plimton, Lyons & Gates
ASA SOKOLOW   Rosenman Colin Kaye Petschek·Freund &
Emil
PAUL TRACTENBERG   Member of the steering committee,
Council of New York Law Associates; Strasser, Spiegelberg,
Fried & Frank

Philadelphia, Pennsylvania
RICHARD BROWN   Morgan, Lewis & Bockius
WINSTON CHURCHILL   Saul, Ewing, Remick & Saul

Appendix

WILLIAM KLAUS   Pepper, Hamilton & Scheetz
PETER SHAW   Saul, Ewing, Remick & Saul

San Francisco, California
JAMES BENNEY   Orrick, Herrington, Rowley & Sutcliffe
CHARLES CLIFFORD   Heller, Ehrman, White & McAuliffe
DAVID GETCHES   Director, Native American Rights Fund (Berkeley)
WILLIS HANNAWALT   Pillsbury, Madison & Sutro
DAVID HEILBRON   McCutchen, Doyle, Brown & Enersen
RICHARD MORRIS   General Counsel, San Francisco Lawyers' Committee for Civil Rights Under Law
DAVID NELSON   Morrison, Foerster, Holloway, Clinton & Clark
C. RICHARD WALKER   Orrick, Herrington, Rowley & Sutcliffe

Washington, D.C.
JOHN BLEVEANS   Executive Director of the District of Columbia, Lawyers' Committee for Civil Rights Under Law
EDGAR CAHN   Director, Citizens Advocate Center
LOUIS COHEN   Wilmer, Cutler & Pickering
WILLIAM DOBROVIR
JOHN FERREN   Hogan & Hartson
MONROE FREEDMAN   Director, Stern Community Law Firm
CHARLES HALPERN   Director, Center for Law and Social Policy
DAVID ISBELL   Covington & Burling
ROBERT KAPP   Hogan & Hartson
GLADYS KESSLER   Berlin, Roisman & Kessler
MICHAEL KLEIN   Wilmer, Cutler & Pickering
ALBERT KRAMER   Executive Director, Citizens Communication Center
CHARLES MILLER   Covington & Burling
BRUCE MONTGOMERY   Arnold & Porter
LOUIS F. OBERDORFER   Co-chairman, National Lawyers'

Committee for Civil Rights Under Law (1967–69); Wilmer, Cutler & Pickering

STEPHEN POLLAK   Shea & Gardner; former Assistant U.S. Attorney General, in charge of Civil Rights Division of the Justice Department

E. BARRETT PRETTYMAN, JR.   Hogan & Hartson

JOHN SAPIENZA   Covington & Burling

LAWRENCE SPEISER   Director, Washington office of national American Civil Liberties Union

RALPH TEMPLE   Director, Capital Area Chapter, American Civil Liberties Union

MICHAEL TRISTER   Staff Attorney, Washington Research Project

The geographic distribution of visible public interest work determined the locale of our field work. The greatest activity appeared to be on the East coast—in Boston, New York, Philadelphia, Baltimore, and particularly, Washington—with only a scattering in the Midwest and on the West coast.

The interviews were conducted in 1970 between the months of May and October. They were unstructured, lasted approximately an hour, and were designed to promote reflection and evaluation on the part of the respondents.

The interviews focused on four distinct areas of concern:

1. What are you (or your firm or organization) doing?
2. Why are you doing it now?
3. Why are you responding in this particular way? (This question had several components: What are your perceptions of the need? What alternatives do you see? What factors affected your choice?)
4. What do you think all this means—both your firm's (or organization's) efforts and the phenomenon generally?

The interviews were conversational, and, in our judgment, the rapport was generally good. In all but one case we received permission to tape-record the interviews. We recognized the possibility of inhibiting candor and alienating the respondents by taping the interviews. On the other hand, we expected that the public nature of the work we were discussing, coupled with the participants' sense of engagement and commitment to that work, made this risk slight. Given the nature of the document we anticipated writing, we did not offer confidentiality, and rarely was it requested. However, we did code all interviews. We used names when the context suggested that some richness of the background or some of the understanding would be obscured by omission.

During the months of our data gathering we also had informal conversations with lawyers who were engaged in public interest work or concerned with the issue. Beyond this we had access to written materials—interfirm names, reports, etc., that were particularly relevant to the public interest activities we were examining. We further supplemented our own data with interview transcripts made available to us by a team from the *Yale Law Journal,* which had recently conducted a study of public interest lawyers. Their study was reported in an excellent Comment, "The New Public Interest Lawyers," 79 *Yale L.J.* 1069 (1970). A list of their interviews appears at pages 1151–52 of that volume.

Finally, we attended two directly pertinent conferences during the period of our field work; one held in Chicago, May 16, 1970, by the Law and Society Association ("Providing Legal Services to Reduce Poverty and Protect the Public Interest"), and the other in St. Louis, August 9, 1970, by the National Legal Aid and Defender Association (a fuller replay of the Atlanta Conference). We obtained transcripts of both conferences and found they provided useful additional data.

Index

Index